Information Systems for Knowledge Management

Information Systems for Knowledge Management

Edited by
Inès Saad
Camille Rosenthal-Sabroux
Faïez Gargouri

Series Editor
Jean-Charles Pomerol

WILEY

First published 2014 in Great Britain and the United States by ISTE Ltd and John Wiley & Sons, Inc.

ISTE Ltd
27-37 St George's Road
London SW19 4EU
UK

www.iste.co.uk

John Wiley & Sons, Inc.
111 River Street
Hoboken, NJ 07030
USA

www.wiley.com

Library of Congress Control Number: 2014930207

British Library Cataloguing-in-Publication Data
A CIP record for this book is available from the British Library
ISBN 978-1-84821-664-8

Printed and bound in Great Britain by CPI Group (UK) Ltd., Croydon, Surrey CR0 4YY

Table of Contents

**Chapter 1. Assessing the Community Maturity from a
Knowledge Management Perspective**   1
Imed BOUGHZALA

    1.1. Introduction.   2
    1.2. Background   4
        1.2.1. Maturity models.   4
        1.2.2. Knowledge-oriented maturity models   5
    1.3. Method   9
    1.4. The CoMM 10
        1.4.1. The development 10
        1.4.2. The description 13
    1.5. Application within a CKO professional association 18
        1.5.1. Overview of need. 18
        1.5.2. Field application steps 19
        1.5.3. Findings 20
        1.5.4. Reflection on the field application of CoMM 23
    1.6. Discussion and implications 24
    1.7. Conclusion 25
    1.8. Bibliography 26
    1.9. Appendix 31

**Chapter 2. Social Networks: Leveraging User Social Data to
Empower Collective Intelligence** 33
Xuan Truong VU, Marie-Hélène ABEL and Pierre MORIZET-MAHOUDEAUX

    2.1. Introduction. 34
    2.2. Collective intelligence by user-centered social network aggregation . . 35
    2.3. Related works 37
    2.4. Proposed system 40

2.4.1. User-centered social network aggregation   41
2.4.2. Personalized information filtering   45
2.4.3. Collaborative knowledge management   48
2.5. Decision support   50
2.6. Use scenario   53
2.7. Prototype   54
2.8. Conclusions and future work   57
2.9. Acknowledgment   58
2.10. Bibliography   58

**Chapter 3. Sociocultural Knowledge Management toward the
Adaptation of a CSCL Environment**   61
Fadoua OUAMANI, Narjès Bellamine Ben SAOUD and
Henda Hajjami Ben GHEZALA

3.1. Introduction   61
3.2. The concept of culture and sociocultural factors   63
3.2.1. Culture in ethnology   64
3.2.2. Culture in psychology   65
3.2.3. Cultural properties   66
3.2.4. Models of national culture   67
3.2.5. Discussion   70
3.3. The relation between sociocultural human
characteristics, KM and CSCL   71
3.3.1. CSCL and knowledge sharing   71
3.3.2. Culture, human mind and KM   73
3.3.3. Discussion   74
3.4. Sociocultural considerations in collaborative environments   75
3.4.1. Study of existing culturally sensitive tools   75
3.4.2. Limitations and findings   76
3.5. The proposed ontology-based sociocultural user profile   78
3.6. The conceptual ontology framework based adaptation approach   82
3.7. The sociocultural aware KM system for CSCL   83
3.8. Conclusion and ongoing work   86
3.9. Bibliography   87

**Chapter 4. An Argumentation-based Rough Set Theory for
Knowledge Management**   93
Sarra BOUZAYANE, Imène BRIGUI-CHTIOUI, Inès SAAD

4.1. Introduction   93
4.2. Background   95
4.2.1. Dominance-based rough set approach (DRSA)   95
4.2.2. Argumentation   97

4.2.3. Multiagent system 104
4.3. Related work 106
4.4. Multiagent argumentative approach 116
4.4.1. Interaction protocol. 116
4.4.2. Arguments 117
4.4.3. Argument and counter-argument evaluation 120
4.4.4. Counter-argument construction. 121
4.5. Example. 123
4.6. Conclusion 126
4.7. Bibliography 126

**Chapter 5. Considering Tacit Knowledge When Bridging
Knowledge Management and Information Systems for
Collaborative Decision-Making**. 131
Pierre-Emmanuel ARDUIN, Camille ROSENTHAL-SABROUX, and
Michel GRUNDSTEIN.

5.1. Introduction. 132
5.2. Background theory 133
5.2.1. A vision of knowledge within the organization 133
5.2.2. Ethnographic workplace study: participation
as a means to observe 134
5.2.3. Incommensurability: when communication breaks down 136
5.3. Proposition. 138
5.3.1. Fieldwork through participant observation 139
5.3.2. Highlighting evidences and levels with ISO/IEC 15504 141
5.3.3. Rating the attributes and assessing tacit knowledge
consideration 146
5.4. Case study 149
5.4.1. Describing the field. 149
5.4.2. Discussing the collected data and the results. 151
5.5. Conclusions. 154
5.6. Acknowledgments. 155
5.7. Bibliography 156

Chapter 6. Relevant Information Management in Microblogs. 159
Soumaya CHERICHI and Rim FAIZ

6.1. Introduction. 160
6.2. Twitter IR 161
6.3. Features for tweet ranking 163
6.3.1. Feature set 164
6.3.2. Metric measure of the impact of criteria to improve search results. 168
6.4. Experimental evaluation 172

6.4.1. Description of the collection 172
6.4.2. Results 173
6.5. Conclusion 176
6.6. Bibliography 177

**Chapter 7. A Legal Knowledge Management System
Based on Core Ontology** 183
Karima DHOUIB and Faïez GARGOURI

7.1. Introduction. 183
7.2. Legal KM 185
7.2.1. Legal portals. 186
7.2.2. Legal decision support systems and legal expert systems 187
7.2.3. Legal case-based reasoning 187
7.2.4. Legal ontology 188
7.3. Functional architecture of the system 188
7.4. Legal ontology construction approach 189
7.4.1. Existing ontology construction methodologies 190
7.4.2. Our approach 193
7.4.3. Our reference ontological framework 196
7.4.4. Our building blocks 198
7.4.5. Discussion 201
7.5. Jurisprudence decision structuring methodology (JDSM) 202
7.5.1. Thematic document structuring: some related works 203
7.5.2. Our methodology 204
7.6. Conclusion 209
7.7. Bibliography 210

**Chapter 8. Foundations for a Core Ontology of
an Organization's Processes**. 215
Mohamed TURKI, Gilles KASSEL, Inès SAAD and Faïez GARGOURI

8.1. Introduction. 216
8.2. Our reference ontological framework 218
8.2.1. DOLCE. 220
8.2.2. Actions, participation roles and participatory capacities 222
8.2.3. Artifacts 224
8.3. A core ontology of an organization's processes 224
8.3.1. Collective phenomena 226
8.3.2. Organizational phenomena 231
8.3.3. Process of organization 234
8.4. Discussion 240
8.5. Conclusion 243
8.6. Bibliography 244

Chapter 9. A Business Process Evaluation Methodology
for Knowledge Management Based on Multicriteria
Decision-Making Approach   249
Mohamed TURKI, Inès SAAD, Faïez GARGOURI and Gilles KASSEL

9.1. Introduction.   249
9.2. Related works   252
9.3. Dominance-based rough set approach   254
9.4. BP evaluation methodology   256
  9.4.1. Phase 1: preference model construction.   257
  9.4.2. Phase 2: exploitation of the preference model   262
9.5. The decision support system for identifying sensitive
  processes OP-DSS.   264
  9.5.1. Graphical interface   264
  9.5.2. Model base.   265
  9.5.3. Database   265
  9.5.4. Knowledge base.   267
  9.5.5. Implementation   268
9.6. Case study   271
9.7. Conclusion and futures works.   272
9.8. Bibliography   273
9.9. Appendix 1. The set of criteria   275
9.10. Appendix 2. Contribution degree computing algorithm   277

Chapter 10. A Collaborative Approach for Optimizing
Continuity between Knowledge Codification with
Knowledge Engineering Methods and Knowledge Transfer.   279
Thierno TOUNKARA

10.1. Introduction   279
10.2. Factors influencing knowledge transfer   280
  10.2.1. Characteristics of knowledge   281
  10.2.2. Knowledge transfer channels   283
  10.2.3. Absorptive capacity of knowledge receivers   284
  10.2.4. Cultural and organizational contexts.   285
10.3. Modes of knowledge transfer   286
  10.3.1. Social exchange versus codification   286
  10.3.2. Knowledge transfer models   286
10.4. Research methodology   290
  10.4.1. Literature review   290
  10.4.2. Focus groups for data collection and generation of
  testable propositions.   290
10.5. Codifying with knowledge engineering methods:
  barriers for knowledge transfer   293

10.5.1. Multiplicity of formalisms.   294
10.5.2. Heterogeneity of readers profiles   295
10.5.3. Background   295
10.5.4. Contexts of use   295
10.5.5. Preferences for logical structuring and
understanding profile   295
10.5.6. Level of description of complex knowledge   296
10.5.7. Level of description of specific knowledge   296
10.5.8. Exchange channels to increase diffusion/transfer   297
10.6. Methodology for knowledge transfer efficiency   298
10.6.1. Capturing and codifying tacit knowledge domain   298
10.6.2. Defining and formalizing exchanges between
groups of actors involved in the knowledge transfer process   298
10.7. Hydro Quebec case study.   302
10.7.1. Approach   303
10.7.2. Results and implications   304
10.8. Discussion.   305
10.8.1. About completeness of knowledge.   305
10.8.2. Exploring ontologies for knowledge transfer   305
10.8.3. About costs.   306
10.9. Conclusion   306
10.10. Bibliography.   307

List of Authors   311

Index   313

Chapter 1

Assessing the Community Maturity from a Knowledge Management Perspective

Knowledge is considered as a strategic resource in the current economic age. Strategies, practices and tools for enhancing knowledge sharing and knowledge management (KM) in general have become a key issue for organizations. Despite the demonstrated role of communities in sharing, capturing and creating knowledge, the literature is still missing standards for assessing their maturity. Even if several knowledge-oriented maturity models are provided at the enterprise level, few are focusing on communities as a mechanism for organizations to manage knowledge. This chapter proposes a new Community Maturity Model (CoMM) that was developed during a series of focus group meetings with professional KM experts. This CoMM assesses members' participation and collaboration, and the KM capacity of any community. The practitioners were involved in all stages of the maturity model's development in order to maximize the resulting model's relevance and applicability. The model was piloted and subsequently applied within a chief knowledge officers' (CKO) professional association, as a community. This chapter discusses the development and application of the initial version of CoMM and the associated method to apply it.

Chapter written by Imed BOUGHZALA.

1.1. Introduction

Knowledge is considered as a key competitive advantage [PEN 59], therefore several knowledge-intensive organizations are investing in methods, techniques and technologies, to enhance their KM, among others through communities. The community-based KM approach has become one of the most effective instruments to manage organizational knowledge [BRO 91]. Indeed, Wenger [WEN 98] argues that knowledge could be shared, organized and created within and among the communities. He posits that communities of practice (CoPs) are the company's most versatile and dynamic knowledge resource. They form the basis of an organization's ability to know and learn. From practical and theoretical perspectives, we can find several types of communities (of practice (CoPs), virtual CoP (VCoP), of interest (CoIN), of project, etc.). Furthermore, since they mostly deal with knowledge, Correa *et al.* [COR 01] call them knowledge communities (KCs) and consider them as a key KM resource through socialization [NON 95, EAR 01].

Nowadays, due to the increasing use of communities in the professional context and the exponential growth of social networks and online communities [RHE 93], it is more important than ever for modern organizations to assess the quality of their outcomes, and to understand their role in intra- and interorganizational KM settings. To establish such an understanding, many questions need to be answered, including but not limited to: how do we determine the type of a community? Under which conditions are communities more productive and useful for organizations? How they can be beneficial to KM: knowledge sharing, capturing and co-creation? Which attitudes and capabilities should individuals develop to better involve themselves within communities? What kind of facilitation means do they need for operating better? Are there different levels of quality that can be recognized and that communities should aim for? Which role should knowledge and collaboration technologies play to foster productivity? How can we measure the impacts of communities on organizational performance? Therefore, it is clear today that organizations urgently need guidance on those issues and on how to take advantage from the KCs' production and to efficiently use and manage them for better sharing, learning and innovating.

Several scholars have proposed models and approaches to assess communities [VER 06, MCD 02]. One way to assess the overall characteristics, management, evolution and performance of a community is through a maturity model approach with a KM-oriented perspective. Maturity models have been used extensively in quality assurance for product development [FRA 02].

Few efforts have been reported on using maturity models to assess communities, especially from a KM perspective. Most of the KM models proposed in the literature (such as Global Knowledge Management Maturity Model (GKMMM [PEE 06]), Knowledge Management Assessment Project (KMAP [GAL 08]), Model for General Knowledge Management within the Enterprise (MGKME [GRU 08]) and Knowledge Navigator Model (KNM [HIS 09])) are either very generic at the enterprise organizational level and/or not enough specific to assess communities. Very few community-oriented KM maturity models have been proposed [GON 01, LEE 10]. Even if these examples of models present an interesting theoretical perspective, little is reported on their application and evaluation. They are not specifically KM oriented and most of them focus only on CoPs. This chapter is an attempt to address this gap and to propose a new model for assessing communities from a KM perspective sufficiently generic to be applied to any community or social network. It addresses the following research question:

How do we determine the maturity level of a community from a KM perspective?

This question can be divided in two subquestions:

– What characteristics describe a community's maturity?

– What steps need to be taken to measure a community's maturity in terms of KM?

This chapter advances a CoMM that was developed in cooperation with a focus group consisting of professional KM experts. The CoMM is intended to be usable by practitioners for conducting self-assessments. This chapter first discusses the development of the initial version of the CoMM and the associated method to apply it, and second an application and evaluation that provide evidence of proof of value and proof of use in the field. The purpose of this chapter is to further serve as a starting point for future research in this area.

The remainder of this chapter is structured as follows. We first present the theoretical background related to maturity models. Next, we introduce our research approach to develop the CoMM, based on the design science perspective. Then, we report on the field application of the CoMM within a CKO professional association. Lastly, we present the implications for research and practice, followed by our conclusion that summarizes the limitations of this ongoing research and presents future research directions.

1.2. Background

The word maturity is equivalent to *"ripeness"*, which means having reached the most advanced stage in a process. Maturity is a quality or state of becoming mature [AND 03]. Paulk *et al.* [PAU 93, p. 21] define process maturity as "the extent to which a specific process is explicitly defined, managed, measured, controlled, and effective". They describe the transition from an initial to a more advanced state, possibly through a number of intermediate states [FRA 02]. Maturity models position all the features of an activity on a scale of performance under the fundamental assumption of ensuring plausible correlation between performance scale and maturity levels. A higher level of maturity will lead to a higher performance [FRA 03]. "At the lowest level, the performance of an activity may be rather *ad hoc* or depend on the initiative of an individual, so that the outcome is unlikely to be predictable or reproducible. As the level increases, activities are performed more systematically and are well defined and managed. At the highest level, 'best practices' are adopted where appropriate and are subject to a continuous improvement process" [FRA 03, p. 1500].

1.2.1. *Maturity models*

Approaches to determine process or capability maturity are increasingly applied to various aspects of product development, both as an assessment instrument and as part of an improvement framework [DOO 01]. Most maturity models define an organization's typical behavior for several key processes or activities at various levels of "maturity" [FRA 03]. Maturity models provide an instantaneous snapshot of a situation and a framework for defining and prioritizing improvement measures. The following are the key strengths of maturity models:

– They are simple to use and often require simple quantitative analysis.

– They can be applied from both functional and cross-functional perspectives.

– They provide opportunities for consensus and team building around a common language and a shared understanding and perception.

– They can be performed by external auditors or through self-assessment.

One of the earliest maturity models is Crosby's Quality Management Maturity Grid (QMMG) [CRO 79], which was developed to evaluate the status and evolution of a firm's approach to quality management. Subsequently, other maturity models have been proposed for a range of activities including quality assurance [CRO 79], software development [PAU 93], supplier relationships [MAC 94], innovation [CHI 96], product design [FRA 02], R&D effectiveness [MCG 96], product reliability [SAN 00] and KM [HSI 09]. One of the best-known maturity models is the Capability Maturity Model (CMM) for software engineering (based on the Process Maturity Framework of Watts Humphrey [PAU 93], and developed at the Software Engineering Institute (SEI)). Unlike the other maturity models, CMM is a more extensive framework in which each maturity level contains a number of key process areas (KPAs) containing common features and key practices to achieve stated goals. A number of studies of the software CMM have shown links between maturity and software quality (e.g. [HAR 00]). This model (with multiple variations) is widely used in the software industry.

Nowadays, several maturity models have been proposed that aim at clearly identifying the organizational competences associated with the best practices [FRA 02]. In practice, however, many maturity models are intended to be used as part of an improvement process, and not primarily as absolute measures of performance [FRA 02]. Few maturity models have been validated in the way of performance assessment. An exception is Dooley *et al.*'s study [DOO 91] that demonstrated a positive correlation between new product development (NPD) process maturity and outcome.

1.2.2. *Knowledge-oriented maturity models*

The interest in KM dates back to the early 1990s when companies realized the strategic value of knowledge as a competitive resource and a factor of stability for their survival [SPE 96]. There is more than one definition of KM. Mentzas [MEN 04, p. 116] defines KM as the "discipline of enabling individuals, teams and entire organizations to collectively and systematically create, share and apply knowledge, to better achieve the business objectives". KM generally refers to how organizations create, retain and share knowledge [ARG 99, HUB 91]. It involves the panoply of procedures and techniques used to get the most from an organization's tacit and codified know and know-how [TEE 00]. According to McDermott [MCD 02], "tacit knowledge is the real gold in knowledge management and CoPs are the key to unlocking this hidden treasure". Wenger [WEN 98] defines CoP as a group of people who share a concern, a set of problems or a passion about a topic and who deepen their knowledge and expertise in this area by interacting on an ongoing basis. It is distinguished by three essential characteristics: a joint enterprise, a mutual commitment and shared repository/capital [WEN 02]. On the one hand and in the broadest sense, Correa *et al.* [COR 01] consider any community as a KC where members share knowledge (tacit or explicit) around an interest, a practice or a project activity. On the other hand, Cummings [CUM 03] posits that knowledge sharing is the means by which an organization obtains access to its own and other organizations' knowledge. In the case of these communities, Bresman *et al.* [BRE 99] argued that individuals will only participate willingly in knowledge sharing once they share a sense of identity (or belonging) with others. This sense of identity is one of the several key factors to reach maturity for a community.

In the context of this research, we define *community maturity as a community's maximum capability to manage knowledge where community members actively interact/participate and effectively collaborate, reach mutual commitment based on a well-shared capital and adjust their efforts and behaviors in fulfilling the community mission by producing high-quality outcomes.*

Recently, a number of maturity models related to KM have been proposed: the GKMMM [PEE 06] is descriptive and normative. It describes the important characteristics of an organization's KM maturity level and offers Key Process Areas that characterize the ideal types of behavior that would be expected in an organization implementing KM. The KMAP [GAL 08] is based on the qualitative GKMMM [PEE 06] and Q-Assess developed by Science Applications International Corporation (SAIC). Q-Assess represented 12 subassessments to assess levels of maturity across three KPAs: people, processes and technology. This model allows assessing workgroups, and it highlights weaknesses and gives recommendations to deal with them. The MGKME [GRU 08] is composed of two levels: the underlying level and the operating level. Under each category, many key issues are focused upon and addressed in the assessment process. They consist of managerial guiding principles, *ad hoc* infrastructures, generic KM processes, organizational learning processes, and methods and supporting tools. The KNM [HSI 09] is developed in order to navigate the KM implementation journey. This maturity model consists of two frameworks, namely: evaluation framework and calculation framework. The first one addresses three management targets: culture, KM process and information technology. The second one is characterized by a four-step algorithm model.

Each of the above maturity models deals with KM evaluation within organization; thus, it correlates maturity levels only with KM evolution stages and do not deal with many characteristics of communities: common values, sense of identity, history, etc. These models are not intended to assess communities in an informal mode in intra- or inter-organizational setting, even less in a holistic manner from a KM perspective. They address, more specifically, a formal project mode context in intra-organizational setting. Many of these models are descriptive and normative (e.g. GKMMM and MGKME), they do not prescribe or present actions to perform in order to address weaknesses revealed by the model.

Very few maturity models related to communities have been proposed. First, the community evolution model proposes five main stages as community maturity levels, which are potential, building, engaged, active and adaptive [GON 01]. For each of these stages, they defined fundamental functions and used three perspectives in order to describe the characteristics of every maturity stage. These perspectives are the behavior of people, degree and type of process support, and types of technology encountered at each stage. Second, the maturity model presents four stages of maturity (building, growth, adaptive and close) [LEE 10]. This model gives a snapshot of the current community maturity level based on a set of critical success factors, analyzes the stage and proposes a guide for improving the CoP. These maturity models are not all knowledge-oriented *per se*. Most are inspired from the five-staged CMM model without trying to focus on the originality of communities and to develop a maturity model that fit exactly with them. These models aim to assess communities in an intra-organizational context under a set of characteristics related to maturity stages. Furthermore, based on these models, we cannot differentiate a community from a social network or even a project team. Moreover, these models may not be generalized on different types of community since they focused mainly on CoPs.

Name	GKMMM	KMAP	MGKME	KNM	CEM	MM	CoMM
Reference	[PEE 06]	[GAL 08]	[GRU 08]	[HSI 09]	[GON 01]	[LEE 10]	Current research
Results focus	Descriptive	Prescriptive	Descriptive	Descriptive	Descriptive	Prescriptive	Prescriptive
Goal	Intra-organizational KM assessment	Intra-organizational KM assessment	Intra-organizational KM assessment	Intra-organizational KM assessment	Intra-organizational CoP assessment	Intra-organizational CoP assessment	Intra- and cross-organizational community assessment
	Enterprise	Enterprise	Enterprise	Enterprise	CoP	CoP	Any community
Work mode	Formal project mode	Formal project mode	Formal project mode	Formal project mode	Informal community mode	Informal community mode	Formal project mode and informal community mode
Assessment focus	KM evolution stages (inspired from CMM)	KM evolution stages (inspired from CMM and based on GKMMM)	Underlying and operating levels (derived from the Nonaka and Takeuchi's SECI model [NON 95])	Evaluation and calculation frameworks (inspired from CMM and other KM maturity models)	Community Evolution stages (community lifecycle)	Community Evolution stages (community lifecycle) basing on a set of critical success factors	Holistically (fitting with communities' characteristics and stages)

Table 1.1. *Comparison of CoMM with other maturity models*

The main objective of the study reported in this chapter is to present the blueprint for a new CoMM based on the literature, which addresses some of the limitations described earlier. This prescriptive model is sufficiently generic to be applied to all types of communities and networks. It aims to assess the KM maturity of a given community holistically. Further, it supports the development of recommendations to improve the quality of outcomes and therefore the performance.

1.3. Method

The present research is based on a design science, an inductive approach. Design science research tries to meet the identified business needs through the building and evaluation of artifacts [HEV 04]. These artifacts are built to address unsolved problems, and are evaluated with respect to the utility they provide in solving these problems. This approach is very suitable for the development and application/evaluation of the CoMM by demonstrating its practical feasibility and utility through pilot and field studies according to Hevner *et al.*'s [HEV 04, p. 86] design evaluation framework.

Constructs, models, methods and instantiations are the four design artifacts produced by design science research in information systems (IS) [MAR 95]. In our research, the CoMM artifacts would be represented as follows:

– *Constructs*: the CoMM structure that describes the community characteristics (areas of concerns or topics) and their related criteria.

– *Model*: the CoMM questionnaire that includes questions, levels of rating and mathematical equations for analysis.

– *Method*: the CoMM method that (1) defines the steps and provides guidance on how to run the CoMM questionnaire in the field and (2) supports the development of recommendations.

– *Instantiation*: the CoMM tool that is a customized MS Excel application that represents the implementation of the above artifacts and enables the execution of a concrete assessment.

The development and application of the CoMM can be summarized as follows. First, based on the literature, we identified the main previous research in the area of maturity models in general and the knowledge-oriented ones in particular. Second, to maximize the proposed maturity model's relevance and practical applicability, KM experts were involved from the early stages (see section 1.4.1) in the development of CoMM artifacts (focus group meetings, see section 1.4.2) and the implementation in the field (pilot studies, see section 1.4.1). Third, the model was field tested within a CKO professional association to evaluate its artifacts on the ground (see section 1.5). Further field studies should be continued to enhance the quality of the CoMM artifacts (structure, questionnaire, method and tool) still under validation.

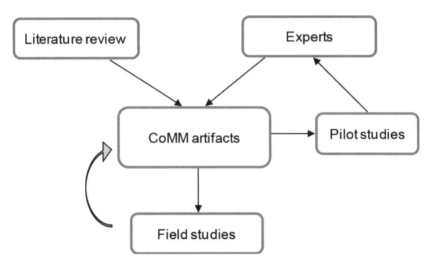

Figure 1.1. *CoMM development and application steps*

1.4. The CoMM

1.4.1. *The development*

The CoMM was developed in cooperation with a focus group consisting of professional KM experts. These experts were accustomed to meeting in the context of a professional association (1) to share their best practices regarding methods, techniques and tools, (2) to get their peers' feedback on case studies and (3) to attend special presentations on the latest trends in the KM area. The involvement of the experts' group enabled us, in the words of Hevner *et al.*'s research framework [HEV 04, p. 80], "to combine relevance and rigor by meeting a business need with applicable knowledge" and so to maximize the resulting artifacts' relevance and applicability. In the following, we report on the focus group meetings on the CoMM development between January 2007 and March 2008. The goals of these meetings were threefold. First, to build a generic CoMM for the holistic assessment of a community based on previous maturity models. Second, to apply the model in practice through pilot and field studies. Finally, to provide guidelines and a tool to enable practitioners for conducting self-assessments with the model.

1.4.1.1. *Participants*

The focus group experts included 12 CKOs working for different companies of different sizes (ranging from 1,000–5,000 to 100,000–200,000 employees, including seven multinational firms) in different sectors (including automotive, software, audiovisual, civil engineering and telecommunications). The participants held at least a Master's degree (MSc or MBA; two held a PhD) from different areas (including industrial design, mechanical engineering, human resources, management, computer science and ergonomics). They had at least 10–15 years of work experience, with 58% of them having 5–9 years as a CKO. The average age of the CKOs was 44 years; 75% were male. Table 1.3 provides more details on participants.

1.4.1.2. *Focus group process*

The development of the CoMM took more than 1 year. The focus group process consisted of 3-h-long monthly meetings. Seven meetings were used to work on the CoMM artifacts, three meetings for participants' feedback on pilot studies and three hosted external presentations related to maturity models and community-based KM approach from professional and research perspectives. The focus group meetings were facilitated by a researcher. The participants expressed the following critical requirements for the CoMM:

– *Resource efficient*: the CoMM should be quick to complete.

– *Rich data*: the CoMM should report on different points of view and concerns from the workplace, using both quantitative and qualitative data.

– *Limited need for further advanced data analysis*: the supporting tool should provide integrated support for the interpretation of the results.

– *Self-assessment*: practitioners should be able to apply the CoMM themselves.

– *Constructive learning*: the CoMM should promote community consolidation and organizational learning rather than control.

The main seven working meetings as the focus group process steps can be summarized as follows:

– The *first step* consisted of the generation of the antecedents to KM within communities. Following this meeting, two thematic presentations were planned on the topic.

– The *second step* was to generate the requirements, analysis levels and topics of analysis for a useful CoMM. One presentation was provided after this meeting on a literature review of KM maturity models.

– The goal of the *third step* was to generate during the meeting the constructs of the CoMM in terms of criteria and levels of assessment.

– The *fourth step* focused on the development of the CoMM questionnaire in terms of items (questions), rating levels, average calculations and weightings.

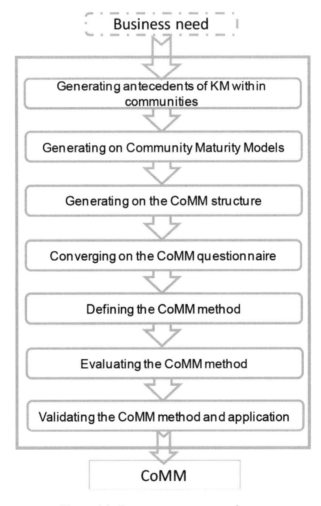

Figure 1.2. *Focus group process and steps*

– The *fifth step* addressed the CoMM method in terms of project scope, respondents' selection and questionnaire running in practice. Following this meeting, the CoMM was tested in two pilot studies (i.e. for a sound engineering community and a sustainable development community) that were organized in the companies of two of the participants (i.e. the audiovisual CKO and the aeronautic CKO, respectively). As a result, two feedback presentations and group discussions were planned.

– In the *sixth step*, the use of the CoMM method was evaluated. Several adjustments and improvements were proposed and discussed in this meeting. After that, the CoMM tool was designed (by a third party) and another pilot study (for a change management community) was presented by the IT consulting CKO.

– In the *final step*, both the CoMM method and tool were approved by the focus group in the presence of the executive president of the association who was interested in applying the CoMM within the association (see section 1.5).

1.4.2. *The description*

The CoMM aims to assess the maturity of a given community holistically from a KM perspective. It supports the development of recommendations in the form of an action plan to reach improved quality and performance. Its applicability is not limited to a particular type of community (of practice, of interest, virtual, etc.) but to any KC. The model can be used for different organizational settings (intra- or inter-organizational).

1.4.2.1. *Structure*

Inspired by the maturity model literature, CoMM distinguishes between four maturity levels: *ad hoc*, exploring, managing and optimizing. At the *ad hoc level*, the community is emerging (but not yet as such) and therefore immature to effectively manage knowledge (emergence or forming stage). Members have many difficulties in interacting/participating and effectively collaborating, reaching mutual commitment based on a shared capital and adjusting their efforts and behaviors in fulfilling the community's mission by producing high-quality outcomes. At the *exploring level*, the community is at the structuring stage and members are well aware of their weaknesses in terms of maturity to manage knowledge. Members try to build mutual commitment based on a shared capital, but are faced with many challenges. Some initiatives to address these are attempted but without major impacts.

At the *managing level*, the maturity of the community is quite good (maturation or performing stage), but there still is room for improvement. In general, members have quite a good sense of community and are able to produce good-quality outcomes. At the *optimizing level*, the community is mature enough to manage (and even to create) knowledge and very well structured (consolidation or norming stage). Members perform/operate together optimally and are able to accomplish high-quality outcomes.

Unlike the other maturity models discussed earlier, CoMM explores the maturity of a given community holistically from a KM perspective related to its basic characteristics. The following areas of concerns (inspired mostly from [WEN 98]) were considered essential by the participants in the focus group meetings to analyze the maturity of a community:

– *Joint enterprise (action):* all that makes a community an autonomous entity: practices, missions/objectives, interests, production, etc.

– *Mutual commitment:* mutual aid relationship among members that is necessary for knowledge sharing [CRA 01]. It is also the realization of actions to maintain coherence, which is necessary within a KC.

– *Shared capital:* it is the whole informational capital created, retained and shared by the community, which allows its members to create new knowledge starting through interaction, participation and collaboration.

– *Collaborative work:* collaborative tasks/activities and processes carried out by members within the community with the goal of sharing and creating knowledge (experiments, know-how, best practices, etc.). It is also methods and technologies that support them [BOU 12].

For each area of concern, a number of criteria were defined (see Table 1.2). These criteria represent the topics for a questionnaire (CoMM questionnaire). Each criterion is represented by an item that is evaluated on a four-level scale. To support the respondents, the levels of each criterion are described briefly, with examples wherever possible.

Respondents are allowed to provide scores such as "0.5", "1.5", "2.5" and "3.5". When a respondent cannot answer, no score is recorded. The calculation of points provides the level of maturity (*ad hoc* (<20%), exploring (20–50%), managing (50–80%) and optimizing (80%–100%)).

Areas of concern	Criteria	References
Joint enterprise	1. Legitimacy	[DOW 75]
	2. Mission	[DRE 87]
	3. Common areas of interest	[WEN 98]
	4. Knowledge creation/construction	[NON 94]
	5. Management endorsement	[KAY 02, MUN 07]
Mutual commitment	6. Admission of members	–
	7. Code of conduct	[PAI 94]
	8. Motivation	[OST 00]
	9. Level of participation	[DRI 78]
	10. Mutual trust	[BAI 86]
Shared capital	11. History	–
	12. Common repository	[BER 94]
	13. Information capital	[ATK 93]
	14. Common values	[MAS 92]
	15. Sense of identity	[GRE 58, BRE 99]
Collaborative work	16. Communication	[SHA 48, KHA 06]
	17. Animation, facilitation and coordination	[CLA 93, MAL 94]
	18. Cooperation and collaboration	[SCH 94, BRI 03, BOU 07]
	19. Knowledge and collaboration technologies	[JOH 91, GRI 03, GRE 08]

Table 1.2. *CoMM structure*

JOINT ENTERPRISE
Mission
What is the nature of the community' mission?

Level 1   Undefined
The community has not clearly identified mission.

Level 2   Blur
Each member within the community defines its own missions, according to his/her perception of the community objectives

Level 3   Clear
The community defines itself its missions collectively.

Level 4   Precise
The missions are in line with a predefined framework/strategy.

Score (from 1 to 4)

Figure 1.3. *Example of criterion in CoMM (captured from the CoMM tool)*

In essence, the CoMM is structured as a library of criteria. Sometimes, not all criteria are relevant. So, the evaluators can decide which criteria fit better with a particular context. They can also decide to expand the set of criteria. Also, for some contexts, certain criteria may be more important than others. In such situations, it is possible to assign different weights to the criteria.

1.4.2.2. Process

The CoMM method defines the steps to perform the analysis. Figure 1.4 shows the seven main steps in the method.

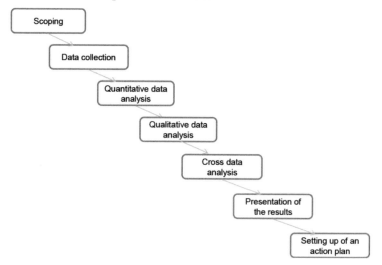

Figure 1.4. *The seven steps in the CoMM method*

At the scoping step, the purpose of the CoMM analysis is defined according to the organizational context and business needs and strategy. The boundaries of the analysis are precisely defined before starting. The reasons for performing the assessment should be communicated to all the community members. It is important to present this as a holistic community assessment to improve the overall performance, rather than as an individual evaluation of members.

The data collection is performed through individual and/or collective interviews based on the CoMM questionnaire (quantitative data). The selection of members should be representative of the target community according to their roles (leader, coordinator, expert, contributor/active member, etc.). During interviews, qualitative observations should be collected to enrich the analysis and gain a deeper understanding of any perception differences that may exist. After the data collection, a first quantitative data analysis is performed using the CoMM tool (see below). This analysis presents individual perceptions about the knowledge-oriented maturity of the community. It also helps us to identify critical perception differences concerning the different criteria. The qualitative data analysis (that could be done with a content analysis method based on statements collected during interviews) helps us to get a more in-depth understanding of these perception differences for each criterion or group of criteria (area of concern or topic). Follow-up discussions and consensus building efforts could be carried out for relevant scores, in order to settle on an acceptable assessment. The cross-analysis may yield additional interpretations by combining criteria for specific measurements of capabilities according to the aim of the assessment, such as knowledge sharing (criteria 8, 9, 12 and 13), social capital (criteria 6, 7, 10, 11, 12, 13, 14 and 15), value creation (criteria 4, 9 and 18) and organizational learning (criteria 12, 13, 17, 18 and 19).

The results can be presented through the CoMM: (1) individual spider diagrams of all criteria scores individually or grouped by topic. (2) Superposition of individual spider diagrams showing the rating gaps on individual criteria or topics. (3) Comparison curves, which allow visualizing perception differences between different respondents regarding the same criterion. This helps us to identify criteria for which it is necessary to collect additional information. (4) Collective spider diagrams of all criteria scores individually or grouped by topic. These represent the collective perception of the maturity of the community. (5) Cloud matrices showing the combination of criteria.

The last step of the CoMM method concerns the definition of an action plan. It helps in the framing of concrete recommendations in terms of actions to improve the community performance and quality of outcomes. Such actions may involve a variety of initiatives, for example the clarification of the community missions, strengthening of the sense of community/identity, developing a charter/code of good conduct, training on virtual facilitation techniques and providing the appropriate collaboration technologies.

1.4.2.3. *The CoMM tool*

CoMM Excel application was customized to allow data collection quantitatively and qualitatively during the interviews and to analyze the quantitative data automatically. It provides different presentations of results and the results' report generation (spiders, curves, etc.).

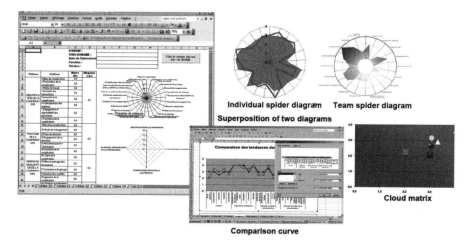

Figure 1.5. *The CoMM tool data collection and analysis*

1.5. Application within a CKO professional association

1.5.1. *Overview of need*

As we mentioned earlier, the CoMM was developed in cooperation with KM experts from a French KM association. This non-profit industrial association of CKOs was founded more than 10 years ago. Its objectives are:

– to develop an activity of cross-sector dialogue and debates between decision makers, practitioners and experts around the KM field;

– to help the managers to locate their action compared to the major evolutions in this strategic field;

– to propose think tanks, meetings (face-to-face and virtual), documents, best practices, etc., allowing to collect rich and global information in a very short time;

– to increase the dialogue between stakeholders and extend networks;

– to provide the members with an operational tool kit and guidelines helping them to implement steps of KM in their organizations.

This association functions by thematic workgroups, which work on topics identified as crucial for KM: economic aspects, change management, human resource and competence management, business intelligence, collaboration, innovation, communities and social networks, etc. Each workgroup, led and facilitated by a chair, produces deliverables that are integrated into the association knowledge capital to be shared by all the members through an Intranet platform (shared space), reports, multimedia CD-ROMs, trainings, etc. Particular and specific events allow gathering all the members for more informal exchanges.

The association is considered first, by players and environment, as a CoP in the KM field since all the developed topics are in the KM field, and second as a KC since its main objective is to share and produce knowledge among members. The CoMM is one of its future deliverables. It is developed in the framework of the communities and social networks workgroup. The executive president of the association was interested to apply the CoMM within the association itself, as a field evaluation, among all members and workgroups to assess whether the association is an efficient KC or not, able to help members and organizations to share knowledge (e.g. best practices), and to see how to improve the association management and quality of outcomes.

1.5.2. *Field application steps*

The field application followed the CoMM method steps. As presented to members, the objectives of the CoMM analysis were to check:

– if the association had all the required characteristics to be qualified as a KC;

– if the association had adequate capabilities and means to effectively support high-quality KM actions, at least good knowledge sharing;

– if the operation and management (animation) of the association are well made;

– if members are interacting well, participating and collaborating;

– if they have a real shared capital;

– if collaboration technologies provided were well selected and effectively used.

All members of the association, 58 persons in total (39 CKOs, 11 CKO surrogates and 8 KM consultants) from different organizations, were asked to participate to this field application. The CoMM questionnaire was sent to the respondents before the meeting with an introduction to the CoMM objectives. Anonymity and confidentiality of the treatment of the responses were formally assured to ensure the authenticity of the opinions. Sixteen individual interviews and six collective interviews (seven persons each) were conducted face-to-face in French. Next, two collective interviews were conducted to examine perception gaps on some criteria. Each interview lasted approximately 90 min.

During the interviews, the CoMM tool was used for data collection. All interviews were recorded for further qualitative data analysis if needed. After the quantitative (through CoMM Excel application), qualitative (on some specific statements) and cross-data (mainly on knowledge sharing capabilities) analyses, a first report was sent to the respondents to solicit any corrections before the final report was prepared. A final presentation to the association board was scheduled in February 2009 to report on the results and provide recommendations in form of a list of suggested future actions. The final report was posted to all the members.

1.5.3. *Findings*

The findings were reported as a discussion of the different perceptions related to the CoMM criteria and topics. Findings reported to the association members according to the four CoMM areas of concern include:

– *Joint enterprise:* we found similar perceptions about legitimacy of the community, its mission, common areas of interest among members and different perceptions regarding knowledge creation. Indeed, the members' seniority positively impacts their perception of this criterion.

– *Mutual commitment*: we noted different perceptions between new members and old members regarding admission of members. A few years ago this relied on co-optation; today, rather, it relies on a simple statement. There is almost a consensus on mutual trust that governs the association, only some exceptions related to the consultant profile.

– *Shared capital:* we found different perceptions on common repository. Even if sharing is one of the most important key elements of the KC, members do not care to share information and knowledge optimally. However, they have the same understanding of concepts and believe in the existence of valuable information capital held by the association.

– *Collaborative work:* we noted different perceptions among members on the community animation and the degree of use of collaboration technologies from workgroup to another. This depends on the generation to which each one belongs. The older generation is more familiar with face-to-face meetings which are expensive and difficult to organize. Facilitation skills in face-to-face situations are different from virtual situations.

Through the qualitative data analysis (in this case, limited to a quick reviewing of respondents' statements), we found some concerns among members about the involvement of consultants in the association. They are sometimes perceived as "lurkers" or opportunists, i.e. people who take much more than they give/share. Turnover among the members is quite common. However, a core has already been formed a few years previously. For some, association activities are more beneficial for former members. In what is shared, we can find different types of information and knowledge. Some are very interesting and others not at all. Knowledge sharing can be further improved and optimized.

The general findings reported can be summarized as follows:

– The KM association is a real KC, which is very useful for sharing best practices between members and organizations. Many means are proposed for this: monthly face-to-face workgroup meetings, meeting minutes, a shared intranet platform based on a content management system (CMS), workgroup-based organization and deliverables, publications (three books and two CD-ROMs), internal and external training, annual seminar, etc.

– From the outside, this association seems closed off especially to small and medium enterprises (SMEs). Membership fees are high.

– The association is mature enough to share knowledge (best practices, guidelines, tools, etc.). Sharing rules and levels are not sufficiently formalized.

– The maturity level of this association was between the exploring level (42 points) and the managing level. The association has reached the structuring stage.

– Knowledge sharing was considered good enough from the internal viewpoint to the association and less good from the outside viewpoint.

– The involvement of researchers is very appreciated by practitioners.

In the final report, various recommendations were proposed, including:

– Giving a new name to the association for highlighting the openness of its structure (e.g. network or community) and offering three levels of participation: for everyone interested by the KM field as a community/network (third level) and for members who pay their membership fees as a club (second level) with a hard core of board and active members (first level).

– Creating a scientific committee for the association bringing together some VIPs (from the world of academia and business), giving it a better image and evaluating its progress and outcomes.

– Clarifying and better balancing the responsibilities of everyone (board members, facilitators, active members) in the functioning of the association.

– Assessing the performance and outcomes of each workgroup annually.

– Using more Web 2.0 technologies to enhance interaction, participation and knowledge sharing among people within and outside the association, e.g. by using wikis, blogs, RSS, social networks, etc.

– Expanding the activities of the association to become a reference in the KM field and a place of socialization for all players: referencing books, white papers, curriculums, services and providers, funding, tools, surveys, etc.; making the bridge between research and business and facilitating partnerships; participating in scientific events such as conferences; and publishing results such as case studies with the assistance of researchers both in French and English.

After 1 year, three of the suggested recommendations were followed up with concrete actions:

– The third recommendation was clearly mentioned in the priorities of the executive board. Tasks and responsibilities were assigned to each board member, and the role of the facilitator was more clarified and formalized. A scale of confidentiality has been created based on access rights and the level of participation of members.

– Following the fourth recommendation, a new system of workgroup assessment was introduced to annually check the outcomes of each workgroup.

– Following the fifth recommendation, a blog for the association was created and a KMpedia project was launched (a specific online Wikipedia for the KM field).

– Following the sixth recommendation, the association with other academic partners has created a new scientific conference on KM.

1.5.4. *Reflection on the field application of CoMM*

During the application of the CoMM among this field study, we gathered various experiences and feedback regarding the appropriateness and usefulness of CoMM. According to the respondents, the CoMM analysis was interesting and correctly represented their perceptions. It focused on real issues and allowed traditionally "unspoken issues" to surface. They were also satisfied with the feedback provided to the executive board and the subsequent actions that were taken related to the assessment's recommendations. According to the workgroup facilitators, the results were relevant.

According to the board members, the study was satisfactory in terms of results and recommendations, as they confirmed and reinforced some of their own perceptions. This allowed them, for example, to focus more on the functioning of the association and participation of members.

We also received feedback and recommendations from the respondents on the CoMM questionnaire such as the possibility to review some criteria and questions. The respondents stated that some criteria were a little bit difficult to understand. Also, the nuances between levels of responses were sometimes subjective or difficult to distinguish. In addition, they proposed to add some criteria, such as practice diversity related to the generational diversity, and to rename some areas of concern, such as "in-house collaboration" instead of "collaborative work". Finally, they suggested putting a stronger focus on collaboration and social media rather than on knowledge and collaboration technologies. Interestingly, this was complementary to the suggestions expressed by the focus group. However, since the CoMM is developed as a library of criteria, the review of the CoMM structure according to a specific context is possible; therefore, the respondents' suggestions can be easily accommodated. In terms of execution, most respondents (since anonymity and confidentiality were not a big deal in this case) expressed that they preferred the use of collective rather than individual interviews as this would enable a faster application of the CoMM process.

1.6. Discussion and implications

In this chapter, we followed the seven guidelines for design science evaluation as proposed by Hevner *et al.* [HEV 04]. To produce new artifacts (CoMM structure, questionnaire, method and tool) to be added as applicable knowledge to the knowledge base (see IS research framework in [HEV 04, p. 80], we developed a purposeful method and application (*Guideline 1: Design as an artifact*) showing, step by step, how to solve a specific problem related to the holistic assessment of the knowledge-oriented maturity of a community. This problem meets a clear business need as expressed by professionals as a means to reach better productivity and performance of communities (*Guideline 2: Problem relevance*). A total of three pilot case studies in three communities within companies and one field application within a CKO professional association using observational methods were executed to evaluate the appropriateness and usefulness of the CoMM, with the active contribution from a focus group of experts (*Guideline 3: Design evaluation*). Our literature review showed that a CoMM does not appear to be well addressed in the field, while concerned experts confirmed a clear business need (*Guideline 4: Research contributions*). The development was rigorously defined (*Guideline 5: Research rigor*) using a combination of research methods including a literature review, an expert focus group, and empirical studies (*Guideline 6: Design as a search process*). Finally, the results of our study are and will be communicated in two steps (*Guideline 7: Communication of research*): first, the method and initial experiences are presented through publications to other researchers who, we hope, will consolidate and extend the CoMM method and application, and to practitioners who could apply the method and provide feedback and recommendations for its future enhancement. Second, after further study of the method and its application in various contexts (other field studies), top managers could decide to use it as a strategic instrument to improve their communities' performance.

1.7. Conclusion

This research tries to achieve an important business objective aimed at knowledge-intensive organizations, by providing them an instrument for assessing their communities' maturity in this direction. The literature provides some KM maturity models, but most of them are dedicated to the enterprise organizational level. In this chapter, we report on the development and a field application of a new CoMM. It was developed in an inductive perspective to meet a real business need as expressed by 12 CKOs and other experts who are regularly confronted with community performance and innovation challenges. Our contribution is both theoretical and practical as we propose a model, an application method, a supporting tool and empirical evidence of their evaluation. The results should be of interest to academic researchers and information systems practitioners interested in the management and performance of communities and/or social networks. Nevertheless, there are limitations related to this work in order to complete the design science evaluation framework. First, our empirical evidence is based on three pilot studies but only a single field application reported here in addition to three others executed by a third party in different sectors (banking, consulting and education alumni). Furthermore, field studies have to be executed to expand the evaluation of the CoMM artifacts and to further enhance the CoMM. Particular care will have to be taken to ensure that CoMM can take into account all characteristics of a given community in different settings and stages. Second, at this stage, the CoMM cannot yet be used to investigate a correlation between community maturity levels and organizational performance. However, it provides a first step in this direction. We recommend several directions for future research to enhance the current version of CoMM. First, the model has to be applied in an intra- and interorganizational context for different types of community. The experiences from these applications will assist in the further development and evaluation of the CoMM artifacts (structure, questionnaire, method and tool). Second, the weighting of criteria, not detailed in this chapter, should be further explored and correlated with the four levels of maturity. Third, organizational and community performance measures have to be developed to enable an analysis of the relationship between community maturity and organizational productivity.

1.8. Bibliography

[AND 03] ANDERSEN E.S., JASSEN S.A., "Project maturity in organisations", *International Journal of Project Management*, vol. 21, pp. 457–461, 2003.

[ARG 99] ARGOTE L., *Organizational Learning: Creating, Retaining and Transferring Knowledge*, Kluwer, Norwell, MA, 1999.

[ATK 93] ATKESON A., KEHOE P.J., "Industry evolution and transition: the role of information capital", 1993. Available at http://minneapolisfed.org/research/SR/SR162.pdf.

[BAI 86] BAIER A., "Trust and antitrust", *Ethics*, vol. 96, no. 2. pp. 231–260, 1986.

[BER 94] BERNSTEIN P.A., DAYAL U., "An overview of repository technology", *Proceedings of the International Conference on Very Large Data Bases*, pp. 707–713, 12–15 September 1994.

[BOU 07] BOUGHZALA I., *Ingénierie de la Collaboration: Théories, Technologies et Pratiques,* Hermes-Lavoisier, Paris, 2007.

[BOU 12] BOUGHZALA I., *Collaboration Engineering: A Contribution to Its Foundations Through the 2.0 Era*, Lambert Academic Publishing, Saarbrücken, Germany, 2012.

[BRE 99] BRESMAN H., BIRKENSHAW J., NOBEL R., "Knowledge transfer in international acquisitions", *Journal of International Business Studies*, vol. 30, no. 3, pp. 439–462, 1999.

[BRI 03] BRIGGS R.O., de VREEDE G.J., NUNAMAKER J.F., "Collaboration engineering with ThinkLets to pursue sustained success with group support systems", *Journal of Management Information Systems*, vol. 19, no. 4, pp.5–8, 2003.

[BRO 91] BROWN J.S, DUGUID P., "Organizational learning and communities of practice: toward a unified view of working", *Learning and Innovation, Organization Science*, vol. 2, no. 1, pp. 40–57, 1991.

[CHI 96] CHIESA V., COUGHLAN P., VOSS C., "Development of a technical innovation audit", *Journal of Product Innovation Management*, vol. 13, no. 2, pp. 105–136, 1996.

[CLA 93] CLAWSON V.K., BOSTROM R.P., "The facilitation role in group support systems environments", *Proceedings of the 1993 Conference on Computer Personnel Research (SIGCPR '93)*, 1993.

[COR 01] CORREA J.S., FINK D., MORAES C.P., *et al.*, "Supporting knowledge communities with online distance learning system platform", in OKAMOTO T., HARTLEY R., KINSHUK N., KLUS J.P. (eds), *Proceedings of the IEEE International Conference on Advanced Learning Technology: Issues, Achievements and Challenges*, IEEE Computer Society, Madison, USA, pp. 6–8 August 2001.

[CRA 01] CRAMTON C.D., "The mutual knowledge problem and its consequences for dispersed collaboration", *Organization Science*, vol. 12, no. 3, pp. 346–371, 2001.

[CRO 79] CROSBY P.B., *Quality is Free*, McGraw-Hill, New York, 1979.

[CUM 03] CUMMINGS J., *Knowledge Sharing: A Review of the Literature*, The World Bank, Washington, DC, 2003. Available at lnweb18.worldbank.org.

[DOO 91] DOOLEY K., SUBRA A., ANDERSEN J., "Maturity and its impact on new product development project performance", *Research in Engineering Design*, vol. 13, pp. 23–29, 2001.

[DOO 01] DOOLEY, K., SUBRA, A., ANDERSON J., "Maturity and its impact on new product development project performance", *Research in Engineering Design*, vol. 13, pp. 23–29, 2001.

[DOW 75] DOWLING J., PFEFFER J., "Organizational legitimacy: social values and organizational behavior", *The Pacific Sociological Review*, vol. 18, no. 1 pp. 122–136, January 1975.

[DRE 87] DRESSEL P.L., "Mission, organization, and leadership", *The Journal of Higher Education*, vol. 58, no. 1, pp. 101–109, 1987.

[DRI 78] DRISCOLL J.W., "Trust and participation in organizational decision making as predictors of satisfaction", *The Academy of Management Journal*, vol. 21, no. 1, pp. 44–56, March 1978.

[EAR 01] EARL M., "Knowledge management strategies: toward a taxonomy", *Journal of Management Information Systems*, vol. 18, no. 1, pp. 215–233, 2001.

[FRA 02] FRASER P., MOULTRIE J., GREGORY M., "The use of maturity models/grids as a tool in assessing product development capability", *IEEE International Engineering Management Conference*, Cambridge, 2002.

[FRA 03] FRASER P., FARRUKH C., GREGORY M., "Managing product development collaborations – a process maturity approach", *Proceedings of the Institution of Mechanical Engineers*, vol. 217, no. 11, pp. 1499–1519, 2003.

[GAL 08] GALLAGHER P.S., ALTALIB H., "Assessing knowledge management maturity within NASA's Johnson Space Center", *Interservice/Industry Training, Simulation, and Education Conference (I/ITSEC)*, 2008.

[GON 01] GONGOLA P., RIZZUTO C.R., "Evolving communities of practice", *IBM Systems Journal*, vol. 40, pp. 842–862, 2001.

[GRE 58] GREENACRE P., "Early physical determinants in the development of the sense of identity", *Journal of the American Psychoanalytic Association*, vol. 6, pp. 612–627, 1958.

[GRE 08] GREAVES M., MIKAA P., "Semantic web and web 2.0" *Web Semantics: Science, Services and Agents on the World Wide Web*, vol. 6, no. 1, pp. 1–3, 2008.

[GRI 03] GRIFFITH T., SAWYER J., NEALE M., "Virtualness and knowledge in teams: managing the love triangle of organizations, individuals and information technology", *MIS Quarterly*, vol. 27, no. 2, pp. 265–287, 2003.

[GRU 08] GRUNDSTEIN M., "Assessing the enterprise's knowledge management maturity level", *International Journal of Knowledge and Learning*, vol. 4, no. 5, pp. 415–426, 2008.

[HAR 00] HARTER D.E., KRISHMAN M.S., SLAUGHTER S.A., "Effects of process maturity on quality, cycle time, and effort in software product development", *Management Science*, vol. 46, no. 4, pp. 451–466, 2000.

[HEV 04] HEVNER A.R., MARCH S.T., PARK J., *et al.,* "Design science in information systems research", *MIS Quarterly*, vol. 28, no. 1, pp. 75–105, 2004.

[HSI 09] HSIEH P.J., LIN B., LIN C., "The construction and application of knowledge navigator model (KNMTM): the evaluation of knowledge management maturity", *Expert Systems with Applications*, vol. 36, pp. 4087–4100, 2009.

[HUB 91] HUBER G.P., "Organizational learning: the contributing processes and literatures", *Organization Science*, vol. 2, no. 1, pp. 88–115, 1991.

[JOH 91] JOHANSON R., SIBBET D., BENSON S., *et al., Leading Business Teams: How Teams Can Use Technology and Group Process Tools to Enhance Performance*, Addison-Wesley, Reading, MA, 1991.

[KAY 02] KAYWORTH T.R., LEIDNER D., "Leadership effectiveness in global virtual teams", *Journal of Management Information Systems*, vol. 18, no. 3, pp. 7–40, 2001–2002.

[KHA 06] KHAZANCHI D., ZIGURS I., "Patterns for effective management of virtual projects: theory and evidence", *International Journal of E-Collaboration*, vol. 2, no. 3, pp. 25–48, 2006.

[LEE 10] LEE J., SUH E., HONG J., "A maturity model based CoP evaluation framework: a case study of strategic CoPs in a Korean company", *Expert Systems with Applications*, vol. 37, pp. 2670–2681, 2010.

[MAC 94] MACBETH D., FERGUSON N., *Partnership Sourcing: An Integrated Supply Chain Management Approach*, Financial Times/Pitman Publishing, London, 1994.

[MAL 94] MALONE T.W., CROWSTON K., "The interdisciplinary study of coordination", *ACM Computing Surveys*, vol. 26, no. 1, pp. 87–119, March 1994.

[MAR 95] MARCH, S.T., SMITH, G., "Design and natural science research on information technology", *Decision Support Systems*, vol. 15, no. 4, pp. 251–266, 1995.

[MAS 92] MASKIN E., TIROLE J., "The principal-agent relationship with an informed principal, II: common values", *Econometrica*, vol. 60, no. 1, pp. 1–42, 1992.

[MCD 02] MCDERMOTT R., "Measuring the impact of communities", *Knowledge Management Review*, vol. 5, no. 2, pp. 25–30, 2002.

[MCG 96] MCGRATH M.E. (ed.), *Setting the PACE in Product Development: A Guide to Product and Cycle-Time Excellence*, Butterworth-Heinemann, Oxford, 1996.

[MEN 04] MENTZAS G., "A strategic management framework for leveraging knowledge asset", *International Journal of Innovation and Learning*, vol. 1, no. 2, pp. 115–142, 2004.

[MUN 07] MUNKVOLD B., ZIGURS I., "Process and technology challenges in swift-starting virtual teams", *Information & Management*, vol. 44, no. 3, pp. 287–299, April 2007.

[NON 94] NONAKA I., "Dynamic theory of organizational knowledge creation", *Organizational Science*, vol. 5, no. 1, pp. 14–37, 1994.

[NON 95] NONAKA I., TAKEUCHI H., *The Knowledge-Creating Company: How Japanese Companies Create the Dynamics of Innovation*, Oxford University Press, Oxford, 1995.

[OST 00] OSTERLOH M., FREY B.S., "Motivation, knowledge transfer, and organizational forms", *Organization Science*, vol. 11, no. 5, pp. 538–550, 2000.

[PAI 94] PAINE L.S., "Managing for organizational integrity", *Harvard Business Review*, Boston, March–April 1994. Available at http://cism.my/upload/article/201106171723110.Managing%20organizational%20integrity.pdf.

[PAU 93] PAULK M.C., CURTIS B., CHRISSIS M.B., *et al.*, "Capability maturity model for software", Version 1.1, Software Engineering Institute Technical Report No. CMU/SEI-93-TR-24, 1993.

[PEE 06] PEE L.G., TEAH H.Y., "Development of a general knowledge management", *The Tenth Pacific Asia Conference on Information Systems (PACIS 2006)*, Kuala Lumpur, Malaysia, 6–9 July 2006.

[PEN 59] PENROSE E., *The Theory of Growth of the Firm*, Basil Blackwell, London, 1959.

[RHE 93] RHEINGOLD H., *The Virtual Community: Homesteading on the Electronic Frontier*, Addison-Wesley, Reading, MA, 1993.

[SAN 00] SANDER P.C., BROMBACHER A.C., "Analysis of quality information flows in the product creation process of high-volume consumer products", *International Journal of Production Economics*, vol. 67, no. 1, pp. 37–52, 2000.

[SCH 94] SCHMIDT K., *The Organization of Cooperative Work Beyond the Leviathan Conception of the Organization of Cooperative Work*, ACM Press, 1994.

[SHA 48] SHANNON C.E., "A mathematical theory of communication", *The Bell System Technical Journal*, vol. 27, pp. 379–423, 623–656, 1948.

[SPE 96] SPENDER J.C., "Making knowledge the basis of a dynamic theory of the firm", *Strategic Management Journal*, Winter special issue, vol. 17, pp. 45–62, 1996.

[TEE 00] TEECE D., "Strategies for managing knowledge assets: the role of firm structure and industrial context", *Long Range Planning*, vol. 33, pp. 35–54, 2000.

[VER 06] VERBRUG R.M., ANDRIESSEN J.H.E., "The assessment of communities of practice", *Knowledge and Process Management*, vol. 13, no. 1, pp. 13–25, 2006.

[WEN 98] WENGER E., *Communities of Practice: The Social Fabric of a Learning Organization*, Cambridge University Press, NY, 1998.

[WEN 02] WENGER E., MCDERMOTT R., SNYDER W.M., *Cultivating Communities of Practice*, Harvard Business School Press, Cambridge, MA, 2002.

1.9. Appendix

Sector	Firm size	Firm type	Person	Nationality	Age	Gender	Background	Level	Years of work experience	Years of work as CKO
Automotive	100,000–200,000	Multinational	P1	FR	45–49	M	Industrial design	MSc	20–24	0–4
Automotive	10,000–20,000	Multinational	P2	FR	50–54	M	Mechanical engineering	MSc	25–29	5–9
Software edition	1,000–5,000	National	P1	FR	35–39	M	Ergonomics	PhD	10–14	0–4
Audiovisual and communications	1,000–5,000	National	P1	FR	55–59	F	Human resources	MBA	30–34	10–14
Civil engineering	5,000–10,000	Multinational	P1	FR	50–54	M	Cognitive sciences	MSc	25–29	5–9
IS/IT consulting	1,000–5,000	Multinational	P1	FR	40–44	M	IT	MSc	15–19	0–4

Table 1.3. *Expert focus group characteristics*

Chapter 2

Social Networks: Leveraging User Social Data to Empower Collective Intelligence

Online social networks such as Facebook, Twitter or LinkedIn have become extremely popular and ubiquitous. Users are actively connected to these services for discussing and sharing news, events as well as contents of interest. However, they are facing problems such as the disconnected nature of social Websites, user privacy issues and the huge amount of information available for browsing. Consequently, a considerable part of interesting information remains ignored by the users. We present in this chapter a possible answer to this problem based on a new approach consisting of aggregating relevant information from social networks to empower the collective intelligence shared by a given group of users. We have built our solution on a user-centered approach, the main benefit of which is that each user can delegate to the system the tasks of aggregating his/her scattered social data and extracting information relevant to the topics of interest of the group. Moreover, the user is provided with helpful features to make the best decisions for choosing the information he/she is ready to share.

Chapter written by Xuan Truong VU, Marie-Hélène ABEL and Pierre MORIZET-MAHOUDEAUX.

2.1. Introduction

Online social networks, commonly known as social networks, such as Facebook[1], Twitter[2] or LinkedIn[3] have become a very important part of our everyday life. Hundreds of millions of users from around the world are connected to these Websites to freely use their services for both personal and professional purposes. They use them to create, publish and share with others a lot of news, events as well as contents of their respective interests.

Current social networks are different from each other in terms of offered services and privacy policies [KIM 10]. They are also disconnected from each other. Therefore, the users must create and maintain different profiles if they want to be connected to different social networks. Consequently, they have to browse each of the corresponding Websites when they need to search for information.

Moreover, the friends that a given user has on each social network are not necessarily the same and can rapidly grow. Each friend has his/her own interests and may share only a small part with the user. Given the large number of friends of the user, it is not realistic for him/her to manually select information from all information relevant to his/her current interest from all information published by his/her friends.

A major consequence is that a considerable part of information, including those relevant to the user's interests, remains ignored by the user. They, furthermore, prevent users, who may share a common interest, from an efficient Internet working knowledge sharing scenario.

In response to such a problem, we present in this chapter a new approach consisting of aggregating user data from different social networks, and filtering and indexing information relevant to the center of interests of the members of a given group. Taking into account user privacy issues, our approach is user centered. It means that the users grant the system-specific permission to aggregate their different social profiles into aggregated profiles and decide which part of their aggregated information should be shared or not.

---

1 https://www.facebook.com.
2 https://www.twitter.com.
3 https://www.linkedin.com.

This chapter is organized as follow. In section 2.2, we introduce our main motivations and the expected benefit of what we will define as a collective intelligence based on our user-centered social network aggregation approach. Then, we present some recent related works in section 2.3. In section 2.4, we describe an extensible architecture supporting our approach. In section 2.5, we introduce a special feature of our proposed system for supporting decision-making. A use scenario is described in section 2.6 for illustrating the system operation. We present our primary prototype in section 2.7. Finally, we conclude and present our future work.

2.2. Collective intelligence by user-centered social network aggregation

There are a lot of social Websites available on the Internet ranging from very general to domain-specific networks[4]. It is very common that the users are simultaneously connected to several Websites. They use them for two main purposes: (1) as a new type of communication platform [CHE 11] and (2) as a new medium of information sharing [KWA 10].

A huge amount of content is generated on social networks every day by the users. A lot of it is conversations between users while others reflect the users' interests. This content, that we call *social data*, therefore includes a lot of updated personal and social information. Since the users may discuss and share with others any topics on social networks, social data can also be considered as a multidomain data source.

Thus, it is difficult and time-consuming for the social networks users to keep track of and to select interesting information from the enormous amount of social data published by their friends on different social networks. Some commercial solutions such as FriendFeed[5] or Gathera[6] allow users to pull their social accounts in one place and subsequently to search information across different accounts. However, this information is not categorized by the users' center of interests and limited to those belonging to the users and their friends.

On the other hand, some social data may match the scope of interests of a given group, which could be a professional team, a collaborative group or

---

4 http://en.wikipedia.org/wiki/List of social networking websites.
5 http://friendfeed.com/.
6 http://www.gathera.com/.

any community of people sharing common interests. It would be very interesting to be able to capture this information and make it available within the group so that its members can easily access the gathered information at a single point. We can also visit different groups for viewing information relevant to one's different interests. However, the disconnected nature of today's social networks and user privacy issues prevent groups from an efficient Internetworking information collection in both manual and automated ways.

We have considered both of these problems that a group of users and single users are, respectively, facing, at the same time in order to propose solutions that could benefit both the group and the user. Our approach, *collective intelligence by user-centered social network aggregation*, consists of allowing the members of a given group to (1) aggregate their different social profiles and (2) share a part of aggregated information with the group according to its center of interests. Each user who is member of a group can therefore access more interesting information, including the information available from other members of the group who are not yet their social network friends.

Collective intelligence: we expect from this approach that the *collective intelligence* including *knowledge sharing* and *knowledge creation* of the group could be collaboratively empowered by the use of its members' social data. Here are some types of information that we have identified as being useful for the group's collective intelligence.

– *Members' additional interests/expertise*: Each member's interests/expertise is evolving and changing over time. Social data can be an alternative source for updating and enriching one's profile by allowing the uncovering of his/her most recent interests and/or expertise [GAO 12, ORL 12]. Therefore, the group will learn more about each member.

– *New web resources*: social networks are intensively used for publishing and spreading news content and web resources. For example, a significant part of tweets, short messages published by Twitter users, can be considered as *information sharing* [NAA 10]. Most of them contain URLs referring to web pages, thus allowing the discovery of new resources matching the interests of the group.

– *Emerging topics*: by watching recently captured members' additional interests and new web resources, emerging topics could be identified.

– *Possible subgroups*: each member can be connected to some other members on one or several social networks. These relationships and their *interaction degree* [VU 12] will provide extra indicators beside the *similarity indicators* [HOR 10] for efficiently locating some possible subgroups.

– *Extended membership*: some external users, who are not currently members of the group, may be considered for extended memberships when they belong to the lists of contacts of several members of the group. These people could be invited to join the group or lent a certain level of trust if other members would like to reach them for information.

User-centered: our approach depends essentially on the motivation and willingness for sharing personal social data with each of the other members of the group. They are the key components of our approach. We must keep in mind that one of the main tasks is to provide them with helpful means to have the best control over the information that they are ready to share. Therefore, we have adopted a *user-centered* approach. This means that the users are solely responsible for aggregating their own social profiles and for sharing some part of their aggregated information with a given group. Such an approach enables us to considerably reduce user privacy issues since social data are now authenticated and authorized by the users.

Moreover, it is obviously impossible to ask each member to copy their relevant information manually, already published on social networks, into the group. An automated process is necessary to save users from making such manual efforts. It provides users with appropriate tools to which they can grant their permission, set their private settings and their preferences for information sharing. All of these elements should be taken into account during the whole process of information collection and sharing.

We will go deeper into these aspects in the remaining part of this chapter, and to start, we will present related works in section 2.3.

2.3. Related works

With the widespread nature of social networks on the Internet, and the large number of users participating and generating an enormous amount of content in these Websites, there is more and more research related to social networks or more precisely interested in their real and complex data sets. On the basis of how social data are modeled and applied, we have grouped related works into the following three main categories:

– social network analytics;

– social data mining for prediction;

– user-oriented systems.

The *social network analytics* category gathers works that have applied graph algorithms for investigating latent social structures and patterns inside online social networks. They allow building real applications such as *detecting community* [LIM 12], *analyzing information propagation* [LER 12] and *identifying influential users* [WEN 10].

The *social data mining for prediction* category takes advantage of the real-time nature and information-sharing characteristic of social Websites for predicting some real-world events. For example, Sakaki *et al.* [SAK 10] have proposed an earthquake reporting system, which is intended to be able to detect an earthquake in Japan with a high probability merely by monitoring tweets from Twitter. Other systems, like [BOL 10], have extracted public mood states from public tweets to improve the accuracy of prediction of the daily closing values of the stock market.

The third category, *user-oriented systems*, regroups works dealing with aggregating the users' social data from different social networks and user modeling to achieve the users' more comprehensive profiles, which may be used for creating more personalized user experiences. Our research mainly belongs to this category.

User-centered social networks aggregation has recently become a trending topic, which has attracted the attention of both researchers and practitioners. This is a non-trivial problem, which can be split into two principal challenges.

The first challenge is how to uniquely identify users across social Websites. One of the most notable efforts is the Google Social Graph API[7]. This service, including a matching technique for cross profiling based on the user homepage, enables an automatic identification. However, it has been

_____

7 https://developers.google.com/social-graph/.

unavailable since 2012. Another effort has been introduced in [CAR 10] where the authors have proposed an automated matching algorithm that, given an initial set of user attributes such as nickname, gender, birthday and city, is able to compute the probable similarity between these initial attributes and crawled data from social Websites. The more data crawled, the more accurate the algorithm. Nevertheless, due to closeness and authentication requirements of most of popular social networks, few of users' data are publicly available. In our user-centered approach, we do not have to tackle this challenge. The users are directly asked for authenticating and authorizing the system to access and recover their social data. Thus, more users' information may be accessible.

The second challenge is how to merge users' heterogeneous data. Many commercial solutions, commonly called *social network aggregators*, such as FriendFeed and Gathera allow users to handle their different social accounts via a single location. Similarly, Zhang *et al.* [ZHA 13] have introduced a personalized social network aggregator allowing users not only to pull together their social content and activities but also to blend and group friends on different social networks, and rate the friends and their activities as favorite, neutral or disliked. However, these systems simply centralize users' social data but do not really integrate them.

The most important requirement for integrating users' social data is to define a common target data model. Several user models have been presented in [CAR 11, ABD 13]. Plumbaum *et al.* [PLU 11] have presented a *social web user model* intended to fit the needs of social applications. The proposed model encompasses the most frequent user dimensions and attributes available in 17 different social Websites. Nevertheless, no final model has been provided and the social relationship aspect was not considered. Kapsammer *et al.* [KAP 11] have introduced a comprehensive and extensive reference model for social user profiles, which provides concepts to represent users' information as well as meta-information. This work is related to an ongoing research project, and the comprehensibility and computational complexity of the model for domain-specific extensions have not yet been discussed.

A popular solution for social user modeling is to use the friend of a friend (FOAF) vocabulary[8], one of the most popular lightweight ontologies on the

---

8 http://xmlns.com/foaf/spec/.

Semantic Web. FOAF makes it possible to represent the users' personal information and social relations. The authors [ABE 10, ORL 12] have used FOAF as a domain-specific vocabulary for integrating users' social data into aggregated profiles. They have also used the *linked data*, in particular, DBpedia[9] as a cross-domain knowledge base [MEN 12] to enrich the users' aggregated information. We have followed this *Semantic Web* approach for modeling users.

Recent research has begun to seek helpful applications by reusing aggregated users social data. It mainly focuses on retrieving users' interests or expertise and users' relationships that could be later served as input of *social network-based recommender systems* for books, movies [SHA 13], news [ABE 11, OBA 12] and people [HOR 10, DE 11, VU 12].

The originality of our work is the new collaborative use of the users' social data. By sharing their aggregated social information with their group, the members are allowed to empower and enrich the collective intelligence within the same group, because more information will be accessible and new knowledge could even emerge. To our knowledge, this is the first time that such a social and collaborative approach has been proposed.

2.4. Proposed system

In this section, we present a flexible and extensible system, which supports our approach of *user-centered social network aggregation for collaborative intelligence*. This system includes different technical components allowing it not only to save the users from making extra efforts of copying information from social networks but also to give the users a reliable control over the information sharing. Basically, the system is made up of three main modules (Figure 2.1): (1) *user-centered social network aggregation*, (2) *personalized information filtering* and (3) *collaborative knowledge management*. The first module retrieves the users' social data from different social networks with specific permissions granted by the users and then outputs preprocessed data. The second module then extracts from the preprocessed data relevant information by the means of a variety of filters. Finally, the collaborative knowledge management module provides the group with an easy access to the centralized knowledge and helpful

---

9 http://dbpedia.org.

features for creating new knowledge. Each of the three modules is detailed in the following sections.

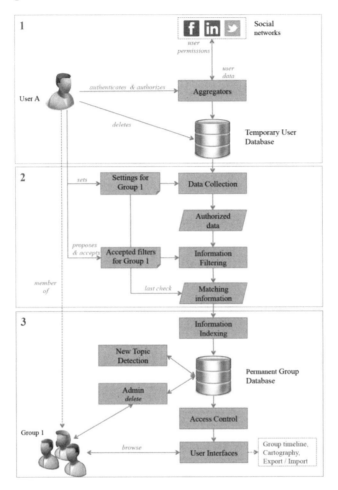

Figure 2.1. *Extensible system for empowering collective intelligence by user-centered social network aggregation: (1) user-centered social network aggregation, (2) personalized information filtering and (3) collaborative knowledge management*

2.4.1. *User-centered social network aggregation*

The user-centered social network aggregation module is designed for gathering, merging and modeling users' social data from various social networks. As mentioned above, we do not have to identify the different social profiles of a unique user, since the user will self-authenticate his/her social profiles and will authorize the system to access these profiles. More personal information, not only limited to publicly available information, can thus become accessible. Nevertheless, we need to define a common user model so that the social data from the user's different profiles can be merged.

A general social user model: we have discussed Facebook, Twitter and LinkedIn, the three most popular social networks in terms of number of users and number of daily-generated content in addition to Google+[10] and OpenSocial[11] Websites for identifying the most frequent user dimensions and properties. So, we have built a *general social user model* including six dimensions as follows:

– The *personal characteristics* dimension includes the user's basic information such as name, bio, current city, gender and so forth.

– The *friends* dimension represents the user's social friendships.

– The *interests* dimension contains the user's declared interests, preferences or expertise.

– The *groups* dimension contains the groups, created by users on social networks, to which the user belongs.

– The *studies* and *works* dimension describes the user's education, such as the schools, colleges or universities that he/she has attended, and the user's workplaces.

– The *user-created contents* or *activities* include conversations and contents produced by the user.

This user model has a twofold function: (1) to indicate to the system which part of the user's social profile may be extracted and then aggregated; (2) to allow the users to choose which information may be shared with their groups.

For representing this user model, we have followed a *Semantic Web* approach. We have mainly based our model on the FOAF vocabulary, which has enough concepts to handle its first five dimensions. Other Semantic Web

10 https://plus.google.com/.
11 http://opensocial.org/.

vocabularies such as Semantically Interlinked Online Communities (SIOC)[12] and Dublin Core[13] have also been used for representing the last dimension, such as presented in the example of Figure 2.2.

```
@prefix sioc: <http://rdfs.org/sioc/spec/> .
@prefix dcterms: <http://purl.org/dc/terms/> .
@prefix twitter: <https://www.twitter.com/>.
<twitter:status_358213711829270528>
  a <sioc:Post> ;
  dcterms:created "2013-07-19T15:16:51+02:00" ;
  sioc:has_creator twitter:user_truongci5 ;
  sioc:content "Intro to Social Media, Monitoring and
  Intelligence http://shar.es/kgSJI  via @sharethis" ;
  sioc:links_to <http://t.co/I6PviiDdyM>
```

Figure 2.2. *Example of the user-created contents and activities dimension*

Moreover, we have managed to match certain users' information to *linked data*, in particular, DBpedia resources. Figure 2.3 illustrates a simplified view of the aggregated user profile where the user is uniquely identified by his/her e-mail. The various social accounts of the same user are represented as separated entities and linked to the user by the *owl:sameAs* concept. Therefore, each social account has its own attributes, which may be duplicated, or even contains conflicting values. Such a representation enables us to preserve in an explicit way the source of any piece of information (e.g. from Facebook or from Twitter). This feature will also ease users' control over their data and the information sharing.

Aggregation process: on the basis of the previous user model, the aggregation process is able to integrate gathered social data into the users' aggregated profiles by the means of a set of automated programs called *aggregators* (see Figure 2.1, part (1)). Each aggregator is dedicated to a specific social network.

These programs are implemented with authentication protocols (e.g. OAuth1.0/2.0[14]) and dedicated APIs (e.g. Facebook Graph API[15] and

---

12 http://sioc-project.org/ontology.
13 http://dublincore.org/documents/dces/.
14 http://oauth.net/.
15 https://developers.facebook.com/docs/reference/api/.

Twitter REST API[16]). So, they can deal with the proprietary social Website for authenticating the users and getting their specific permission to access their social profiles and then for collecting user data.

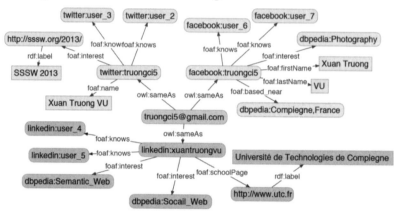

Figure 2.3. *FOAF-based user aggregated profile*

The aggregators are scheduled to regularly (e.g. once or twice a day) recover new user information matching the user model. Otherwise, several Websites such as Facebook and Twitter provide a very helpful feature called *real-time update*, to which our aggregators can subscribe to receive certain changes in user data (e.g. feed, friends and likes) within a couple of minutes of their occurrence.

Gathered user social data will then be put in the aggregated profiles by the same aggregators. For this purpose, they reply on a set of handcrafted mapping rules. These rules enable us to map straightforwardly gathered information to specific FOAF, SIOC concepts, for example:

– facebook:User.name = twitter:User.name = foaf:name

– facebook:User.photo = twitter:User.profile image = foaf.img

– facebook.User.friends = (twitter:User.friends ∧ twitter:User.followers) = foaf:knows

– facebook.User.likes = foaf:interests

– facebook.User.post = twitter:status = sioc:Post

---

16 https://dev.twitter.com/docs/api/1.1.

Most of the properties of *personal characteristics* belong to a range of literals except current location, which will be matched to a related DBpedia place entity. The studies and works dimension is described by two properties *foaf:schoolHomepage* and *foaf:workplaceHomepage* the values of which are web page identifiers (i.e. URL). We have also used prefixes such as *facebook:* or *twitter:* to indicate instances of social networks, for example *facebook:user_truongci5* denotes a Facebook user having "truongci5" as a username or *twitter:status_358213711829270528* denotes a Twitter post identified by the number string "358213711829270528".

Unlike other kinds of user information, the user's interests are less explicit and need additional processing steps before being merged into the unified profiles. In our case, the user's interests are extracted from a list of unstructured texts representing things that users have claimed as belonging to their interest. We have used DBpedia Spotlight[17]and DBpedia keyword search API[18] for searching related DBpedia resources from these texts. Matched DBpedia resources will be inserted instead of the initial texts.

The users' aggregated profiles are then stored in a database called *temporary user database* (see Figure 2.1, part (1)). Each gathered piece of information is stored. In the case of duplicates or conflicts between different social profiles, the user will later be prompted to decide which information should be kept or deleted. The user is also able to delete any of his/her aggregated information stored in the *temporary user database*. In addition, some kind of information such as user activities can be automatically removed out of the temporary user database after a certain time stamp for space-saving reasons.

2.4.2. *Personalized information filtering*

The *information filtering* process is a crucial step of the whole data integration process since it must simultaneously address the user privacy and the information matching issues (see Figure 2.1, part (2)). The first issue is how to give the users better control over their own information so that they can make informed decisions for sharing information. This is a challenging problem considering existing privacy laws of lawful authorities. The second

---

17 https://github.com/dbpedia-spotlight/dbpedia-spotlight.
18 https://github.com/dbpedia/lookup.

issue is how to extract information relevant to the center of interests of a given group from all authorized social data. The two problems are linked. We have chosen a personalized approach in which the users are free to customize their preferences for information sharing including *user settings* and *personalized information filtering*.

User settings: before using our system, each user is informed about its objectives and its operations. The users are asked to grant suitable permission to the system so that the system can access, collect and process his/her social data. The users can revoke granted access whenever they feel it necessary.

As a member of a group, the user shares his/her aggregated profile with other members. It is not necessary to share everything but only the relevant part of the aggregated profile. Before any contribution to the group, the user is therefore required to set the following personal settings:

– which *social profiles* can be applied to the information filtering, for example only information gathered from Facebook or only information gathered from Twitter or both will be considered;

– which information *dimensions* can be applied to the information filtering, for example all dimensions or only *friends* and *interests* dimensions will be analyzed;

– a *final review*, with the possibility of removing undesired information even when it is considered matching the group's interests by the system. If enabled, this option prevents the information from being immediately shared with others but leaves it waiting for the user's validation. If the user does not validate it, then it will be definitively deleted. Otherwise, the information will be accessible within the group.

The two first settings correspond to different scopes (i.e. horizontal and vertical views) of information available for sharing. They are required while the last setting is optional and disabled by default. The users can also modify these settings whenever they want to. The modifications will be taken into account for the next filtering launch.

Personalized information filtering: the information filtering process is also scheduled (e.g. twice a day). At each launch, the social data of all members of a given group is selected from the temporary user database taking into consideration the user settings of each member. This authorized social data must be processed to determine whether it matches to the group's interests. Each group interest is embodied in a specific filter. We have therefore developed different filtering techniques including hashtag-based, keyword-based, ontology-based and empirical methods.

Hashtag-based method: a hashtag is a word or a phrase prefixed with the symbol "#". For example, #UTC could stand for the University of Technology of Compiegne. Hashtags have become very popular and efficient means for grouping and retrieving messages related to a given topic on social Websites, particularly on Twitter. The members of a group are thus encouraged to use their commonly defined hashtags across social networks. It could be a good practice to use hashtags reflecting the name or the main characteristics of the group. Gathered contents including such hashtags will be directly considered pertinent for the group without any processing.

Keyword-based method: keywords can be used for representing the group's interests. Natural language processing techniques can be applied to improve the retrieval quality, for example, by extending a keyword by its derived forms (i.e. singularized and pluralized) and/or its synonyms. However, the keywords should be finely chosen such as specific terms (e.g. "collective intelligence") or named entities (e.g. "UTC") to avoid ambiguity and high recall.

Ontology-based method: an interest can also be represented by a semantic concept/resource of a given ontology. Compared to keywords, semantic concepts give more powerful performance for matching information. First, they provide multilanguage labels for a single concept. Second, it is not necessary to list all concepts semantically linked to each other, in particular those belonging to a same category. DBpedia is appropriate for this task, according to its multidomain knowledge and its large number of resources. Let us consider an example from DBpedia in which the social networking services category[19] is the subject (i.e. *dcterms:subject*) of a lot of networking services such as *dbpedia:Facebook*, *dbpedia:Twitter*, *dbpedia:Myspace*, *dbpedia:Instagram* and *dbpedia:FOAF (software)*. In such a case, only the category will be needed in order to match information related to one of its members.

---

19 http://dbpedia.org/resource/Social_networking_service.

Empirical methods: additional methods can be used before the previous methods in order to reduce the amount of information to be processed. They tend to remove special messages such as self-describing messages or messages replying to a given person. They rely on some simple detection patterns such as emoticons (e.g. "tired and upset :(")) or other usernames (e.g. "take a look at these photos http://bit.ly/Ywg7p6@truongci5") are present.

To comply with the user data control priority, we have adopted a *personalized filters* approach. Each member is free to propose his/her own filters, if they do not yet exist, and that he/she feels it relevant to the group. Furthermore, he/she may accept or ignore the filters proposed by others. He/she can later disable one or some of his/her filters. Only personalized filters, proposed or accepted by the user, are applied for matching his/her social data while others are simply ignored.

At the end of this filtering process, matching information is ready to be transferred into the group's memory except those waiting for the user's last check.

2.4.3. *Collaborative knowledge management*

The collaborative knowledge management module can be considered as a simplified collaborative system since it provides the users with different features to access, to manage and to analyze centralized information. This module contains some important components such as *information indexing*, *new topic detection* and *access control*.

Information indexing: the information-indexing component indexes the information output by the filtering module while storing them into the *permanent group database*. It is very important for two reasons: (1) to keep track of the origin of any piece of information (i.e. which part of the aggregated information   belongs to which person) and (2) to have an efficient access control over centralized information.

Each piece of information contains its original identity (i.e. its attributed identity on its original social network), its content, the time of creation, its source (i.e. a social network) and its included links. The original identity and the source allow referring to the original information on the corresponding social network. Moreover, we will embed in these properties three additional properties: the user who owns the piece of information, the group with which it is shared and the filter that it is matching. Each piece of information relevant to the interests of a given group is therefore indexed by a tuple as follows:

```
<a piece of information, a user, a group, a
filter>
```

With such an indexing technique, it is very easy and quick to answer certain kinds of queries, in the context of a given group, for example:

– all shared information;

– all information shared by a given member;

– all information shared by a given member matching a given filter;

– all information matching a given filter;

– last interests (filters) a given member has been interested in.

Access control: the access control feature is designed to provide a given user with appropriate access to a piece of information. There are two levels of control. The first level checks whether the user is a member of the group to which he/she is trying to access. If the user does not belong to the group, he/she will be refused access. The second level checks whether a member is authorized to view a given piece of information. This complies with our *personalized filters* approach where each member is free to choose the filters that he/she feels necessary. Accordingly, he/she can only view the information matching with the filters that he/she has accepted. Moreover, this access is limited to the information discovered since his/her acceptance of the corresponding filters.

This feature of access control is not an obstacle for information sharing. However, it contributes to creating a fair environment between all members so that they feel more natural and motivated to share their own information.

New topic detection: this feature allows the discovery of new topics of interest from shared information. It uses natural language processing techniques to detect topics (i.e. keywords or key phrases) that repeatedly cooccur with the group's interests in gathered contents. When a new topic exceeds a certain threshold, the system will propose it to all members of the group so that they can set it as a new filter. Consequently, more interesting information can be captured.

In addition, we have considered two useful features for the users. The first feature offers the user the possibility of deleting a piece of information, which was originally his/hers. The second feature allows the user to export a part of shared information so that he/she can use it elsewhere.

2.5. Decision support

As mentioned before, our user-centered approach for social network aggregation attempts not only to facilitate the knowledge sharing inside a given group of people sharing common interests but also to promote knowledge creation. The new topic-discovering feature previously introduced already offers a kind of knowledge creation. However, our main focus is to provide the group with tools supporting group-related decision-making.

Our approach, centered on users and articulated around topics of interests, made it possible to support some group-related decisions such as (1) *expert finding*, (2) *project team building*, (3) *membership admission*, (4) *weak and strong point identification*.

Expert finding consists of finding the right person or people with specific skills and knowledge for archiving a given task. In our proposed system, a member of the group is known for his/her respective interests/expertise. We can also know his/her interest level for each of the topics shared by the group, just by looking the number of his/her late shared information matching the topic.

Project team building is a subsequent task of *expert finding*. Once people with the right expertise are identified for a project, it is interesting to select the best candidates among them to form a good team. We can base the decision on their mutual affinity with the assumption that the more they interact, the more they know each other and could work efficiently together. Using the members' shared information, especially the *friends* dimension, we know whether or not a member is connected to another member on social networks and even if they are connected on more than one social network. Such information gives a primary indicator for computing the users' mutual affinity. Furthermore, to improve this indicator, the system can also consider the *interaction degree* (i.e. how much they talk, mention, reply to each other over their published contents) between the members.

Membership admission is to accept or to deny a membership application of an external user to the group. As this user is not yet a member, the system is not allowed to uncover his/her entire information to the group but only his/her social network relationships (i.e. friends dimension). So if he/she seems to be already connected to several members of the group, he/she could be a credible person.

The last type of decision, *weak and strong point identification*, is the most interesting and really strategic for any professional group. If all members of the group and their respective interests/expertise can be put on the same level, we obtain an overview of the group's available competency. We therefore know the topic for which we have the best expertise and the topic for which we have the weakest expertise according to the number of members specialized in the topic.

Visualization: to deal with these kinds of decisions, we have chosen a visual approach in which the users and the topics of interests, the two most important elements of our systems, can be represented in a dynamic cartography.

Specially, the users and the topics of interests are represented as nodes of an oriented graph and can be linked with each other: (1) by a bidirectional edge between two users if they are connected on at least one social network, (2) by an unidirectional edge from a user to a topic if the user has lately shared something about this topic. The user can visualize the entire graph or focus on a specific node.

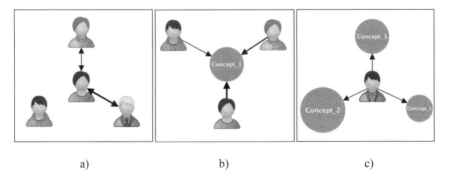

a)   b)   c)

Figure 2.4. *Visualization features: a) one's relationship, b) members who are interested in a given topic, c) one's interested topics*

Figure 2.4 shows some focuses on our cartography. Figure 2.4(a) shows one's relationships with other members of the group. There is not an edge between two members if they are not connected on a social network. The edge thickness reflects the interaction degree between two members. Figure 2.4(b) shows the interest/expertise degree of some members for a given topic. The thicker the edge is, the more the member is interested in (i.e. has shared) the topic. Figure 2.4(c) shows a member's interested topics. The bigger the circle of a topic, the more the member interested in this topic.

On the other hand, each node, both user and topic, is intended to be clickable. The clicked node will become the central subject of the graph. Moreover, shared information related to it is also shown not directly in the graph but in the next information palette like the one illustrated in Figure 2.5.

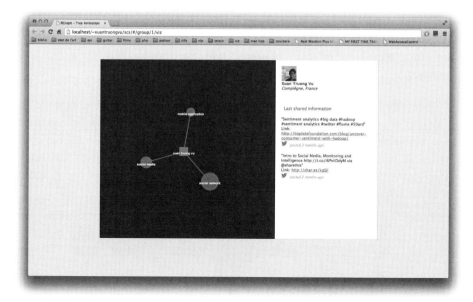

Figure 2.5. *Example of cartography: focus on a member*

We also intend to implement advanced visualization features like the one inspired from bipartite graph[20], which allow us to identify subsets of users

---

20 http://en.wikipedia.org/wiki/Bipartite_graph.

and topics of interest in which every user is linked to every topic. It allows detecting very similar members in terms of shared interests.

With these visualization features, we expect that it will be easier to locate and reach the information needed for making the decisions discussed above.

2.6. Use scenario

In this section, we present a detailed scenario of our system use. Let us consider that Xuan is a user of online social networks and is a member of a group called 50A. The group has other members who are also connected to social networks. They share common interests on social networks, social media and mobile applications. They begin to use the system.

Xuan first creates a profile on the system by only setting up an e-mail and a password. He then decides to give the system *permissions* to access his Facebook and Twitter profiles. Once the valid permission is obtained, the two *aggregators* dedicated to Facebook and Twitter Websites are launched for the first time. They attempt to gather information corresponding to the *general social user model*. Gathered information is integrated into Xuan's *aggregated profile*, which is stored in the *user temporary database*. Xuan checks his aggregated profile and discovers some undesired pieces of information. So he deletes them.

Before beginning to share a part of his aggregated information with the group 50A, Xuan has to set his *settings*. He allows the system to collect information aggregated from both profiles Facebook and Twitter. However, he only accepts that the information of the *basic*, *friends* and *activities* dimensions are shared. He also enables the *last check* option.

He visits the space of the group 50A. There are already several filters: "#50ard" for a *hashtag-based filter* and "social media", "mobile application", "user data" for *keyword-based filters*. Xuan accepts "#50ard", "social media", "user data" but not "mobile application" and proposes his two own filters: "social network" and "http://dbpedia.org/resource/Social_networking_service" for a *concept-based filter*. Consequently, Xuan can only see information matching these accepted and self-proposed filters.

In the background, the system is scheduled to be self-launched, for aggregating social data of each member of the group on the one hand and filtering relevant information from authorized data on the other hand. Let us see the case of Xuan, the *aggregation module* of the system aggregates his new social data, since the last launch, shared on Facebook and Twitter. The *filtering module* selects new information, since the last filtering, of the *activities* dimension and applies Xuan's filters on this information. It then discovers two interesting pieces of information:

– Sentiment analytics #bigdata #hadoop #sentiment analytics #twitter #flume #50ard http://t.co/FxCuVnTRFC.

– Intro to Social Medias, Monitoring and Intelligence http://t.co/ I6PviiDdyM via @sharethis http://shar.es/kgSJI.

The first piece of information is detected by containing the hashtag "50ard" while the second one is detected by including the "social media" keyword. Both are not immediately inserted into the *permanent group database* as Xuan chose *last check* option. Then, the system shows a warning message indicating that there are two pieces of information relevant to the group 50A, which need to be validated. Xuan chooses to validate both so that they are inserted into the database and visible to other members of the group.

The *new topic detection* module is also launched in the background for discovering emerging topics. Regarding Xuan's two pieces of information, "big data" or "sentiment analytics", they could be taken in consideration if they appear repeatedly in others' shared information.

Xuan goes to the group 50A to look for interesting information. He can furthermore choose between the group's *timeline* and the *cartography* to visualize information related to his personalized filters. The timeline displays information one by one in a chronological order while the cartography shows information in a graph. Eventually, Xuan is also able to export the information that he is shared with.

2.7. Prototype

We have developed a first prototype implementing our proposed approach. This is a web-based application that allows the users to use their Facebook, Twitter or LinkedIn accounts to empower and enrich the collective knowledge of a given group to which they belong. The prototype has supported the user's *basic, friends, interests and activities* dimensions.

Figures 2.6–2.8 are screenshots of this prototype illustrating the main implemented features. Figure 2.6 shows the aggregated profile of a user. The user can see his/her connected social profile that he/she has allowed the system to access and to aggregate social data. The user can also visualize his/her aggregated information, which is arranged into four views: (1) profile containing profile information such as name, photo, bio and current city; (2) friends containing the user's social network friends; (3) activities including the user's last published contents; (4) interests including the user's favorite things. There is a small icon beside every piece of information to indicate its provenance (e.g. from Facebook profile or from Twitter profile). The user can decide to delete any undesired piece of information.

Figure 2.7 shows the user settings page. The user can allow the system to access his/her social profiles and can revoke the granted permission. Moreover, the user is able to leave a group or modify his/her personal settings: *authorized profiles, authorized information, last check*.

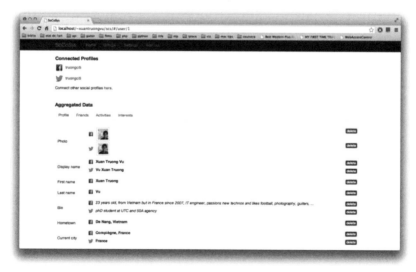

Figure 2.6. *The user's aggregated profile page*

Figure 2.8 is the group space where the user can visualize shared information. The user is also shown the list of filters that he/she has accepted and those proposed by others but not yet validated. He/she can propose his/her own filters. Shared information is displayed one by one in the order of publication date. The user can see the information with his/her owner and its provenance. It is also possible to filter information by clicking on any filter.

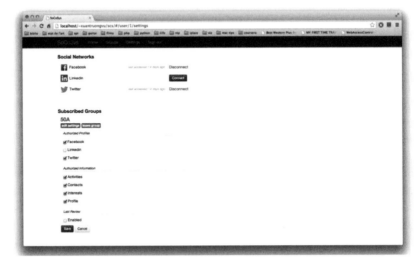

Figure 2.7. *The user's settings page*

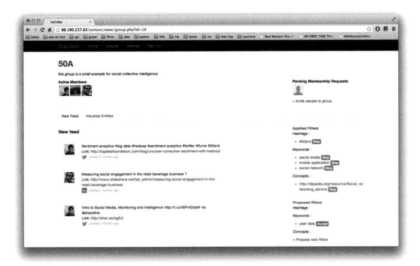

Figure 2.8. *Group page*

2.8. Conclusions and future work

In this chapter, we have introduced a new approach for empowering the collective intelligence by user-centered social network aggregation. We have presented the problems that the users of today's social networks and the group interested in social data are facing. They are the disconnected social Websites, the huge amount of data and the user privacy concerns. We have been convinced that a user-centered approach is an efficient way to deal with these challenges. The users authenticate themselves and authorize the system to access and to uncover their social profiles. According to their own interests, they also have to choose their settings and preference for sharing information with a given group.

We have shown the interests of the collective intelligence empowered by social data: (1) knowledge sharing and (2) knowledge creation. The knowledge sharing features save the users from aggregating, selecting social data and filtering relevant information tasks. They also allow the users to have easy access to more interesting information in a single place. The knowledge creation in our case means the group-related decision-making process. We have discussed several kinds of helpful decisions such as expert finding, project team building, membership admission, and weak and strong point identification. We have not considered creating any tool for automating the decision but to provide an efficient support for that. Therefore, we have presented a visual approach using cartography features to show important information including users and topics of interests.

An extensible system implementing our approach has also been detailed in this chapter. It includes modules for aggregating the users' social data, filtering information appropriate to a given group, and indexing and managing shared knowledge within the group. It is extensible in several ways: increasing the number of supported social networks, adding finer user settings, implementing more reliable types of filters, creating advanced features dedicated to knowledge creation.

Ongoing work will focus on two main tasks. The first one consists of finding out additional methods besides the *user sharing settings* and *personalized filters* features for enhancing the users' control over their shared information. The users should be offered more reliable means to make informed decisions. The second task deals with enhancing our primary prototype. This requires some different efforts. First, we want to improve the information indexing taking into account all essential features that allow the users to easily reach the information needed. Moreover, our user model and shared information model could be updated and the amount of data could rapidly grow. Consequently, we will also consider more efficient database management approaches such as triple-store [ROH 07] or NOSQL database [POK 11]. Lastly, we will implement the cartography features as described earlier.

We also intend to test our final prototype with a real group of users to obtain more social data and feedback. We will then be able to evaluate our approach on three criteria: (1) How motivated are the users for sharing their social data? (2) How do they define and use their topics of interest? (3) How much information is relevant to their common interests?

2.9. Acknowledgments

Part of this work has been developed in cooperation with the 50A Company[21], which has funded this work.

2.10. Bibliography

[ABE 10] ABEL F., HENZE N., HERDER E., *et al.*, "Linkage, aggregation, alignment and enrichment of public user profiles with mypes", *Proceedings of the 6th International Conference on Semantic Systems*, New York, pp. 11:1–11:8, 2010.

[ABE 11] ABEL F., GAO Q., HOUBEN G.-J., *et al.*, "Analyzing temporal dynamics in twitter profiles for personalized recommendations in the social web", *Proceedings of ACM WebSci '11, 3rd International Conference on Web Science*, ACM, Koblenz, Germany, June 2011.

[ABD 13] ABDEL-HAFEZ A., XU Y., "A survey of user modelling in social media websites", *Computer and Information Science*, vol. 6, no. 4, pp. 59–71, 2013.

[OBA 12] O'BANION S., BIRNBAUM L., HAMMOND K., "Social media-driven news personalization", *Proceedings of the 4th ACM RecSys Workshop on Recommender Systems and the Social Web (RSWeb '12)*, ACM, New York, NY, pp. 45–52, 2012.

[BOL 10] BOLLEN J., MAO H., ZENG X.-J., "Twitter mood predicts the stock market", *Journal of Computational Science*, vol. 2, no. 1, pp. 1–8, March 2011. Doi:10.1016/j.jocs.2010.12.007.

---

21 http://50a.fr/.

[CAR 10] CARMAGNOLA F., OSBORNE F., TORRE I., "User data distributed on the social web: how to identify users on different social systems and collecting data about them", *Proceedings of the 1st International Workshop on Information Heterogeneity and Fusion in Recommender Systems, (HetRec '10)*, ACM, New York, NY, pp. 9–15, 2010.

[CAR 11] CARMAGNOLA F., CENA F., GENA C., "User model interoperability: a survey", *User Modeling and User-Adapted Interaction*, vol. 21, no. 3, pp. 285–331, February 2011.

[CHE 11] CHEUNG C.M.K., CHIU P.-Y., LEE M.K.O., "Online social networks: Why do "we" use facebook?" *Computers in Human Behavior*, vol. 27, no. 4, pp. 1337–1343, 2011. Doi:10.1016/j.chb.2010.07.028.

[GAO 11] GAO G., ABEL F., HOUBEN G., "GeniUS: generic user modeling library for the social semantic Web", *Proceedings of the 2011 Joint International Conference on The Semantic Web,* Berlin, Heidelberg, Springer-Verlag, pp. 160–175, 2011. Doi:10.1007/978-3-642-29923-0_11.

[HOR 10] HOROWITZ D., KAMVAR S.D., "The anatomy of a large-scale social search engine", *Proceedings of the 19th International Conference on World Wide Web, (WWW '10)*, ACM, New York, NY, pp. 431–440, 2010.

[KAP 11] KAPSAMMER E., MITSCH S., PROLL B., *et al.*, "Towards a reference model for social user profiles: concept & implementation", *International Workshop on Personalized Access, Profile Management, and Context Awareness in Databases (PersDB) at VLDB 2011*, 2011.

[KIM 10] KIM W., JEONG O.-R., LEE S.-W., "On social web sites", *Information Systems*, vol. 35, no. 2, pp. 215–236, 2010.

[KWA 10] KWAK H., LEE C., PARK H., *et al.*, "What is Twitter, a social network or a news media?", *Proceedings of the 19th International Conference on World Wide Web*, New York, NY, pp. 591–600, 2010.

[LER 12] LERMAN K., GHOSH R., SURACHAWALA T., "Social contagion: an empirical study of information spread on digg and twitter follower graphs", *Journal of CoRR*, 2012. Retrieved from http://arxiv.org/abs/1202.3162.

[LIM 12] LIM K.H., DATTA A., "Finding twitter communities with common interests using following links of celebrities", *Proceedings of the 3rd International Workshop on Modeling Social Media (MSM '12)*, ACM, New York, NY, pp. 25–32, 2012.

[MEN 12] MENDES P.N., JAKOB M., BIZER C., "Dbpedia for NLP: a multilingual cross-domain knowledge base", *Proceedings of the 8th International Conference on Language Resources and Evaluation (LREC '12)*, Istanbul, Turkey, May 2012.

[DE 11] DE MEO P., NOCERA A., TERRACINA G., *et al.*, "Recommendation of similar users, resources and social networks in a social internetworking scenario", *Information Sciences*, vol. 181, no. 7, pp. 1285–1305, April 2011.

[NAA 10] NAAMAN M., BOASE J., LAI C., "Is it really about me?: message content in social awareness streams", *Proceedings of the 2010 ACM Conference on Computer Supported Cooperative Work*, pp. 189–192, 2010.

[ORL 12] ORLANDI F., BRESLIN J., PASSANT A., "Aggregated, interoperable and multi-domain user profiles for the social web", *In Proceedings of the 8th International Conference on Semantic Systems*. New York, NY, USA: ACM, pp. 41–48, 2012. Doi:10.1145/2362499.2362506.

[PLU 11] PLUMBAUM T., WU S., "User modeling for the social semantic Web", *In Proceedings of ISWC,* pp. 1–12, 2011.

[POK 11] POKORNY J., "NoSQL databases: a step to database scalability in web environment", *Proceedings of the 13th International Conference on Information Integration and Web-based Applications and Services (iiWAS '11)*, ACM, New York, NY, pp. 278–283, 2011.

[ROH 07] ROHLOFF K., DEAN M., EMMONS I., *et al.*, "An evaluation of triple-store technologies for large data stores", *Proceedings of the 2007 OTM Confederated International Conference on the Move to Meaningful Internet Systems (OTM '07)*, MEERSMAN R., TARI Z., HERRERO P. (eds), Part II, Springer-Verlag, Berlin, Heidelberg, pp. 1105–1114, 2007.

[SAK 10] SAKAKI T., OKAZAKI M., MATUSO Y., "Earthquake shakes twitter users: real-time event detection by social sensors", *Proceedings of the 19th International Conference on World Wide Web, (WWW '10)*, ACM, New York, NY, pp. 851–860, 2010.

[SHA 13] SHAPIRA B., ROKACH L., FREILIKHMAN S., "Facebook single and cross domain data for recommendation systems", *User Modeling and User-Adapted Interaction*, vol. 23, nos. 2–3, pp. 211–247, 2013.

[VU 12] VU T., BAID A., "Ask, don't search: a social help engine for online social network mobile users", *35th IEEE Sarnoff Symposium*, pp. 1–5, 2012.

[WEN 10] WENG J., LIM E.-P., JIANG J., *et al.*, "Twitterrank: finding topic-sensitive influential twitterers", *Proceedings of the 3rd ACM International Conference on Web Search and Data Mining, (WSDM '10)*, ACM, New York, NY, pp. 261–270, 2010.

[ZHA 13] ZHANG J., WANG Y., VASSILEVA J., "Socconnect: a personalized social network aggregator and recommender", *Information Processing and Management*, vol. 49, no. 3, pp. 721–737, May 2013.

Chapter 3

Sociocultural Knowledge Management toward the Adaptation of a CSCL Environment

3.1. Introduction

Learning together with the use of computers and new technology of information and communications (NTICs) has become very important all around the world whether in organizations or in educational institutions. This is intended to facilitate information access and knowledge sharing. So, the major challenge of computer-supported collaborative learning (CSCL) field is to combine these two facts: learning together while using computer technologies to enhance distant or face-to-face learning. In recent years, the CSCL field has known a widespread deployment. However, despite the existence of a plethora of tools and systems developed in this field, they were not really adopted by institutions and organizations because these systems do not seem to fit well with their practices. To deal with this problem, the researchers in the CSCL field focused on understanding the basic characteristics of human activities during learning, within humanities and social sciences. One of the main issues to arise, which is inspired by the sociocultural theory of Vygotsky [VYG 34], focuses on studying the place of culture and the social side in a human cognitive activity, including the technological dimension. Vygotsky [VYG 34] states that

Chapter written by Fadoua OUAMANI, Narjès Bellamine BEN SAOUD and Henda Hajjami BEN GHÉZALA.

"mental functioning of an individual is intrinsically located in historical institutional, cultural and social contexts". Therefore, to understand human thinking and learning, we must consider their sociocultural contexts.

In fact, the collaborative learning activities involve intensive interactions among collaborators such as articulating knowledge into written, verbal or symbolic forms, authoring articles or posting messages and responding or adding comments to messages posted by others [YAN 04b] and also require the constant generation, transfer and understanding of shared knowledge [LIA 08]. Knowledge collaborators' capabilities to provide knowledge and the motivation to collaborate in the learning process influence the quantity and quality of the knowledge to flow into the virtual learning community [YAN 04b] and are strongly influenced by their social and cultural contexts [NIS 02]. However, the extent to which these benefits are realized depends largely on the effectiveness of group interaction. In other words, understanding and considering learner's cognitive, social, cultural, physical and personal characteristics in intercultural collaboration may enhance or promote their satisfaction with the CSCL environment and therefore their interaction in collaborative learning.

To make collaboration efficient, to enhance the learning procedure and outcomes and to promote knowledge access and sharing, we need to pay attention to the cultural differences between learners. We need to adapt these environments to the sociocultural specificities (national culture and social context) of learners and many of other socioculturally sensitive characteristics (such as personality, cognition, emotion and motivation). In fact, adapting the CSCL environment to sociocultural characteristics of its users is a challenging task [BLA 10]. First, it is a multidisciplinary task that needs to carry studies within humanities and social sciences, educational sciences and computer sciences in order to determine and define two types of variables: (1) sociocultural characteristics of a user, which influence his/her behavior, personality and different states and (2) CSCL variables that are socioculturally sensible. Second, in such environments, the knowledge handled by such adaptation is very specific, semantically rich and holds various relationships among them. So, in order to achieve such a goal (the adaptation of CSCL system to the sociocultural characteristics of its users), we propose an ontology framework based adaptation. This conceptual framework consists of two ontologies: the first one models user sociocultural characteristics and is domain independent. The second one specifies the main collaborative learning concepts. These two ontologies communicate together and share knowledge about the user in order to perform appropriate adaptation tasks through the use of adaptation rules, which are built such that concept values of the first ontology trigger concept values in the second ontology.

The use of ontology allows us to develop a generic conceptualization of sociocultural human characteristics by identifying the sociocultural dynamics of human beings (different cultural and social concepts and relations as well as different concepts and relations that are socioculturally sensible). This generic conceptualization will be considered as a generic profile that can be used in several disciplines. This generic ontology-based profile will promote both the interoperability by enforcing the consistency of cultural data modeling between systems, thus facilitating the reuse of computerized data and cultural automatic reasoning, and therefore allowing systems to take culturally informed decision that may impact on their internal processing as well as on human computer interaction (HCI) [BLA 10].

This chapter is organized as follows: in section 3.2, we will introduce the concept of culture and the sociocultural factors. Then, in section 3.3, we will show the relationship between CSCL, knowledge management (KM) and sociocultural human characteristics. After this, we will provide a number of research that consider the culture discussed in section 3.4. Section 3.5 will be dedicated to the description of the proposed ontology-based sociocultural user profile. Then, in section 3.6, we will depict the proposed ontology framework composed of the latter ontology and the sociocultural aware CSCL domain ontology. In sections 3.5 and 3.6, we will give a detailed description of the concepts and relations of the two ontologies, their sources, their construction processes and how they communicate together to share sociocultural knowledge about the user in order to make the adaptation to the CSCL environment. This will lead us to describe in section 3.7 our adaptation system integrating the ontologies to manage and use the sociocultural knowledge about the user. Finally, we will summarize and discuss our contributions and we will give an overview of our ongoing work.

3.2. The concept of culture and sociocultural factors

The study of culture is important for many disciplines such as psychology, sociology, anthropology, archeology, communication, management and business. However, there are various approaches and methods that have been developed to deal with and discuss cultural matters in these domains. In this section, as we want to define the sociocultural characteristics that distinguish individuals from different cultures, we give a brief overview of our literature study within ethnology and psychology.

3.2.1. *Culture in ethnology*

Ethnology is the branch of anthropology that compares and analyzes the origins, distribution, technology, religion, language and social structure of the ethnic, racial and/or national divisions of humanity [NEW 08]. It offers many definitions of culture. A list of more than 200 different definitions of culture can be found in [KRO 52], classified into six groups (see Table 3.1)

Group	Content
Descriptive	"Enumeration of content"
Historical	"Social heritage and traditions"
Normative	"Rule or way"
Psychological	"Culture as a problem-solving device"
Structural	"Pattern or organization of culture"
Genetic	"Culture as a product or artifact"

Table 3.1. *Classification of culture definitions*

The anthropologist Edward Tylor [TYL 24] is widely known as the first to have given a definition of culture in anthropology. According to him, culture in its wide ethnographic sense is "a complex whole which includes knowledge, beliefs, arts, morals, law, customs and any other capabilities and habits acquired by (wo)man as a member of society".

Anthropologists Agar and Hall [AGA 94, HAL 90] make a link of synonymy between culture and communication; according to them, the concept of culture cannot be understood only through the concept of communication and a communication strategy. Culture is thus defined gradually through dialogue with each other by organizing in a coherent whole all the differences found between two cultures.

The definition of Hofstede [HOF 97] for culture has a great influence on organizational communications and business literatures. In fact, for Hofstede, culture is "the collective programming of the mind which distinguishes the members of a group or class of persons". This definition underlines the fact that culture is a collective activity, which must be conceived as a dynamic process of group identity construction and its conservation. Hofstede [HOF 97] also lists several types of cultures that may be related to ethnic groups, countries, religious groups, tribes and minority groups.

These studies show that culture is considered and defined on the group level. This is not sufficient because individuals can be influenced and inherit characteristics from the group but (s)he can develop his/her own sociocultural particularities. So, in order to study culture at the individual level, we analyze psychology contributions to culture definition and study.

3.2.2. *Culture in psychology*

Cultural psychology is a field of psychology that assumes the idea that culture and mind are inseparable, and that psychological theories grounded in one culture are likely to be limited in applicability when applied to a different culture [SHW 90]. This field includes many other fields, such as social psychology, the culture of development and cognitive psychology. In these fields, many authors [LUR 79, VYG 34, LEO 72, BAK 84] state that the development of thought is mediated by "cultural tools" (material objects and signs) and historically constituted as particular group. The use of these tools enables companies to grow and individuals to control their environment and regulate and develop their thinking. These authors also examine the role of these tools in the reasoning and the articulation of individual consciousness and collective activity. Many other works have shown cultural influences on personality, goals and preferences [OIS 04, ALL 61]. Culture also influences individual needs, motivational states [LIN 77], cognitive states [NIS 02], emotional states [OIS 03, SAN 93, BOE 04] and social roles and situations [ALL 61].

3.2.3. Cultural properties

The above studies have shown that culture is global (it includes all the elements that characterize the group life), shared (individuals of a social group adhere to a set of values and norms to resolve the problems caused by their environment), transmissible (from one generation to another to ensure its continuity over time) and evolutionary (not static to maintain its adaptation to the world).

On the basis of these studies, we present Figure 3.1, which shows that culture has two big dimensions: the individual dimension (which includes individual particularities) and the collective dimension (which includes group characteristics). The two dimensions are complementary: the individual dimension tries to adapt, integrate the collective dimension and build an identity regarding it, and the collective dimension tries to accept, melt and enrich the individual dimension. This is what we call the cultural dynamics.

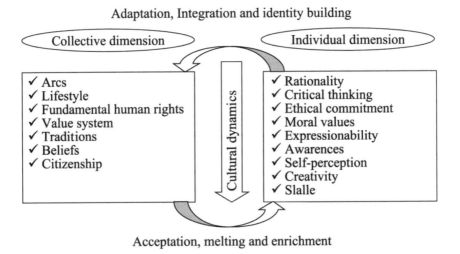

Figure 3.1. *The cultural properties*

The characteristics of the two dimensions show the cultural differences between cultural groups or between two or more individuals belonging to different cultural groups. So, to measure these differences, there are, in the literature, models of culture, especially national culture.

3.2.4. *Models of national culture*

As we have seen above, given the differences between cultures and their different natures, there are models of specific cultural behaviors depending on the degree of importance of the meanings in each culture. Most models for measuring culture are built on the basis of cultural dimensions that best reflect a culture. These dimensions are the realities of cultural cues that convey crucial meanings in cultures. These models offer useful templates for comparing cultures in many ways. A model of culture can be defined according to Herskovitz [HER 50] as a pattern that depicts the forms taken by the elements of a civilization, where models of behavior, which occur among members of society, converge and create a consistent, continuous and distinct lifestyle.

Our study includes models proposed by Kluckhohn and Strodtbeck [KLU 61], Hofstede [HOF 80], Hall [HAL 76], Schwartz [SCH 92], Trompenaars and Hampden-Turner [TRO 93] and House *et al.* [HOU 04]. Each model highlights different aspects of social beliefs, norms and/or values. Thus, we talk about sociocultural factors because they all contain a social side; they find their way and their meaning within a society. The authors [KLU 61] proposed a value-oriented theory of culture. It was one of the earlier models of culture based on value orientations within a social group. They used anthropological theories to identify their five values, which are the relationship with nature, relationship with people, human activities, relationship with time and human nature.

Hofstede [HOF 80] developed a multidimensional model of culture in the late 1970s from a study on the cultural values of IBM employees in over 75 countries. The five dimensions of the model are related to the authority (or power distance), the relationship between group and individual (individualism vs. collectivism), the concepts of masculinity and femininity, management of ambiguity and uncertainty and the long-term orientation opposed to a short-term orientation. The author assigned scores by countries to measure the intensity of each cultural dimension present in the culture of this country.

Another multidimensional model for studying the cultural influences on communication was proposed by Hall [HAL 76]. In his model, we find three cultural dimensions, namely context, time and space. From a psychological perspective, Schwartz [SCH 92] offered a basic human values model, in which he identified universal human values, which are power, achievement, hedonism (behavior is motivated by the desire for pleasure and the avoidance of pain), stimulation, self-direction, universalism, benevolence, tradition, conformity and security.

In [TRO 93], the authors did a survey on cultural differences that arise in professional contexts. On the basis of this survey, they developed their model of seven cultural dimensions that contain universalism and particularism, individualism or collectivism, objectivity or subjectivity, degree of commitment – diffuse or specific – to a person or situation, status assigned or acquired status (achievement vs. ascription), time perspective and relationship with nature.

We provide in this section a comparative and critical study of these models to determine the sociocultural factors needed in our study. Rather than advocating one model or another, we suggest that all models contain important factors that contribute to our understanding of culture. To take advantage of all these theories of culture, we believe that the most productive approach is to integrate and adapt the different models according to their usefulness for a better understanding of the cultural and intercultural context. To do so, we look for common topics that collectively represent the main differences between cultures. Although no single model can cover all aspects of a culture, we believe it is possible to highlight the key cultural features through such an analysis.

Table 3.2 represents the results of our study: five relatively distinct topics emerge from this comparison and the divergence lies in a few dimensions (see other topics) not included in common topics. These dimensions relate to emotions, communication and roles, and we consider that such topics are concepts and characteristics influenced by the cultural dimension.

The power distance determines how power and authority are distributed in a society, whether this distribution is based on concepts of hierarchy or egalitarianism; if social beliefs concern equality or privilege. It is a sociocultural factor that reflects the way in which a culture directs and makes things (values, needs, relationships, professional hierarchies, etc.). So the way that humans behave is structured in culturally defined environments. This factor is crucial both in the organization of tasks in the execution of roles and individual freedom. The implications of such a factor is observed in the way in which individuals take possession of a new artifact and its manipulation in their coordination of a set of artifacts, in adapting them to changes, autonomy, harmony in maintaining relationships with others and the construction of meanings.

Common topics	Model of national culture					
	[KLU 67]	[HOF 80]	[HAL 76]	[SCH 92]	[TRO 93]	[HOU 04]
Power distance		Power distance	Space	Universalism Particularism	Hierarchy Egalitarism	Power distance Gender Egalitarism
Belonging	Relationship with people	Individualism Collectivism		Individualism Collectivism	Conservatism Autonomy	Institutional collectivism In-group collectivism
Relationship with environment	Relationship with nature Human nature	Masculinity Femininity		Relationship with environment	Master harmony	Human orientation Assertiveness Performance orientation
Attitude toward time	Relationship with time	Long term/short term orientation	Time	Time perspective		Future orientation
Control	Human activities	Uncertainty avoidance		Achievement ascription		Uncertainty avoidance
Other topics			Context	Neutral affective Specific diffuse		

Table 3.2. *Comparison of models of national culture*

The belonging defines the fundamental building block of a society, if it is individual or group and determines how a society organizes its collective action. It is also a sociocultural factor that reflects the membership of an individual; it can be political, social, institutional or religious membership. This membership measures the degree of individualism or collectivism of the individual; it takes into account the way in which the individual receives the benefits and values the public interest (community societies) rather than personal interests (individualistic societies). The implications of such a factor will be observed in the handling of artifacts with shared and collective use or with personal use.

The relationship with the environment is also a sociocultural factor. On a social level, it defines how people view the world around them and the nature of their relationship with the natural and social environment, if their goal is to control the environment and events around them or to live in harmony with these external realities

The attitude toward time shows how people in society organize and manage their time to carry out their professional activities and their leisure time activities and how they do their work (in a linear or a nonlinear manner). So this factor occurs in many ways in the way in which cultures perceive the concept of "time" and manage it and structure their activities in time. It also includes the time of change adaptation, time of decision-making, respect for the concept of time, etc. There are two models of behaviors characterized as monochronic (by doing one activity at a time) and polychronic (doing different activities together). However, it should be noted that this factor may vary from one individual to another within the same culture depending on the situation in which it is located and its adaptability.

The control is a mechanism that shows how societies try to insure predictability in the behavior of their members, if they work to control people through uniformly applied rules, policies, laws and social norms or rely more on personal ties or unique circumstances. It involves keeping the political balance at all levels and compensation of behaviors. It includes both uncertainty control and risk control. The uncertainty avoidance reflects the behavior and actions caused by companies to face any future events, especially when changes occur while risk control takes into account behaviors caused and measures undertaken to address a potential for social, financial, physical or moral level. The implications of such a factor are observed in the level of commitment and acceptance both with respect to events, risks or new artifacts.

3.2.5. *Discussion*

The study provided above should be validated by a specialist from the field. The models of culture discussed earlier provide information about well-defined cultural groups such as a nation or a region. When we only use these studies, we risk ignoring the cultural characteristics of an individual, by assigning to him/her the same characteristics of the group to which he/she belongs [OIS 04]. For example, if we simply use the Hofstede scores, we can say that because the Arab countries are countries with high collectivism (low individualism score), then no Arab person will ever have an individualistic tendency. This is totally wrong. These scores reflect general trends of a cultural group of a nation or group of nations. It would be reasonable to speculate that an Arab would be more likely to have a collectivist attitude than an American.

To take culture into account, we need to have a good understanding of this individual and all internal processes of his/her personality, his/her cognition and his/her psychological, emotional, motivational states, as shown in the psychological view discussed earlier.

3.3. The relation between sociocultural human characteristics, KM and CSCL

3.3.1. *CSCL and knowledge sharing*

Collaborative learning reflects the constructivist [ANN 11] and the socioconstructivist [VYG 34] learning theories, where the learner is autonomous and active; he/she actively classifies, analyzes, predicts and creates their own meaning when learning something new, in a collaborative and social dialogue with others. These theories emphasize that collaboration is essential for the development of logical and critical thinking. In this way, instead of being based on information assimilation and memorization, collaborative learning is based on learners of different performance levels, from different cultures, working in groups, sharing a common goal.

Papert's constructionist learning theory [PAP 84] cited in emphasizes the importance of sharing knowledge using concrete artifacts. He states that learning effectively occurs when the learner is "engaged in the construction of something external or at least shareable... a sand castle, a machine, a computer program, a book". According to him, building meaningful and sharable knowledge leads to a cyclic process of externalization of knowledge that is in the mind of the learner and internalization of new structures, as a result of the social interaction around this external artifact. This externalization and internalization cycle seems to coincide with Nonaka and

Takeushi's KM theory [NON 95]. According to them, there are two types of knowledge: explicit and tacit. The first one refers to components that we can codify, and which can be disembodied and transmitted, while the second one refers to knowledge that is "confined in people's mind", which is difficult to articulate and disseminate. However, through social interaction and collaboration, tacit knowledge is transformed into explicit, and individual knowledge is transformed into organizational. Organizational knowledge creation is a result of a continuous and dynamic process of conversion between these two knowledge types.

In fact, collaborative learning communities can be considered as organizations in which the members share the two types of knowledge. However, in an intercultural collaborative learning community, there are two types of challenges: the first one concerns the identification, gathering, analyzing, constructing, sharing and application of sociocultural knowledge and sociocultural practices (sociocultural KM). The second one concerning the externalization of knowledge in an intercultural context seems to be intrinsically difficult. Thus, the system should play two important roles: on the one hand, it should give help to the learner who has difficulties collaborating with a learner from a different culture, and on the other hand, it should create a common ground between learners from different cultures and give mechanisms that enable the sharing of common understanding and conflict resolution.

The ultimate goal of sharing knowledge is the attempt to transfer all individuals' experiences and knowledge to organizational assets and resources [YAN 04a]. In fact, sharing knowledge occurs when an individual is willing to assist as well as learn from others in developing new competencies [SAW 00]. From the idea of sharing-and-retaining knowledge, if individuals share what they have learned, they become more experienced and knowledgeable. By having access to more useful and applicable information from a group, individuals have a greater chance of making decisions more effectively and efficiently. Thus, knowledge accumulates its value when it is shared [SIL 00]. So, intercultural collaborative learning should promote and enhance the sharing of sociocultural knowledge about the learners in order to learn also about the cultures of each other.

3.3.2. *Culture, human mind and KM*

In essence, the human mind is similar to a computer process, which explains psychological events in terms of input, storage and output. Based on the information processing point of view, KM should include five different stages: information definition, information acquisition, information transformation, knowledge construction and knowledge sharing [LIA 05]. Trying to find similarities between the human mind knowledge construction process and the KM process, the authors of [LIA 08] state that "The information definition stage is similar to the stage of knowledge objective. In this stage, the purpose of knowledge construction is to define and clarify the needed knowledge. In other words, the needed knowledge should be defined and confirmed at first before an individual establishes new knowledge. The information acquisition stage is equal to the stage of knowledge gathering, in which an individual expresses his/her interests in finding useful information and attempts to explore and transform external stimuli by reviewing his/her own knowledge structures. The information transformation stage can be viewed as the stage of knowledge analysis whereby an individual selects appropriate information, organizes and integrates it with existing knowledge. The knowledge construction stage is similar to the stage of task knowledge structure. Here, an individual constructs his/her knowledge that is not limited to the results of rote memorization, but also a kind of new knowledge that could be applied in unknown circumstances and used to solve problems. And the last stage is the knowledge sharing stage. The knowledge sharing stage is to share and exchange individual knowledge based on collaborative activities".

However, cultural psychology is a field of psychology that assumes the idea that culture and mind are inseparable, and that psychological theories grounded in one culture are likely to be limited in applicability when applied to a different culture [SHW 90]. This field includes many other fields such as social psychology, the culture of development and cognitive psychology. In these fields, many authors [LUR 79, VYG 34, LEO 72, BAK 84] state that the development of thought is mediated by "cultural tools" (material objects and signs) and historically constituted as a particular group. The use of these tools enables companies to grow and individuals to control their environment and to regulate and develop their thinking. These authors also examine the role of these tools in the reasoning and the articulation of individual consciousness and collective activity. Many other works have shown cultural influences on personality, goals and preferences [OIS 04,

ALL 61]. Culture also influences individual needs, motivational state [LIN 77], cognitive state [NIS 02], emotional state [OIS 03, SAN 93, BOE 04] and social role and situation [ALL 61].

3.3.3. *Discussion*

In this section, we have shown, based on studies found in psychology, anthropology and learning sciences, that we have complementary relationships and cause–effect relationships between sociocultural user characteristics, CSCL domain and KM process: since we are concerned with knowledge, specifically a sociocultural one, we should specify how this knowledge is acquired and learned, how it can be externalized in a collaborative learning activity. To do that, we referred to Nonaka and Takeushi KM theory, which can be also applied to sociocultural knowledge. In fact, as has been proved by studies in cultural psychology (for example, the studies of Vygotsky, Leont'ev and Luria), sociocultural knowledge is transmitted through a socialization process according to which this knowledge is learning in the family, in institutions and mainly through social interactions. It is externalized when learners provide knowledge to others through communication and contribution in a collaborative activity.

Through intercultural interaction, learners from different cultures externalize and share their sociocultural specificities with others and learn about others' culture. The new knowledge is combined with the existing knowledge. This new knowledge is then internalized, for example, as new structures or new patterns of behavior. This kind of knowledge raises an important issue that deals with gathering, analyzing, constructing, sharing and applying sociocultural knowledge, which represents the steps of sociocultural KM. To address this issue, we need to model the sociocultural knowledge.

Moreover, knowledge is created in individual minds and according to constructivism theory the human mind reflection process is similar to knowledge construction and management process. According to this quotation, the human mind does the same activities: first, it should clarify the knowledge needed; then gather this knowledge; after that, it analyzes this knowledge and tries to find new structures and finally the constructed knowledge will be shared in a collaborative activity.

However, as proven by psychological research mentioned above, this process is strongly influenced by culture because mind and culture are inseparable. So, all these tasks are mediated by cultural tools which are material objects and signs provided to each individual by the culture in which he/she evolves. For example, we mention: language tools, cultural symbols and heroes. These tools convey meanings which are different from one culture to another.

This raises two important issues: first, what knowledge is to be modeled and second; how to get sociocultural-aware CSCL systems based on this knowledge.

3.4. Sociocultural considerations in collaborative environments

Little research in collaborative environments, mainly in CSCL and computer-supported collaborative work (CSCW) has addressed the sociocultural issues. Most of this research is empirical investigation, which studies the cultural influences on different characteristics of these environments such as collaboration, negotiation and appropriation of the collaborative tool. This research is often carried out with dyads from the same culture or from different cultures in order to determine the differences between the two cultures concerning these characteristics.

In this section, we give, first, a survey of the existing culturally sensitive collaborative tools. Then, we discuss their limitations.

3.4.1. *Study of existing culturally sensitive tools*

We have studied the few existing collaborative tools developed recently and which are culturally sensitive in different ways (see Table 3.3). For each research work, we determine the application domain, the cultural knowledge taken into account and managed, the approach or technique used to integrate and manage them, whether there is a process of adaptation to cultural characteristics or not and finally the type of the collaboration group studied.

The Alelo project by Johnson and Valente [JOH 08a, JOH 08b, JOH 09] was interested in design and development of pedagogical technologies for language learning. They provide serious games that use intelligent tutoring systems composed of socially intelligent virtual humans. These agents recognize and respond to the user's speech, intent, gesture and behavior. They encapsulate models of cultures [TRA 09] that allow them to imitate the human cultural behavior. Another work [ROS 07] dealing with the exploration of the influence of culture on collaborative learning is in the TagHelper project. This project aims to develop automatic online assessment technologies and adaptive support technologies as infrastructure for supporting and studying collaborative learning in multiple cultures. They develop TagHelper tools, which have been developed to support the analysis of verbal data using text classification technology. TagHelper is an intelligent tutor that assists students during collaborative problem resolution, taking into account their cultural contexts by analyzing their verbal data. Vatrapu [VAT 07a, VAT 07b, VAT 08] has done much research on the cultural effects on human interaction, especially in the field of CSCL, but his research was an almost empirical investigations that show how cultural factors can influence the progress of collaborative problem resolution of participants from different cultures. Along with Suthers [VAT 09b], they designed a research prototype called CollabReps for studying representational guidance [VAT 09a] in computer-supported intercultural collaboration. This prototype is based on the notion of representational guidance that refers to representational tools in support of collaborative learning. They believe that the variation of representational tools which are culturally relative, used by learners working in small groups can have a significant effect on the learners' knowledge building discourse and on learning outcomes. There is also a recent work [MON 10], in which the authors present a simulator that permits active training, with which students can learn by interacting with virtual agents (VAs) and can confront typical language and cultural problems, thus avoiding the impact of mistakes in real settings. VAs are characterized by a particular culture and will place learners in global software development (GSD) scenarios specifically designed to improve their capabilities with regard to cultural and language differences.

3.4.2. *Limitations and findings*

The study above (see Table 3.3) shows that the majority of studies on cultural effects do not handle the collaboration phenomena in the true sense of the term and even if they do, it is with small groups of two members. The collaboration as we have seen above is a crucial phenomenon, which takes place between persons who can be from different cultures and interacting through a computer, so we should focus more on the technological intersubjectivity [VAT 08] issue in practices.

Research	Study criteria					
	Application domain	Prototype	Cultural knowledge	Techniques	Adaptation	Group
[JOH 08a] [JOH 08b] [JOH 09]	Collaborative games for language and foreign culture training	Tactical Iraqi	Non verbal gesture Etiquette Norms of politeness Motivation Personality Emotion Intent	Intelligent tutoring systems Learner model Speech recognition Avatars	Communi-cation Human computer interaction	Dyad
[ROS 07]	Collaborative problem resolution	TagHelper	Language Argumenta-tion style	Intelligent tutoring systems Text mining	No adaptation	Dyad
[VAT 07a] [VAT 07b] [VAT 08]	Collaborative problem resolution	Collabrep	Hofstede and Hall models of culture	Representa-tional guidance [VAT 07b]	No adaptation	Dyad
[MON 10]	Collaborative language training	VENTURE	Hofstede and Hall models of culture Language Skill	Pedagogical agent	No adaptation	Dyad

Table 3.3. *Study of existing culturally aware collaborative tools*

Furthermore, the majority of studies are largely limited to samples drawn from single countries. So, they ignore the individual particularities, his/her social context and the cultural dynamics, which govern all these characteristics. The individual inherits from different national cultures (for example in the case where his/her mother and his/her father are of different nationalities) but he/she develops his/her self-identity and particularities, which distinguish him/her from others. He/she also comes from different social contexts where he/she plays different roles and experiences different situations.

Because of the important role of sociocultural processes, in particular processes of communication that are heavily influenced by culturally based expectations and norms, the collaborative environment is an ideal field in which investigations of multinational experimental studies are necessary.

Thus, what is needed is a detailed process analysis of collaborative behavior with and without support as well as a large-scale effort to explore the relationships between the cultural variables and the collaboration outcomes. Such an analysis would allow researchers to build strong hypotheses about how external processes, such as sociocultural processes, are related to and influence internal processes of an individual and thus his/her behaviors at all levels.

Finally, we conclude that all these systems do not offer a complete solution to the effective integration and operationalization of the sociocultural factors while designing collaborative systems because they partially consider the sociocultural issues. Even if they do, it is with the use of VAs (in form of avatars), which try to imitate individual cultural behaviors to compensate for the cultural gap between collaborators. Otherwise, this imitation is limited and does not reflect the real cultural behaviors.

So, all these limitations and findings lead us to believe that an optimal solution should integrate the following issues: the adaptation of these environments by the use of sociocultural user models that represent the sociocultural dynamics of an individual: all his/her sociocultural characteristics; what he/she knows and can do and his/her cultural, social, emotional and motivational contexts. All these characteristics hold different semantic relations as was shown in the humanities and social sciences.

3.5. The proposed ontology-based sociocultural user profile

The goal of this ontology is to represent sociocultural characteristics of a user, independently of the area in which it can be used. To collect and define its concepts as well as relations between them, we conducted a multidisciplinary study in several disciplines within the humanities and social sciences (anthropology, ethnology, sociology, psychology, etc.), education science and computer science (user modeling, adaptation and personalization, HCI, etc.). These works studied sociocultural issues, their impact on humans and the necessity to take them into account in several areas. So, this ontology built from scratch. Once the concepts and their relationships were defined, we realized the first conceptualization of this ontology, called sociocultural domain ontology (SOCUDO). In [OUA 12], there is a detailed description and sources of SOCUDO concepts and relations. As a way of validating this ontology, we find specialization links between our ontology and existing top ontologies to justify the foundation of the concepts of our ontology. We studied this with the YAMATO ontology [MIZ 09] (see Figure 3.2). The choice of Yamato, among others, is based on the following arguments: first, this ontology deeply addresses some issues and concepts compared to other existing top ontologies (Dolce, BFO, GFO, SUMO, CYC), such as the notion of quality, representation and the difference between object, process and event [MIZ 09]. Second, it addresses sociocultural issues so we find concepts in relation to culture and context. Finally, it is a rich and fine-grained ontology compared to other top ontologies mentioned above.

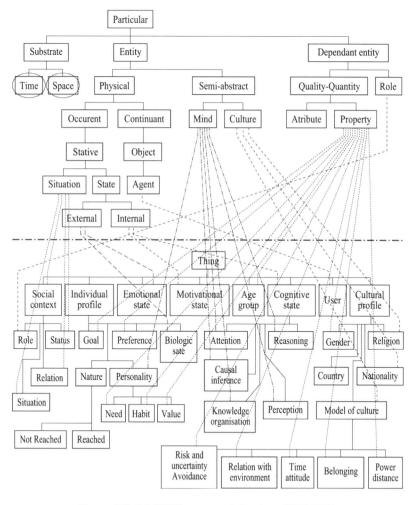

Figure 3.2. *SOCUDO as a specialization of YAMATO*

This ontology is instantiated for each user to represent his/her sociocultural profile. This profile will be used by the system to adapt its functionalities and interfaces to the sociocultural specificities of the user and his/her collaborators. A user can inherit from different models of national cultures (a comparative study of these models was made in [OUA 12] in order to define sociocultural factors presented here in the cultural profile). He/she has one individual profile, one social context, one motivational state, one emotional state, one cognitive state and one age group. These dimensions are necessary to model any user since the interaction between the individual, his/her society and his/her culture allows the formation of behavior patterns and even the deepest affective responses [LIN 77]. We consider the concepts of age as classes because this concept influences the values of the attributes of each dimension.

The user cultural profile (see Figure 3.3) is the set of characteristics inherited from one or more models of national culture. This model is composed of the common topics found in the comparison study of the national culture models that we have done in [OUA 12]. Each topic represents a cultural characteristic that defines a national culture, and it is characterized by a type and score (here we use Hofstede scores [HOF 97]). These characteristics allow us to derive one or more patterns of behavior inherited by the user and which can positively or negatively influence the other characteristics of the other dimensions. So, the proposed cultural profile defines common behavior patterns of given society members even though there are many variations in the individual responses to the same event or in the responses of the same individual to the same event at different moments [LIN 77]. The social dimension describes the social characteristics of the social context and situation of the user. In [OIS 04], the author affirms that the effect of both social status and roles is different from one individual to another. There are those who like their respective statuses and consider them as their central self-concept and do their roles properly to preserve them and those who hate them and avoid doing their roles. These concepts are culturally sensitive because the culture gives meaning to them [ALL 61]. The roles are necessary to preserve a status and these two concepts are given to an individual according to their age, gender and family situation [LIN 77].

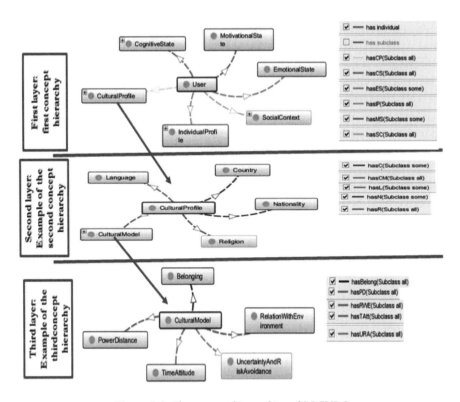

Figure 3.3. *The concept hierarchies of SOCUDO*

The cognitive dimension is composed of three closely related states: the motivational state, the emotional state and the cognitive state. The cognitive state is composed of the perception, the attention, the knowledge organization, the reasoning and the causal inference (this model is borrowed from Nisbett and Norenzayan's psychological study [NIS 02]). The individual is the product of his/her social environment, his/her surrounding culture and a progressive self-construction; he/she inherits real culture from this and constructs his/her own culture [LIN 77]. Thus, our individual profile represents this constructed culture. Each user is characterized by his/her individual profile, which is composed of his/her personality, his/her biologic state, one or different preferences and one or different goals. The personality is defined by different values, different needs and different habits. The needs are important because they represent the motivation, which drives individuals to adopt some behaviors (roles and status) to meet his/her needs [LIN 77]. Individuals select their own lifestyle that goes with their temperament, their values and life philosophy. Personality must be understood as the product of active negotiation between biological predispositions and cultural requirements [OIS 04]. It includes the following properties: individual temperament, values, life philosophy, self-concept and needs. They develop their self-concepts and life philosophies over time by observing their own behaviors and the reaction of others toward them. Culture plays a very important role in limiting the amplification and expression of personality. Individual temperaments and personality restrict degrees of cultural influence on individuals and on cultural aspects that people internalize [OIS 04]. The satisfaction of goals is a crucial characteristic, it influences the measure of subjective well-being of the user [SAN 93].

3.6. The conceptual ontology framework based adaptation approach

To adapt CSCL environments to sociocultural characteristics of its users, we have proposed a conceptual ontology framework composed of two ontologies: the ontology-based sociocultural profile and the sociocultural aware CSCL ontology. This ontology is designed to represent computer-supported learning collaborative variables, influenced by the sociocultural characteristics of the user represented by the first ontology (see Figure 3.4). The definition of the concepts and relation of this ontology is founded on the same multidisciplinary study mentioned above, specifically on the research focused in studying the cultural influences on learning and collaborative learning (CSCL, education science, etc.) [BON 02, ZAI 04, ECO 08, SCH 09, ZHU 12]. This study has allowed us to achieve a first conceptualization of our ontology. This ontology contains concepts related to the field of CSCL, which are influenced by culture. Subsequently, we tried to compare our ontology with existing ontologies representing the same domain subject, trying to find similarities or a possibility of extension. We have found that the more appropriate one is the CSCL ontology [BAR 02] (see Figure 3.4).

The adaptation is based on the ontologies described below for sociocultural adaptivity and adaptability of a collaborative learning environment. The adaptation rules will use instances of the ontology-based user profile to infer instances of the sociocultural aware CSCL ontology and trigger recommendations to the users (learners, tutors or any other type of user using the system). Example of adaptation rules: if (power distance = hierarchical) and (belonging = collective) then assistance degree = high show wizard.

As we have said above, the two ontologies are closely related. They communicate to share sociocultural knowledge about the user in order to trigger the appropriate adaptation tasks. The SOCUDO ontology is instantiated for one user after his/her information is input via the forms; this instance of SOCUDO triggers an instance of SCACO (see Figure 3.5) for this user based on adaptation rules (for example if power distance = hierarchical and belonging = collective, then assistance degree= high show wizard). Then, the adaptation process will use this instance to trigger the right adaptations tasks for this user. Figure 3.3 shows an example of an instantiation part of the two ontologies based on some adaptation rules. If the user "Sarah Ben Foulen" is from Tunisia and lives in Tunisia, then he has a cultural profile characterized by a "collectivism" belonging, "hierarchic" power distance, "monochromic" time attitude, "dominance" relationship with the environment and "uncomfortable" risk and uncertainty avoidance. These concept values trigger specific concept values in the second ontology: for example, "hierarchic" power distance triggers a "pushy" assistance manner, "teacher" help initiator, "formal/structured" activity structure, "hierarchical" control type, etc.

3.7. The sociocultural aware KM system for CSCL

The system collects cultural data (information acquisition module) from users via forms in the client side, these data will be analyzed and used to instantiate a user profile and from knowledge in the user profile, it instantiates the sociocultural aware CSCL ontology.

The adaptation process is composed of two steps: the first adaptation will be done when the user first registers to the system for the first time. The system adapts the collaboration and gives recommendations that suit the cultural parameters of the cultural group to which the user belongs. The system offers a discrete button in the interface to give the possibility to the user of ignoring the recommendation given by the system and explicitly requesting other recommendations. At the active request of recommendations, the system activates a wizard in which the user can review the recommendations provided by the system, decline or accept them or change the settings of recommendation that will be automatically triggered the next time. The second adaptation is done while the users are interacting with the system by inference (observation and recording of user interaction with the system and with other participants and making inferences: need help, need some changes), notifying the user who can accept or reject the proposition. Inferences are made after observing the user interaction with the system (user interaction tracking). So, the system will offer two types of adaptations: computer-supported adaptation (adaptability), when the user initiates the adaptation, the system offers recommendation to the user and he/she declines or accepts it and self-adaptation (adaptivity), when the system automatically applies the adaptation

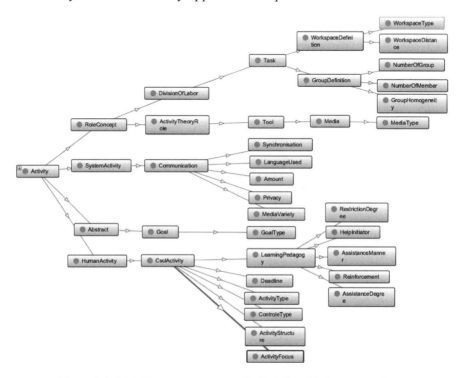

Figure 3.4. *SCACO as an extension of [BAR 01] CSCL domain ontology*

In the following activity diagram (see Figure 3.6.), we show how, when and where the sociocultural KM process is performed:

– We are in the sociocultural knowledge gathering step when the user inputs sociocultural data via forms displayed by the system to collect these data. This step also occurs when the system observes and learns from the user interaction to get additional sociocultural knowledge.

– The second step, which is sociocultural knowledge analysis, occurs once data are gathered and the analysis procedure is started.

– Then, using the analyzed data, the system performs the appropriate tasks to instantiate the two ontologies as we have explained previously to construct sociocultural knowledge.

– Finally, this knowledge is applied through the adaptation process also explained previously.

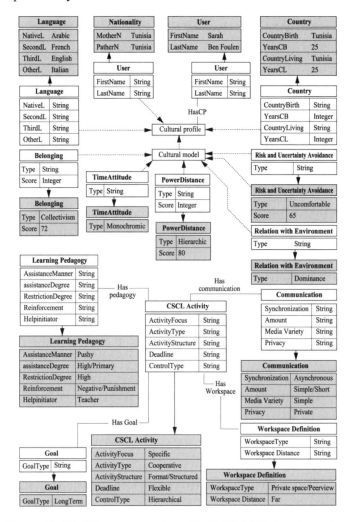

Figure 3.5. *SCACO as an extension of [BAR 01] CSCL domain ontology*

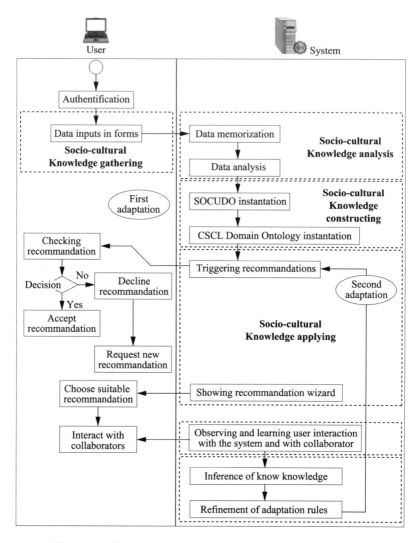

Figure 3.6. *The sociocultural knowledge management within our proposed system of sociocultural CSCL adaptation*

3.8. Conclusion and ongoing work

In this chapter, we have presented our conceptual ontology framework to socioculturally adapt CSCL environment and for the management of the sociocultural knowledge about the learners. The use of this framework will allow our system to offer to the learners communication and collaboration tools designed for their social and cultural characteristics. This may enhance and promote the interaction between learners from different cultures and the knowledge construction and sharing.

We wish later to finalize the following:

– The implementation of a web-based CSCL system, which would include all these solutions. We will use an existing CSCL system in which we will implement our main contributions.

– Then we will incept the experimentation: as a first step, we will do that in two colleges in Tunisia located at two different social contexts then in different national culture settings.

3.9. Bibliography

[AGA 94] AGAR M., *Language Shock: Understanding the Culture of Conversation*, Perennial, New York, 1994.

[ALL 61] ALLPORT G.W., *Pattern and Growth in Personality*, Holt, Rinehart & Winston, New York, 1961.

[ANN 11] ANNIE C.B., *Piaget. Constructivisme Intelligence. L'avenir d'une théorie*, Presses universitaires du Septentrion, Villeneuve d'Ascq, 2011.

[BAK 84] BAKHTIN M., *Esthétique de la création verbale*, Gallimard, Paris, 1984.

[BAR 02] BARROS B., VERDEJO M.F., READ T., *et al.,* "Applications of a collaborative learning ontology", Mexican International Conference on Artificial Intelligence MICAI, LNAI, Springer-Verlag, pp. 301–310, 2002.

[BLA 10] BLANCHARD E.G., MIZOGUCHI R., LAJOIE S.P., "Structuring the cultural domain with an upper ontology of culture", in BLANCHARD E.G., ALLARD D. (eds), *Handbook of Research on Culturally Aware Information Technology: Perspectives and Models*, Information Science Publishing, Hershey, PA, 2010.

[BOE 04] BOELLSTORFF T., LINDQUIST J., "Bodies of emotion: rethinking culture and emotion through southeast Asia", *Ethnos*, vol. 69, no. 4, pp. 437–444, 2004.

[BON 02] BONK C.J., CUNNINGHAM D.J., "Searching for learner-centered, constructivist, and sociocultural components of collaborative educational learning tool", *Electronic Collaborators: Learner-Centered Technologies for Literacy, Apprenticeship, and Discourse*, Lawrence Erlbaum Associates Publishers, pp. 25–50, 2002.

[DOY 03] DOYLE W.D., "Magnetization reversal in films with biaxial anisotropy", *1987 Proceeding INTERMAG Conference*, pp. 221–226, 2003.

[ECO 08] ECONOMIDES A.A., "Culture-aware collaborative learning", *Multicultural Education & Technology Journal*, vol. 2, pp. 243–267, 2008.

[HAL 76] HALL E., *Beyond Culture*, Anchor Press, New York, 1976.

[HAL 90] HALL E., *The Silent Language*, Anchor Books, New York, 1990.

[HER 50] HERSKOVITZ M.J., *Les bases de l'anthropologie culturelle*, François Maspero Éditeur, Paris, 1967. Collection: Petite collection Maspero, 106, 1950.

[HOF 80] HOFSTEDE G., *Culture's Consequences: International Differences in Work-Related Values*, Sage, Beverly Hills, CA, 1980.

[HOF 97] HOFSTEDE G., "Cultures and organizations: software of the mind", *Intercultural Cooperation and its Importance for Survival*, McGraw-Hill, 1997.

[HOU 04] HOUSE R.J., HANGES P.J., JAVIDAN M., *et al., Culture, Leadership, and Organizations: The GLOBE Study of 62 Societies*, Sage Publications, Thousand Oaks, CA, 2004.

[JOH 08a] JOHNSON W.L., VALENTE A., "Collaborative authoring of serious games for language and culture", *Proceeding of Simulation Conference and Exhibition (SimTect 2008)*, Melbourne, Australia, 12–15 May 2008.

[JOH 08b] JOHNSON W.L., VALENTE A., "Tactical language and culture training systems: using artificial intelligence to teach foreign languages and cultures", *Proceeding of Innovative Applications and Artificial Intelligence Conference (IAAI 2008)*, March 2008.

[JOH 09] JOHNSON W.L., "A simulation-based approach to training operational cultural competence", *Proceedings of ModSIM 2009*, Cairns, Australia 13–17 July 2009.

[KLU 61] KLUCKHOHN F.R., STRODTBECK F.L., *Variations in Value Orientations*, Row, Peterson, Evanston, IL, 1961.

[KRO 52] KROEBER A.L., KLUCKHOHN C., *Culture: A Critical Review of Concepts and Definitions*, Peabody Museum of American Archeology and Ethnology, Harvard University, 1952.

[LEO 72] LEONT'EV A.N., *Activity, consciousness and personality*, Prentice-Hall 1972. Available at http://www.marxists.org/archive/leontev/works/1978/index.htm.

[LIA 05] LIAW S.S., "Developing a web assisted knowledge construction system based on the approach of constructivist knowledge analysis of tasks", *Computers in Human Behavior Journal*, vol. 21, no. 1, pp. 29–44, 2005.

[LIA 08] LIAW S.S., CHEN G.D., HUANG H.M., "Users' attitudes toward web-based collaborative learning systems for knowledge management", *Computer & Education Journal*, vol. 50, pp. 950–961, 2008.

[LIN 77] LINTON R., *Le fondement culturel de la personnalité*, LEOTARD A. (trans.), Bordas, Paris, 1977.

[LUR 79] LURIA A.R., *The making of mind: a personal account of Soviet psychology*, in COLE M., COLE S. (eds), Harvard University Press, Cambridge, MA/London, 1979.

[MIZ 09] MIZOGUCHI R., "Yet another top-level ontology: YATO", *Proceeding of the 2nd Interdisciplinary Ontology Meeting*, Tokyo, Japan: Keio University Press, pp. 91–101, 2009.

[MON 10] MONASOR M., VIZCAINO A., PIATTINI M., "An educational environment for training skills for global software development", *ICALT 2010*, Sousse, Tunisia, pp. 99–101, 2010.

[NEW 08] NEWMAN G.G., GRAHAM E., MCLUHAN E., *et al., Echoes from the Past: World History to the 16th Century*, McGraw-Hill, Toronto, 2008.

[NIS 02] NISBETT R.E., NORENZAYAN A., "Culture and cognition", in MEDIN D.L. (ed.), *Stevens' Handbook of Experimental Psychology*, John Wiley & Sons, New York, pp. 561–597, 2002.

[NON 95] NONAKA I., TAKEUCHI H., *The knowledge-creating company*, New York, Oxford University Press, 1995.

[OIS 03] OISHI S., DIENER E., "Culture and well-being: the cycle of action, evaluation and decision", *Personality and Social Psychology Bulletin*, vol. 29, pp. 939–949, 2003.

[OIS 04] OISHI S. "Personality in culture: a neo allportian view", *Journal of Research in Personality*, vol. 38, pp. 68–74, 2004.

[OUA 12] OUAMANI F., HADJ MTIR R., BELLAMINE N., *et al.,* "Proposal of a generic and multidimensional socio-cultural user profile for collaborative environments", *Proceeding of the 5th International Conference on Information Systems and Economic Intelligence SIIE*, Djerba, Tunisia, pp. 75–83, 2012.

[PAP 84] PAPERT S., "New theories for new learnings: a transcript from the National Association of School Psychologists Conference", *School Psychology Review*, vol. 13, no. 4, pp. 422–428, 1984.

[ROS 07] ROSE C.P., FISCHER F., CHANG C.Y., "Exploring the influence of culture on collaborative learning", *Working Notes of the ACM SIG-CHI Workshop on Culture and Collaborative Technologies*, 2007.

[SAN 93] SANDVIK E., DIENER E., SEIDLITZ L., "Subjective well-being: the convergence and stability of self-report and non-self-report measures", *Journal of Personality*, vol. 61, pp. 317–342, 1993.

[SAW 00] SAWHNEY M., PRANDELLI E., "Communities of creation: managing distributed innovation in turbulent markets", *California Management Review*, vol. 42, no. 4, pp. 24–54, 2000.

[SCH 92] SCHWARTZ S.H., Value dimension of culture and national difference, 1992. Available at http://www.uib.no/psyfa/isp/diversity/content/reseach/multicultur/Workshop/Schwartz%20.pdf.

[SCH 09] SCHADEWITZ N., JACHNA T., "Design patterns for cross-cultural computer supported collaboration", *International Journal of Design*, vol 3, no 3, pp. 37–53, 2009. Available at http://www.ijdesign.org/ojs/index.php/IJDesign/article/view/276/273.

[SHW 90] SHWEDER R., SULLIVAN M., "The semiotic subject of cultural psychology", in PERVIN L. (ed.), *Handbook of Personality: Theory and Research*, Guilford Press, New York, pp. 399-416, 1990.

[SIL 00] SILVER C.A., "Where technology and knowledge meet", *The Journal of Business Strategy*, vol. 21, no. 6, pp. 28–33, 2000.

[TRA 09] TRAUM D., "Models of culture for virtual human conversation", *Human Computer Interaction International (HCII)*, San Diego, July 2009.

[TRO 93] TROMPENAARS F., HAMPDEN-TURNER C., *The Seven Cultures of Capitalism: Value Systems for Creating Wealth in the United States, Japan, Germany, France, Britain, Sweden, and the Netherlands*, McGraw-Hill, 1993.

[TYL 24] TYLOR E.B., "Primitive culture: the science of culture", in BOHANNAN P., GLAZER M. (eds), *High Points in Anthropology*, McGraw-Hill, New York, 1924.

[VAT 07a] VATRAPU R., SUTHERS D., "Culture and computers: a review of the concept of culture and its analytical usage", *Paper Presented at the Culture and Collaborative Technologies Workshop at CHI (CHI-2007)*, San Jose, CA, 28–29 April 2007.

[VAT 07b] VATRAPU R., SUTHERS D., "Culture and computers: a review of the concept of culture and implications for intercultural collaborative online learning", in ISHIDA T., FUSSELL S.R., VOSSEN P.T.J.M. (eds.), *Intercultural Collaboration I, Lecture Notes in Computer Science*, Springer-Verlag, pp. 260–275, 2007.

[VAT 08] VATRAPU R., "Cultural usability and computer supported collaboration", *Paper Presented at the Cultural Usability and Human Work Interaction Design – Techniques that Connects Workshop*, 2008 NordiCHI Conference, Lund, Sweden, 2008.

[VAT 09a] VATRAPU R., SUTHERS D., "Is representational guidance culturally relative?", in O'MALLEY C., SUTHERS D., REIMANN P., DIMITRACOPOULOU A. (eds), *Computer Supported Collaborative Learning Practices: CSCL2009 Conference Proceedings, International Society of the Learning Sciences*, Rhodes, Greece, pp. 542–551, 8–13 June 2009.

[VAT 09b] VATRAPU R., SUTHERS D., MEDINA R., "Notational effects on use of collaboratively constructed representations during individual essay writing", in O'MALLEY C., SUTHERS D., REIMANN P., DIMITRACOPOULOU A., (eds), *Computer Supported Collaborative Learning Practices: CSCL2009 Conference Proceedings, International Society of the Learning Sciences*, Rhodes, Greece, pp. 165–169, 8–13 June 2009.

[VYG 34] VYGOTSKY L., *Mind in Society*, Harvard University Press, 1934.

[YAN 04a] YANG J.T., WAN C.S., "Advancing organizational effectiveness and knowledge management implementation", *Tourism Management Journal*, vol. 25, pp. 593–601, 2004.

[YAN 04b] YANG S.J.H., CHEN I.Y.L., SHAO N.W.Y., "Ontology enabled annotation and knowledge management for collaborative learning in virtual learning community", *Educational Technology & Society*, vol. 7, no. 4, pp. 70–81, 2004.

[ZAI 04] ZAITSEVA E., SHAYLOR J., WHATLEY J., "Collaboration across border: benefits and pitfalls of an international collaborative project", *Proceeding of the Education in a Changing Environment*, University of Salford, 2004. Available at: http://usir.salford.ac.uk/id/eprint/2079.

[ZHU 12] ZHU C., "Student satisfaction, performance, and knowledge construction in online collaborative learning", *Educational Technology & Society*, vol. 15, no. 1, pp. 127–136, 2012.

Chapter 4

An Argumentation-based Rough Set Theory for Knowledge Management

Agent-KC platform is devoted to the automation of collaborative multicriteria classification for the identification of crucial knowledge for the sake of knowledge capitalization. It is based on a multiagent argumentative approach to automate the conflict resolution between decision makers (DMs). In a conflictual situation, an agent mediator intervenes to make an objective decision. In this chapter, we propose an argumentative approach for the DMs of the Agent-KC platform. This approach is based on a communication protocol characterized by strategies allowing agents to exchange arguments and counter-arguments in order to have a mutual effect on their preferences and to reach an agreement.

4.1. Introduction

The necessity to manage knowledge mobilized in organizations has increased rapidly in the last few years. Research in knowledge engineering and knowledge management has been focusing on the problems of the acquisition, the preservation and the transfer of knowledge. However, considering the large amount of knowledge to be preserved, the firm must first determine the specific knowledge that should be targeted by capitalization.

Chapter written by Sarra BOUZAYANE, Imène BRIGUI-CHTIOUI and Inès SAAD.

Indeed, we should focus on only the so-called "crucial knowledge" whose risk of loss and cost of (re)creation is considered to be important. In [CHA 12, SAA 09, BRI 11], multicriteria methods have been proposed to take into account the preferences of DMs, which can be different or even contradictory while exploiting and managing their multiple points of view to identify crucial knowledge. However, because of the large amount of knowledge to be analyzed, the large number of DMs involved in the assignments process and the contradictory opinions that they can have, it is necessary to automate the resolution of conflicts between them. The Agent-KC platform (see Figure 4.1) is proposed in [BRI 11] to automate the resolution of conflicts between DMs for identifying knowledge that needs to be capitalized and that we call "crucial knowledge". This process relies on two types of agents: an agent mediator and a set of DM agents. The agent mediator is supposed to be external to this platform since it does not participate in the classification process. In a conflictual state, the Agent-KC platform relies on the mediator agent in order to elicit the preferences of contradictory DMs to make an objective decision. Thus, the aim of this chapter is to propose an argumentative approach based on dominance rough set theory to identify crucial knowledge. Such an approach minimizes the role of the agent mediator and allows the DMs to argue their choices.

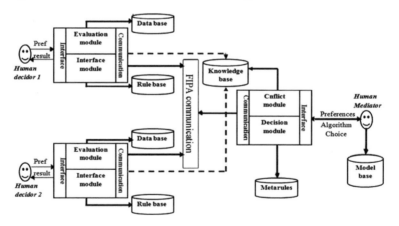

Figure 4.1. *Agent-KC architecture [BRI 11]*

This chapter is structured as follow: section 4.2 discusses the background. Section 4.3 presents a multiagent argumentative approach. Section 4.4 presents an illustrative example and section 4.5 summarizes our contribution.

4.2. Background

4.2.1. *Dominance-based rough set approach (DRSA)*

The DRSA method was proposed by Greco *et al.* [GRE 01] and inspired from the theory of rough sets [PAW 92]. It allows us to compare actions through a dominance relation and takes into account the preferences of a DM to extract decision rules. According to the DRSA method, a data table is a four tuple $S = \langle K, F, V, f \rangle$, where K is a finite set of reference actions, F is a finite set of criteria, $V = \cup_{g \in F} V_g$ is the set of possible values of criteria and f denotes information function $f : F \times K \longrightarrow V$ such that $f(x, g) \in V_g$, $\forall x \in K, \forall g \in F$.

The set F is, generally, divided into a set C of condition attributes and a decision attribute d. In a multicriteria classification, condition attributes are criteria. The notion of criterion involves a preference order in its domain while the domains of attributes, usually considered in machine discovery, are not in an order of preference.

Furthermore, decision attribute d makes a partition of K into a finite number of classes Cl = $\{Cl_t; t \in T\}$, T = $\{1..n\}$. Each x $\in$ K belongs to one and only one class $Cl_t \in Cl$. The classes from Cl are in a preference order following the increasing order of class indices, i.e. for all $r, s \in$ T, such that $r>s$, the objects from Cl_r are preferred to the objects from Cl_s.

In multicriteria classification, because of the preference order in the set of classes Cl, the sets to be approximated are not particular classes but upward and downward unions of classes, thus:

$$Cl_t^{\geq} = \cup_{s \leq t} Cl_s, Cl_t^{\geq} = \cup_{s \geq t} Cl_s; t = 1...n$$

DEFINITION 4.1.– DOMINANCE RELATION.– *Let* $P \subseteq F$ *be a subset of criteria. The dominance relation* D_P *associated with P is defined for each pair of objects x and y, such that:*

$$\forall (x, y) \in K, x D_P y \Leftrightarrow f(x, g_j) \succcurlyeq f(x, g_j) \forall g_j \in P$$

The following are associated with each object $x \in K$:

– *a set of objects dominating x, called P-dominating set,* $D_P^+(x) = \{y \in K : yD_Px\};$

– *a set of objects dominated by x, called P-dominated set,* $D_P^-(x) = \{y \in K : xD_Py\}.$

DEFINITION 4.2.– LOWER APPROXIMATION.– *Lower approximation of unions of classes represents a certain knowledge provided by criteria* $P \subseteq F.$

– $\underline{P}(Cl_t^{\geq}) = \{ x \in K : D_P^+(x) \subseteq Cl_t^{\geq}, \forall t = 1...n \}$: *the set of all objects belonging to* $Cl_t^{\geq}$ *without any ambiguity. It contains all objects with P-dominating set assigned with certainty to classes that are at most as good as* $Cl_t.$

– $\underline{P}(Cl_t^{\leq}) = \{ x \in K : D_P^-(x) \subseteq Cl_t^{\leq}, \forall t = 1...n \}$: *the set of all objects belonging to* $Cl_t^{\leq}$ *without any ambiguity. It contains all objects with P-dominated set assigned with certainty to classes that are at most as good as* $Cl_t.$

DEFINITION 4.3.– UPPER APPROXIMATION.– *Upper approximation of unions of classes represents possible knowledge provided by criteria* $P \subseteq F.$

– $\bar{P}(Cl_t^{\geq}) = \cup_{x \in Cl_t}^{\geq} D_P^+(x) = \{x \in K : D_P^-(x) \cap Cl_t^{\geq} \neq \varnothing\}, \forall t = 1...n\}$: *the set of all objects that could belong to* $Cl_t^{\geq}$. *It contains all objects with P-dominating set assigned to a class at least as good as* $Cl_t.$

– $\bar{P}(Cl_t^{\leq}) = \cup_{x \in Cl_t}^{\leq} D_P^-(x) = \{x \in K : D_P^+(x) \cap Cl_t^{\leq} \neq \varnothing\}, \forall t = 1...n\}$: *the set of all objects that could belong to* $Cl_t^{\leq}$. *It contains all objects with P-dominated set assigned to a class at least as good as* $Cl_t.$

DEFINITION 4.4.– BOUNDARY.– *We call the boundary of agent* a_s, *denoted by* $[Bn_P(Cl_t)]^{a_s}$, *the set of actions that are uncertainly classified in the decision class* Cl_t. *It can be represented in terms of upper and lower approximations as follow:*

– $Bn_p(Cl_t^{\geq}) = \bar{P}(Cl_t^{\geq}) - \underline{P}(Cl_t^{\geq})$: *set of all objects belonging to* $Cl_t^{\geq}$ *with some ambiguity.*

– $Bn_p(Cl_t^{\leq}) = \bar{P}(Cl_t^{\leq}) - \underline{P}(Cl_t^{\leq})$: *set of all objects belonging to* $Cl_t^{\leq}$ *with some ambiguity.*

DEFINITION 4.5.– QUALITY OF APPROXIMATION.– *For every $P \subseteq F$, the quality of approximation of the multicriteria classification Cl by set of criteria P is defined as the ratio between the number of P-correctly classified objects and the number of all the objects in the data sample set. Since the objects P-correctly classified are those ones that do not belong to any boundary of unions $Cl_t^{\geq}$ and $Cl_t^{\leq}$, $\forall t = 1...n$. The quality of approximation of multicriteria Cl by set of attributes P can be written as:*

$$\gamma_P = \frac{|K - (\cup_{t=1...n} Bn_p(Cl_t^{\leq})) \cup (\cup_{t=1...n} Bn_p(Cl_t^{\geq}))|}{|K|}$$

DEFINITION 4.6.– CORE.– *For a given set of decision examples, it is possible to determine which criteria are relevant for the approximation of the attribution made by the DM agent. We call such subsets of relevant criteria the "reducts" and we call their intersection the "core". Otherwise, for each minimal subset of criteria $P \subseteq F$ such as γ_P (Cl)= γ_F (Cl), P is called reduct of F. A decision table can contain several reducts and their intersection set is the "core".*

DEFINITION 4.7.– STRENGTH OR FORCE.– *The strength of a decision rule is the ratio of the set of actions supporting this rule, compared with the number of all knowledge that was classified in a certain way in a given class.*

DEFINITION 4.8.– DECISION RULE.– *Decision rules used in this chapter are generated from the lower approximation. They are represented as follows:*

if $f(x, g_1) \geq r_1 \wedge ... \wedge f(x, g_n) \geq r_n$ **then** $x \in Cl_t^{\geq}$;

such that $(r_1...r_n) \in (v_{g_1}...v_{g_n})$.

4.2.2. *Argumentation*

Argumentation is considered as *a reasoning model based on the construction and evaluation of interacting arguments*. These arguments are intended to support/attack statements that can be decisions, opinions and so on [AMG 12]. Also, in [EEM 96], argumentation is defined *as a verbal and a social activity of reason aiming at increasing (or decreasing) the acceptability of a controversial standpoint for the listener or reader, by putting forward a constellation of propositions intended to justify (or refute) the standpoint before a rational judge.* In the literature, many works proposed different arguments' typologies and structures. In this chapter, we distinguish between four structures (sequence of deduction, tree of rules, triple and pair) and, also, four types of arguments (explanatory, threat, reward and decision).

4.2.2.1. *Argument structures*

Several structures have been identified in the literature to construct and present an argument. Below, we propose a brief description of the four main structures.

– Sequence of deductions: This structure considers an argument as a sequence of rules linked one another. The construction of an argument is done through two steps, and is based on three premises and two conclusions [VER 96]. This form addresses as input two premises to reach a conclusion, called intermediate conclusion (CI). The intermediate conclusion is provided as a premise with a third premise to derive the final conclusion of the argument (see Figure 4.2). Then, an argument having the structure of a sequence of deductions contains, respectively:

- premises that are not derived from other proposals;

- intermediate conclusions derived from certain proposals and allowing in their turn to derive other proposals;

- a conclusion from which no other proposal is derived.

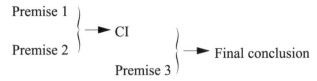

Figure 4.2. *Argument of the form sequence of deductions*

The stages of the inferences are based on the rule of consequence of modus ponens. This form was used and developed in [LIN 89].

– Tree of rules: This structure is presented in [VRE 97]. The author considers that an argument is made by linking rules together into trees. An argument is characterized by certain premises, sentences, assumptions, a

length, a size and a conclusion. In Figure 4.3, three arguments are displayed. The premises of the first, second and third argument are {p, q}, {q, r} and {p}, respectively. The conclusions are s, p and r; the sentences are {p, q, r, s}, {p, q, r, s} and {p, q, r}; the assumptions are {s}, {s} and ∅; the length of all three arguments is equal to 3 (not 2); the size of the arguments is 6, 5 and 4, respectively. The first two arguments are defeasible and the third argument is strict ($\Longrightarrow$ used for defeasible argument and → for strict argument).

– *Triple* $\langle S, C, d \rangle$: This structure takes into consideration both the available information about the universe and the preferences of agents involved in the argumentation process [AMG 04]. Two bases (K and G) are distinguished:

- K: the set of available knowledge about the universe;

- G: DM preferences in the form of priority objectives.

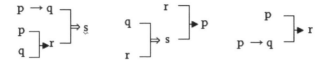

Figure 4.3. *Three arguments with tree structure*

We denote by:

- D: the set of all allowed decisions;

- d = Conclusion (A): the conclusion of the argument A;

- S = Support (A): the support of the argument A;

- C = Consequences (A): the consequences of the argument A (the goals that are reached by the decision d).

Thus, an argument in favor of a decision "d" is a triple A = $\langle S, C, d \rangle$ such that:

– $d \in D$;

– $S \subseteq K^*$;

– $C \in G^*$;

– $S \cup \{d\}$ is consistent;

– $S \cup \{d\} \vdash C$;

– S is minimal and C is maximal (for set inclusion) among the sets satisfying the above conditions.

The triple structure is oriented to an argument of a practical type (Q is the goal, P → Q, then P) and not to the epistemic type (P, P →Q; then Q).

– *Pair* $\langle H, h \rangle$: An argument is a pair $\langle H, h \rangle$ such that h is a basic literal of $P = (\Pi, \Delta)$. Π is a set of strict knowledge and Δ is a set of reviewable knowledge. h is said the conclusion and H is the support of conclusion h [CHE 04].

A pair $\langle H, h \rangle$ is an argument, for the literal h, that satisfies the above conditions:

   - there is a reviewable derivation for h since $\Pi \cup H$ ($\Pi \cup H \longrightarrow h$);

   - $\Pi \cup H$ is consistent;

   - H is minimal compared to the set of inclusion.

In this context, we keep arguments whose structure is a pair $\langle H, h \rangle$ such as H which represents not only reviewable rules possessed by each DM agent, but also evaluations on which rules have been built. Literal h is the decision selected from the set H, which can be either "$K_i \in Cl_1$" or "$K_i \in Cl_2$".

4.2.2.2. *Argument types*

In the literature, several studies have focused on the identification of different types that may have an argument. Among these works, we cite [KRA 98], [AMG 06] and [BEL 07]. Five types of arguments have been distinguished: explanatory argument, request argument, threat argument, reward argument and decision argument. The different types of arguments are briefly explained below (see Table 4.1).

– *Explanatory argument:*   explanations constitute the most common category of arguments. In classical argumentation-based frameworks, which have been developed for handling inconsistency in knowledge bases, each conclusion is justified by arguments. They represent the reasons to believe in the fact. Indeed, from premises, a fact or a goal is entailed [AMG 04].

	Characteristics	Example
Explanatory argument [BEL 07]	- Is used in non-monotonic reasoning, - Manipulates the inconsistency in a knowledge base, - Takes a deductive form, - The premises are composed of beliefs.	-Premise: Tweety is a bird - Conclusion: Tweety flies.
Request argument [KRA 98]	- Is inspired from negotiations between humans, - Has a persuasive purpose, - Encourages one to perform an action, - Is built only from beliefs, - Justifies a belief or goal, - Is composed of several types (practice, promise).	- Knowledge 1: Success. - Knowledge 2: Success $\rightarrow$ gift. - Conclusion: gift, (argument for promise).
Threat argument [KRA 98]	- Is used for human interactions, - It is of a persuasive nature, - Is built from beliefs, goals and actions.	- You should do α otherwise I will do β. - β is a negative consequence for the person to threaten.
Reward argument [KRA 98]	- Is similar to a threat, but it takes a positive direction, - Has a persuasive nature, - Is built from beliefs, goals and actions.	- If you do α, I will do β. - β is a positive consequence for the person to reward.
Decision argument [AMG 04]	- Is used in the context of decision making under uncertainty, - Selects alternative from the set of possible decisions constructed from beliefs and goals justifying a considered decision.	- Belief: If I take my umbrella, I will not be wet. - Purpose: I do not want to get wet. - Decision: I take my umbrella.

Table 4.1. *Arguments types*

Also Belabbes [BEL 07] defined this type of argument as a non-monotonous reasoning for irrelevance manipulation in a knowledge base. This type, whose premises are made of beliefs, takes a deductive shape.

– *Threat argument:* This type is used for human interaction. It has also a persuasive character but is made up of beliefs, goals and actions [KRA 98].

In the same context, Amgoud and Prade [AMG 04] considered that threats are very common in human negotiation. Also, they have a negative character and are used to force an agent to behave in a certain way. Two forms of threats can be distinguished:

    - You should do α otherwise I will do β.

    - You should not do α otherwise I will do β.

The first case occurs when an agent P needs an agent C to do α and C refuses. P threatens then C by doing β that – according to its beliefs– will have bad consequences for the agent C.

– Reward argument: It is similar to that of threat. Yet, it takes a positive sense. During a negotiation, an agent P can entice agent C to do α by offering to do an action β as a reward. Of course, agent P believes that β will contribute to the goals of C. Hence, a reward has generally, at least from the point of view of its sender, a positive character. As for threats, two forms of rewards can be distinguished: "If you do α then I will do β" and "If you don't do α then I will do β" [AMG 04].

– Decision argument: Decision argument is used in the context of decision process under uncertainty. It consists of selecting an alternative among the possible decisions built upon beliefs and goals, justifying a considered decision [AMG 06].

In this chapter, we are located within the same context. In fact, DM agents have to choose only one alternative among two possible decisions: that is to classify knowledge K_i either in the class Cl_1 of non-crucial knowledge or in the class Cl_2 of crucial knowledge. The type of argument kept in this context is, thus, that of a decision, defined in [AMG 06].

4.2.2.3. *Relation between arguments*

We distinguish two types of relations between the predefined arguments: support relation and attack relation.

– Support relation: support between arguments is represented by a binary relation on the set of arguments. Let $A_1 = \langle H_1, h_1 \rangle$ and $A_2 = \langle H_2, h_2 \rangle$ be two arguments. A_1 and A_2 are said to be in a support relation at the conclusion if $h_1 \equiv h_2$; in other words, if their supports H_1 and H_2 support the same conclusion. As well, A_1 and A_2 are said in a support relation to

their assumptions level if $\exists h \in H_2$ such that $h = h_1$ [CAY 05]. This type of relationship is more expressive in the context of an argumentation among, at least, three agents. Indeed, the use of such relationship allows defining two groups of DMs: those who have a support argument supporting the conclusion "h" and those who deny the conclusion.

– *Attack relation:* different forms of attack relationships have been defined [DUN 95] and [VER 96]. We distinguish three conflict relations: the rebutting attack, the assumption attack and the undercutting attack.

- *Rebutting attack:* it is used in [KRA 98] and considered as a symmetrical relationship where both arguments have two contradictory conclusions (see Figure 4.4(a)). An argument $A_1 = \langle H_1, h_1 \rangle$ rebuts an argument $A_2 = \langle H_2, h_2 \rangle$ if and only if (iif)$h_1 = \neg h_2$.

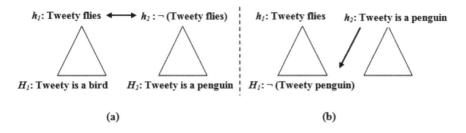

Figure 4.4. *Attack relations*

- *Assumption attack:* it is defined in [BON 97]. It represents the case where an argument contradicts an assumption of another argument (see Figure 4.4(b)).

- *Undercutting attack:* as introduced in [POL 74], it represents the case where the conclusion of an argument contradicts the premises of another argument supporting its conclusion. This conflict concerns the connection between the premises and the conclusion, then the inference rule and not the premises themselves (see Figure 4.5). An argument $A_1 = \langle II_1, h_1 \rangle$ undermines $A_2 = \langle H_2, h_2 \rangle$ if $\exists h \in H_2$ such that $h = h_2$.

The DMs of our study do not share the same opinions. They propose, thus, conflicting arguments. The type of relationship that we retain in this work is that of attack, and more precisely that of the undercutting attack.

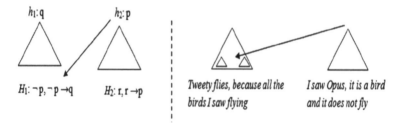

Figure 4.5. *Undercut conflict*

4.2.3. *Multiagent system*

To describe multiagent systems, we need to explain the notion of agent. According to Woolridge [WOO 01], *an agent is a software tool that operates in an environment and that is able to interact with the same to achieve its objectives already prefixed.* More precisely, it is described as an entity making a proof of the following:

– *Reactivity:* intelligent agents are able to perceive their environment and respond in a timely fashion to changes that occur in it in order to satisfy their design objectives.

– *Proactiveness:* intelligent agents are able to exhibit goal-directed behavior by taking the initiative in order to satisfy their design objectives.

– *Social ability:* intelligent agents are capable of interacting with other agents (and possibly humans) in order to satisfy their design objectives.

– *Autonomy* ([CAS 94, WOO 02]): intelligent agents are able to make and receive changes autonomously without direct intervention of other agents (human or artificial). They are led to a kind of control over their actions and internal states.

According to Woolridge and Jennings [WOO 95], an agent with these four characteristics can still have a "weakness". Indeed, the two researchers have identified two notions of agents: the "weak" notion and the "strong" notion. The "weak" notion is described above. The "strong" notion tries to give an intelligent aspect to an agent to fit the context defined in the field of "artificial intelligence". Intelligent behavior is achieved through the integration of "mentalistic" notions [SHO 93] in the "weak" notion of an agent. Thus, the "strong" notion describes an agent as *a computer system characterized by a required intentional orientation.*

After studying the attitudes appropriate for the representation of an agent, two categories were specified: information attitudes and pro-attitudes. Information attitudes are those related to the information that an agent has about the world it occupies such as knowledge and beliefs. Pro-attitudes are those whose purpose is to guide the various actions of an agent such as desires, intentions and commitment.

Beliefs, desires and intentions have been the subject of a new architecture called the beliefs, desires, intentions (BDI) architecture, introduced in [RAO 93] to model the mental states and the rational activity of a cognitive agent.

A cognitive agent is an agent with reasoning capabilities that allow it to achieve its objectives. It has a symbolic representation of the environment as well as of its mental state. It is organized by the BDI architecture into three distinct parts:

– *Beliefs*: the information that the agent has on the environment and on other agents that exist in the same environment;

– *Desires*: the state of the environment, and sometimes of itself, that the agent would like to see made;

– *Intentions*: desires or actions that the agent decided to do in order to fulfill its desires.

Two other types of agents have been identified by researchers, which are the reactive agent which merely react to stimuli coming from the environment and the hybrid agent that brings both.

The BDI architecture has been enriched by Parsons and Jennings [PAR 98] by complementing the classical logic with a degree of belief in the sense of Dempster–Shafer theory [BRA 96] that can explicitly represent the uncertainty of knowledge using mathematical tools. This knowledge representation is installed in the system of reasoning based on the argument theorized in [ELV 93]. The new architecture aims to design DM agents that can both inherit from the BDI architecture and the decision-making under uncertainty.

From these concepts, a multiagent system is defined as an organized set of agents that act and interact together in a common environment. Each agent system is able, first, to act on itself and its environment and, second to communicate with other agents. The behavior of an agent is the result of its observations, knowledge and interactions with other agents.

The argumentation and the multiagent system are two concepts that we needed to achieve our objective. Indeed, we plan to define an argumentative approach applied in a system composed of several decision-making agents having conflicting opinions and aiming to reach a compromise that satisfies their desires and preferences.

4.3. Related work

Crucial knowledge identification is a relatively recent research topic and only few theoretical and empirical works are available in the literature.

The first work that we will discuss in this section is [GRU 04], which proposes global analysis methodology (GAMETH) to develop a decision support approach to identify and locate potential crucial knowledge [SAA 03]. The GAMETH framework can be seen as a decision support tool, which can be applied in the "investigation" phase [SIM 77] of a decision-making process in order to identify potential actions [ROY 00] with respect to the choice problem [ROY 85] concerning the capitalization of knowledge. This proposed methodology relies on three preordered steps:

– *The modeling of the company:* which is based on the concept of activity as having been defined by Lorino [LOR 92]. This leads to a modeling principle in which the company, as conceived by the knowledge that it produces, can be represented by the set of activities that make up the processes that are part of the company's mission. The activity model has been inspired by the system analysis and design technic (SADT) method [JAU 94].

– *The knowledge analysis model:* it is based on the so-called "sensitive processes". A sensitive process is a process, which represents the important issues that are collectively acknowledged. It is obtained through creativity sessions, building on the knowledge that is being held by the responsible persons within the intervention domain. Therefore, the sensitive processes are submitted to a risk assessment. This assessment helps to determine the "critical activities". The problems related to these activities are called "determining problems". The identification of the remaining determining problems leads to the identification of the knowledge that is required for their resolution. This knowledge can be qualified as "crucial knowledge" depending on its actual value.

– *The process modeling approach:* this approach, based on constructivist logic, consists of the construction of a process representation following from the partial knowledge that stakeholders have acquired through the activities that they are supposed to perform. Throughout the analysis, the problems encountered provide the possibilities for the identification of information and communication relations between stakeholders, not recorded in documents, and the identification of the knowledge required for the resolution of these problems. The advantage of this constructivist approach is that it stimulates collective engagement, which is primordial for a successful outcome of a knowledge management initiative.

This approach, which is based on process, has an informal character aiming at a knowledge structure sufficient for their exploitation by an individual and not by an automated system. GAMETH identifies a set of knowledge that is more informative than those identified by other approaches. Indeed, the identification of each knowledge is justified by its role in the resolution of a major problem. In addition, it does not require strategic analysis, which makes it useful at any hierarchical level of an organization. However, this method has major limitations. This is because it involves all stakeholders of the studied process that makes its implementation very complicated. GAMETH does not mention, also, any particular tool to the reification of explicit knowledge, already generated, for their eventual sharing.

In [CAC 08], the author proposed a method that deals with only the issue of knowledge storage and extraction in project-based firms. He develops the notion of "memory objects", which is classified into two types: objects of a static nature containing knowledge that remain unchanged from project to project, and objects of a reconfigurable nature that are "constructed through the recombination of relatively immutable components". This type enriches dialogue between project stakeholders with a well-defined context. The objective of the first type was to enable the individual to construct his/her knowledge without the systematic assistance of the people who hold this knowledge. The objective of the second type was to enable firms to build on experience, while maintaining the flexibility necessary to adapt to the specificities of each project. The author demonstrates how strategic knowledge can be formally expressed and used by means of an Excel workbook that has a crucial impact on how it functioned as a support for knowledge exchange, and therefore how the participants' expertise was retrieved.

Then, we present the paper of Zha *et al.*, [ZHA 08], which develops a practical compromise-based design decision model. It is based on a multiagent framework for collaborative decision and a hybrid approach that combines both, the qualitative and quantitative decision support. This proposed hybrid decision is basically data centric and aims to rank algorithms and inference mechanisms for engineering design evaluation and selection. This model is built upon a computerized platform for cross-functional, highly effective and well-supported engineering decision-making.

In this chapter, we focus on methods of knowledge identification-based processes, especially on the phase of resolution of conflicts that DMs can make when identifying knowledge on which it is necessary to capitalize. Among the existing methods, we chose those of [SAA 09], [CHA 12] and [BRI 11].

The research work [SAA 05] revealed the interest for identifying crucial knowledge. The authors propose a method to locate the company's crucial knowledge for improving the quality of decision-making in a design project. In fact, the method is based, essentially, on two dependent phases. The first phase is that of collecting a set of knowledge – as learning examples – called "reference knowledge" and then the identification of a set of criteria. The first phase is concluded by inferring a preference model that will be useful as an input for the second phase to access the classification of knowledge that can be crucial, called "potentially crucial knowledge".

–Phase 1: Construction of a preferences model

This phase is the succession of four steps starting with identifying and analyzing the "knowledge of reference" and the criteria to finish by the construction of a preference model that permits us to classify – with a coherent manner – all knowledge that may be crucial.

–Step 1: Defining a set of "reference knowledge"

A set of "reference knowledge" is a learning sample that includes an adequate number of examples (knowledge) representative for each determined decision class: "class of non-crucial knowledge" denoted by Cl_1 and "class of crucial knowledge" denoted by Cl_2. Both classes Cl_1 and Cl_2 are subject to an increasing order of preference, in fact, the Cl_2 class is preferable to the Cl_1 class. This set is used to infer decision rules, through the algorithm DOMLEM defined by the DRSA method, from DM preferences. The approach used to the identification of reference knowledge is the GAMETH framework. The choice of this method was justified by the diversity of its application areas and the approach used for the identification of knowledge.

–Step 2: In-depth analysis of "reference knowledge"

This is the step of characterization of knowledge. It seeks to determine – for each knowledge – depth, tacit/explicit [POL 96], specificity, accessibility, level of validation, efficiency and portability [DAV 98].

–Step 3: Construction of a coherent family of evaluation criteria

Three subfamilies of criteria were constructed: (1) knowledge vulnerability family that is devoted to measuring the risk of knowledge lost and the cost of its (re-)creation; (2) knowledge role family that is used to measure the contribution of the knowledge in the project objectives. Each criterion of this family corresponds to an objective; and (3) use duration family that is devoted to measuring the use duration of the knowledge based on the company average and long-term objectives. The evaluation of knowledge with respect to criteria of families (1) and (3) is normally provided by the DM. However, in practice, the DMs may show some difficulty in directly evaluating knowledge due to the complexity of some criteria. To overcome this problem, complex criteria are decomposed into several more simple indicators so that DMs can easily evaluate these indictors.

–Step 4: Construction of a preferences model

During this stage, the researcher involves every DM to determine the assignment examples. Indeed, based on assessments assigned to each reference knowledge on different criteria, each DM assigns each knowledge in the class Cl_1, class of non-crucial knowledge, or in the class Cl_2, class of crucial knowledge. The output of this operation is a number equal to the number of DMs, of decision tables. The decision table corresponding to a DM is made up of 32 lines and 15 columns. Each line is associated with one of the 32 "reference knowledges" that we want to classify and that is characterized by 15 criteria. The last column is reserved to the decision made by the DM concerning each "reference knowledge". So, the researcher, from the set of decision tables, infers, using an inference algorithm (DOMLEM, Explore) proposed in the DRSA method, for each DM, the decision rules corresponding to his/her assignment examples, and then the researcher checks, in an iterative manner, with every one of these DMs the inconsistency of his/her decision rules in order to reach, for each one, a consistent individual rule base. An inconsistency in a rule base can be caused due to a hesitation of a DM, a change of his/her point of view or an inconsistency in the family of criteria. Once the source of inconsistency is determined, the reaearcher corrects it with the concerned DM. This iterative process can be done in individual meetings with an average of 2 h. Finally, the researcher is charged with a single set of decision rules collectively accepted from consistent sets of individual rules. The construction of the collective set is based on a *constructive* approach based on the work of Belton and Pictet [BEL 97] using the technique of "comparison" that they have proposed. The quality of all of these rules must be verified by testing on assignment examples of new knowledge by the same DMs.

–*Phase 2*: Classifying potential crucial knowledge

The term "potential crucial knowledge" should be mapped to the concept of "potential alternatives" as defined in the multicriteria decision-making, that is, "a real or virtual alternative of action considered by at least one DM as a realistic one" [ROY 96]. Thus, "potential crucial knowledge" is the knowledge that has been identified as crucial by at least one DM. In this phase, a multicriteria classification of "potential crucial knowledge" is performed on the basis of the preferences model translated by the decision rules that have been collectively identified by the DMs in the first phase. It consists of four stages. The first stage consists of identifying a set of knowledge likely to be the object of an operation of capitalization, called potentially crucial knowledge. Then, in a second stage, this knowledge will be the object of an in-depth analysis. The third stage consists of evaluating this knowledge on the set of all criteria already identified in phase 1. Finally, the fourth stage is to assign, based on the preference model of the phase 1, the knowledge to a decision class in order to obtain all the effectively crucial knowledge. Knowledge, evaluations, criteria and decisions are grouped in a single table called "performance table", completed by the analyst or the reaearcher.

In our work, we focus on step 4 of the first phase. Step in which DMs can have different or even conflicting preferences, which prevents them from reaching a collective base of rules for the construction of a preference model. Indeed, we must reason about methods dedicated to conflict resolution. The iterative procedure adapted in [SAA 05] for the resolution of the conflicts between the DMs is not easily applicable in a distributed organizational context, when geographical distance and time constraints are added to a growing mass of knowledge and a significant number of DMs.

So to overcome these geotemporal constraints, authors in [CHA 12] have proposed a procedure based on the principle of majority defined through the *concordance* and *discordance* power, which no longer depends on the physical presence of stakeholders but rather on the quality of approximation. In fact, the *concordance* (respectively, *discordance*) power is defined based on the lower (respectively, boundary) class approximation and is calculated as follows:

Let H be the set of DMs and $^{i}\gamma'_{P}$ is the standardized approximation quality such that:

$$^{i}\gamma'_{P} = \frac{\gamma^{i}_{P}}{\Sigma^{h}_{r=1}\gamma^{i}_{r}}$$

Concordance power:

For each $x \in U$ and $Cl_{t} \in Cl$, two sets are defined:

$- L(x, Cl_{t}^{\leq}) = \{i : i \in H \wedge x \in \underline{P}(Cl_{t,i}^{\leq})\}$: set represents the DMs for whom object x belongs to the lower approximation of $Cl_{t}^{\leq}$.

$- L(x, Cl_{t}^{\geq}) = \{i : i \in H \wedge x \in \underline{P}(Cl_{t,i}^{\geq})\}$: set represents the DMs for whom object x belongs to the lower approximation of $Cl_{t}^{\geq}$.

The concordance powers for assigning x to $Cl_{t}^{\leq}$ and $Cl_{t}^{\geq}$ are computed as:

– $L^+(x, Cl_t^{\leq}) = \sum_{i \in L(x, Cl_t^{\leq})} {}^i\gamma'_P$: measures the coalition power of the DMs who assign x to the lower approximation of $Cl_t^{\leq}$.

– $L^+(x, Cl_t^{\geq}) = \sum_{i \in L(x, Cl_t^{\geq})} {}^i\gamma'_P$: measures the coalition power of the DMs who assign x to the lower approximation of $Cl_t^{\geq}$.

The concordance power is based on the lower class approximation, which contains objects that are assigned with certainty.

Discordance power:

For each $x \in U$ and $Cl_t \in Cl$, two sets are defined:

– $B(x, Cl_t^{\leq}) = \{i : i \in H \land x \in Bn_p(Cl_{t,i}^{\leq})\}$: set represents the DMs for whom object x belongs to the boundary $Cl_t^{\leq}$.

– $B(x, Cl_t^{\geq}) = \{i : i \in H \land x \in Bn_p(Cl_{t,i}^{\geq})\}$: set represents the DMs for whom object x belongs to the boundary of $Cl_t^{\geq}$.

The discordance powers for assigning x to $Cl_t^{\leq}$ and $Cl_t^{\geq}$ are computed as:

– $B^+(x, Cl_t^{\leq}) = \sum_{i \in B(x, Cl_t^{\leq})} {}^i\gamma'_P$: measures the coalition power of the DMs who assign x to the boundary of $Cl_t^{\leq}$.

– $B^+(x, Cl_t^{\geq}) = \sum_{i \in B(x, Cl_t^{\geq})} {}^i\gamma'_P$: measures the coalition power of the DMs who assign x to the boundary of $Cl_t^{\geq}$.

The discordance power is based on class boundaries, which contain objects that can be ruled neither in nor out as class members.

Object x is assigned to $Cl_t^{\leq}$ (respectively, $Cl_t^{\geq}$) iif:

i) there is a "sufficient" majority of DMs, using their classification quality, who assign x to $Cl_t^{\leq}$ (respectively, $Cl_t^{\geq}$) and

ii) when the first condition holds, no minority of DMs shows an "important" opposition in assigning x to $Cl_t^{\leq}$ (respectively, $Cl_t^{\geq}$).

However, despite its simplicity, this method remains objective and non-autonomous in the sense that we still talk of human stakeholders. It is for this reason that in the model Agent-KC (see Figure 4.1) proposed in [BRI 11], researchers replaced human DMs with artificial agents. This work proposes an argumentative multiagent model to automate the resolution of conflicts between DMs. Here, we no longer speak of a human decision maker, but rather of two types of artificial agents: DM agents, which replace the field stakeholders, and a mediator agent, which replaces – in some way – researcher. This approach is based both on a multiagent system and an argumentative approach allowing it to be less sensitive to any change in the amount of treated knowledge. The teamwork uses the K-DSS system to infer the inference model, and then the multiagent approach to conflict resolution.

K-DSS is a decision support system designed to identify and assess crucial knowledge. It consists of four components as follows:

– *Database:* contains all the data on the "KNOWLEDGE" class that is identified by a unique number, a name, a type and 11 attributes. Thus, eight of these attributes compose the knowledge vulnerability family. The ninth attribute represents its use duration. The last two attributes represent, respectively, the contribution of a process in a project and a project in an objective.

– *Knowledge base:* contains facts and rules officials to affect potentially crucial knowledge to the class of crucial knowledge.

– *Base model:* contains three types of algorithms that measure the contribution of knowledge to achieve various objectives, and both induction algorithms that ensure the inference of decision rules.

– *Graphic interface:* represents the description and the linking of the three components mentioned earlier.

In a first step, decision makers give their assessments of all knowledge on the set of all criteria that are entered by the analyst in the decision table, already stored in the database. Once the table is completely filled by the criteria, knowledge and assessments of all knowledge on all the criteria, the analyst intervenes again to complete the table for each DM with the classification that he/she assigned to each of this reference knowledge.

This complete table will be provided as input of the induction algorithm chosen by the analyst and that generates after the execution – as output – an initial list of decision rules for each DM agent. Different DM agents may have contradictory or, even, conflicting decision rules. The goal is to reach a list of rules collectively agreed, which fits a group decision.

This work is based on two types of agents:

– The mediator agent that is responsible for the knowledge base management. Its goal is to solve conflicts in order to have a consistent knowledge base. It detects conflicts and connects agents that are the source of these conflicts, and then prompts them to reach an agreement. If an agreement is not reached, the mediator agent makes an objective decision using its meta-rules. Note that only the mediator agent is allowed to modify the collective knowledge base. The mediator agent is supposed to be external to this platform since it does not participate in the classification process.

– The DM agents that are responsible for the knowledge classification on the basis of their beliefs. Each DM agent represents a human DM and manages an individual rule base allowing it to perform classification and argumentation. Agents involved in the knowledge classification process have the same goal: sharing a consistent knowledge base.

In case of conflict between DM agents, the mediator agent intervenes to identify those who are in conflict. It sends them, in pairs, a message *"call-for-arguments"* to inform them of this conflict and it remains in silence, waiting for a response that can be a "reject" or "accept". DM agents, upon receipt of this message, start exchanging messages, in order to reach an agreement. This process runs iteratively until a rejection or an agreement. At this point, the mediator reprised the role. If it is an agreement, so it updates the knowledge base to be consistent, otherwise it uses the method based on its meta-rules, which usually leads to an objective solution. The meta-rules that the mediator agent has are based on a weight associated with each criterion. The idea is to think about the comparison of the number of DM agents supporting the classification of knowledge subject of conflict, the quality of approximation of each of them, the number of rules inducing this classification and the average strength of these rules.

These various studies are summarized in Table 4.2.

Our work is inspired by the method of Brigui-Chtioui and Saad [BRI 11]. Indeed, we use a multicriteria decision approach, an argumentative approach and a multiagent system. Our goal is to enable DM agents to apply argumentative process to resolve the conflict announced without using an external agent such as the mediator.

	Studied Facet	Characteristics	Advantages	Limitations
[GRU 04]	Identification locating	- Mobilization of all the players who contribute to the project - Common validation by experts of the list of identified knowledge	- Constructive approach - More informative knowledge	- *Non-automated* method that may face temporal constraints - Complicated to implement
[CAC 08]	Storing, retrieving adapting	- Integration of the *memory object* notion: object of static nature and objects of *reconfigurable* nature - Well-defined context project	- *Automated* tool - Simplicity of knowledge exchange between projects	- Reserved for experts - Applicable only in projects-based firms
[ZHA 08]	Identification (design selection and evaluation)	- *Multiagent* platform - *Hybrid* approach - *Qualitative* and quantitative knowledge	- *Automated* framework - *Collaborative* model decision based-compromise	- Difficulties to maintain the consistency and validity of product by the repository management system - High costs and long development cycles
[SAA 09]	Identification preservation (conflicts resolution)	Mobilization of human decision makers and human studies	-*Group decision* that satisfies every decision maker - Constructive approach	Non-automated method that may face *geographical and temporal* constraints
[CHA 12]	Identification preservation (conflicts resolution)	*Automated* approach based on majority rule	- Simplicity of use - Non-compensatory aggregation model	-Solution based on objective calculations. - Centralized algorithm with *non-reviewable* parameters
[BRI 11]	Identification preservation (conflicts resolution)	- *Automated* approach based on a multiagent system - *Repetitive recourse* to a mediator agent	- Completely distributed system - Autonomous decision maker agents	- Compensatory aggregation model - *Objective* solution but not suitable for group decisions

Table 4.2. *Previous work characteristics*

4.4. Multiagent argumentative approach

To minimize the recurrent call for a mediator agent, we present multiple argumentation strategies for Agent-KC platform agents. In [AMG 06], argumentation theory is defined as the study of discursive techniques to induce or increase the adherence of minds to the theses that are presented for agreement. In this chapter, multiagent theory has been combined with an argumentative approach to cope with inconsistency in decision rule sets. Our multiagent system is made up of a set of autonomous behavior-based agents that act on behalf of their beliefs based on the interaction protocol. We propose agent strategies for arguments' construction based on agents' rule strength and criteria cores. Once transmitted, the argument is subject to an evaluation by the receiving agent. We conclude with a counter-argument construction algorithm to refine the selection of the counter-argument, in case of counter-argumentation.

4.4.1. *Interaction protocol*

The argumentative process is initiated by the mediator agent as soon as it detects a conflicting state. It is executed as follows:

– *Conflict detection*: once the agents' classifications are introduced in the collective knowledge base, the mediator agent checks consistency. In the case of contradictory classifications, the mediator agent declares a conflict state.

– *Argumentative process between two conflictual agents*: using chronological order of access to collective knowledge base, the mediator agent identifies the initiator agent and several receiving agents. For each knowledge, only one initiator agent is identified. It is the last one that classifies the knowledge subject of conflict in the collective knowledge base. It is called to conduct, sequentially, an argumentative process with each agent in conflict with it concerning the designated classification.

– *Collective knowledge base updating*: if, following the argumentative process, a unanimous agreement was reached, the mediator agent would be informed by the initiator agent and update the collective knowledge base with the new classification. Otherwise, mediator agent should come to an objective solution based on its private meta-rules.

4.4.1.1. *Argumentative process of the initiator agent*

The argumentative process is made up of three steps (see Figure 4.6). It is initiated by the receipt of a message *call-for-argument* from the mediator agent, after which the initiator agent constructs its first argument. Once constructed, the argument is sent to the receiving agent already identified by the mediator agent. The initiator agent waits for a response. It can receive three types of messages: *accept*, *reject* or counter-argument (message *justify*). If it is about a counter-argument, the initiator agent conducts an evaluation phase in order to consider the action to be undertaken.

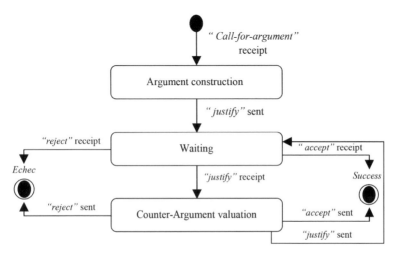

Figure 4.6. *Argumentative process*

4.4.1.2. *Argumentative process of the receiving agent*

The receiving agent argumentative process is launched by the reception of a *justify* message from the initiator agent. The receiving agent evaluates the argument in order to decide if it rejects, accepts or counter-argues.

4.4.2. *Arguments*

The argumentative approach is based on the exchange of arguments and counter-arguments. DM agents have to select a solution among two possible decisions: classify a knowledge K_i in the class Cl_1 of "no crucial knowledge" or in the class Cl_2 of "crucial knowledge". An argument is based on a decision rule and a set of evaluations. To introduce our arguments, we chose the pair structure (support, conclusion) introduced in [CHE 04]. Thus, an argument p proposed by an agent a_j is represented as follows:

$$- Arg_p^{a_j} = \langle \{f(x, g_i) = v_i \wedge ... \wedge f(x, g_n) = v_n; \text{ if } f(x, g_i) \geq v_i \wedge ... \wedge f(x, g_n) \geq v_n, \text{ then } x \in Cl_2\}, x \in Cl_2 \rangle$$

The initiator agent follows a given strategy to build an argument. We call strategy all tactics used by an agent to choose an argument among the set of arguments in its individual rules base, based on the power of its rules, its criteria core and its boundary. The strategy we defined is composed of three stages, subject to a pre-ascending order (see Figure 4.7), denoted by:

- ∂_i: a step i of the strategy, such as $i \in \{1..3\}$;

- R^{a_s}: the individual rules base of the agent a_s;

- $r_t^{a_s}$: the rule t part of the individual rules base of the agent a_s, i.e. ($r_t^{a_s} \in R^{a_s}$);

- $\alpha(a_s, k, Cl_t)$: the classification of knowledge k by the agent a_s in the class Cl_t.

NOTE.– A stage ∂_{i+1} is applied only if the cardinality of the set constructed from the application of the stage ∂_i is greater than 1, otherwise strategy stops at stage ∂_i.

PROPOSITION 4.1. – Let R^{a_s} be the individual rules base of the agent a_s and $K_i \in K$ a given knowledge from the knowledge base K. We call *rs* the function that returns the set of rules from R^{a_s} and supports the classification of K_i in class Cl_t.

$$rs : R^{a_s} \times K \rightarrow R^{a_s}$$

$$R^{a_s} \times K_i \rightarrow \{r_t^{a_s}, t \in \{1...n\}\}$$

where n is the number of rules involving the classification $\alpha(a_s, K_i, Cl_t)$.

PROPOSITION 4.2. – Let $r_t^{a_s}$ be a rule t from the individual rules base R^{a_s} of the agent a_s and F is a finite set of criteria. We called *crit* the function that returns the set of criteria contained in the premise of a rule.

$$crit: R^{a_s} \rightarrow F$$

$$r_t^{a_s} \rightarrow \{g_i, i \in \{1...m\}\}$$

where m is the number of criteria from F forming the premise of the rule $r_t^{a_s}$. We denote by a_{init} the initiator agent. Thus, we apply the strategy (see Figure 4.7):

– Step ∂_1: the initiator agent, a_{init}, selects one or several rules of maximum force among rules supporting the defended classification of K_i. The set of all chosen rules is denoted by Φ:

$$-\forall r_t^{a_{init}} \in \Phi, \nexists r_{t'}^{a_{init}} \in rs(R^{a_{init}}, K_i) \setminus \Phi \text{ such that } force(r_{t'}^{a_{init}}) \geq force(r_t^{a_{init}}); \text{ and}$$

$$-\forall r_t^{a_{init}}, r_{t'}^{a_{init}} \in \Phi, force(r_{t'}^{a_{init}}) = force(r_t^{a_{init}}).$$

If $|\Phi|=1$, the rule is selected to make the object of an argument. Else, go to stage ∂_2.

– Step ∂_2: the initiator agent chooses among the rules set Φ one or several rules with maximum criteria in common with its core. The set of rules constructed from stage ∂_2 is named Φ'. Thus, a rule $r_t^{a_{init}}$ is selected iif :

$$-\forall r_t^{a_{init}} \in \Phi', \nexists r_{t'}^{a_{init}} \in \Phi \setminus \Phi', \text{ such that } |CORE(a_{init}) \cap crit(r_{t'}^{a_{init}})| \geq |CORE(a_{init}) \cap crit(r_t^{a_{init}})|; \text{ and}$$

$$-\forall r_t^{a_{init}}, r_{t'}^{a_{init}} \in \Phi', |CORE(a_{init}) \cap crit(r_t^{a_{init}})| = |CORE(a_{init}) \cap crit(r_{t'}^{a_{init}})|.$$

If $|\Phi'|=1$, the unique rule is selected. Else, go to stage ∂_3.

– Step ∂_3: a rule $r_t^{a_{init}}$ is chosen if it contains a maximum number of criteria in its premise. The group constructed is denoted by Φ''. So, a rule $r_t^{a_{init}}$ is chosen iif:

$$-\forall r_t^{a_{init}} \in \Phi'', \nexists r_{t'}^{a_{init}} \in \Phi' \setminus \Phi'', \text{ such that } |crit(r_{t'}^{a_{init}})| \geq |crit(r_t^{a_{init}})|;$$

$$-\forall r_t^{a_{init}}, r_{t'}^{a_{init}} \in \Phi'', |crit(r_t^{a_{init}})| = |crit(r_{t'}^{a_{init}})|.$$

If $|\Phi''|=1$, the unique rule is selected. Else, the initiator agent selects randomly a rule from the most selective rules set, Φ''.

4.4.3. *Argument and counter-argument evaluation*

Argument or counter-argument evaluation depends mainly on the impact of the rule used in the argument and on the level of certainty of the knowledge classification. By the impact of the rule, we mean the violation rate of the rule on the individual rule base of the receiving agent.

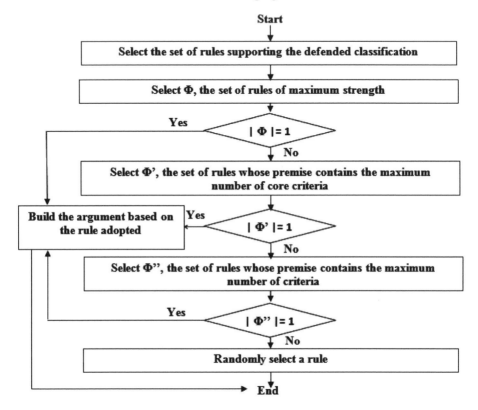

Figure 4.7. *Strategy of an argument construction*

4.4.3.1. *Violation rate*

By accepting a new rule from an agent with conflicting opinions, the DM agent accepts, indirectly, to change its priorities. It promises to change some classifications as well as a part of its rules. We call the rules impacted by the approval of the argument after evaluation violated rules.

PROPOSITION 4.3.– Let R^{a_s} be the individual rules base of the agent a_s and $Arg_p^{a_t}$ the argument p sent by the agent a_t. We denote by rv the function that returns the set of rules from R^{a_s} that are violated in the case of argument acceptance.

$$rv : R^{a_s} \times Arg_p^{a_t} \to R^{a_s}$$

$$R^{a_s} \times Arg_p^{a_t} \to \{r_i^{a_s}, i \in \{1..k\}\}$$

such that $\forall i \in \{1..k\}, r_i^{a_s} \in rv(R^{a_s}, Arg_p^{a_t})$ is violated by the argument $Arg_p^{a_t}$.

The agent must reason about what action to take by calculating the violation rate of the argument received. The violation rate resulting from an argument acceptance p advanced by an agent a_t, denoted by $Arg_p^{a_t}$, is based on the number of rules that are violated by the argument received and the total number of rules contained in the agent's individual rule base. It is calculated as follows:

$$\tau_{Arg_p^{a_t}} = \frac{|rv(R^{a_s}, Arg_p^{a_t})|}{|R^{a_s}|}$$

4.4.3.2. *Argument evaluation process*

The evaluation of an argument or a counter-argument is based on two criteria: the violation rate and the boundary. Each agent a_s fixes its acceptable violation rate, denoted by $\bar{\tau}^{a_s}$. Thus, the receiving agent does not accept an argument whose violation rate is greater than its acceptable violation rate. If the violation rate is less than the acceptable violation rate, the receiving agent accepts the argument and sends an accept message to the initiator agent. Otherwise, if the violation rate is greater than the acceptable violation rate, the concerned agent can either counter-argue or reject. If knowledge does not belong to the boundary of the receiving agent, i.e. if it was classified with certainty, the agent rejects the argument, otherwise it counter-argues (see Figure 4.8).

4.4.4. *Counter-argument construction*

To construct a counter-argument, the agent takes into account its local information and the argument received by the initiator agent $Arg_p^{a_{init}}$. The strategy consists of three steps:

– Step ∂_1: a receiving agent selects, from the rules that support the concerned classification, one or several rules with the maximum number of criteria in common with the premise of the rule $r_t^{a_{init}}$ contained in the received argument $Arg_t^{a_{init}}$. The resulting set of rules is called Φ .

$$-\forall r_{t'}^{a_{rec}} \in \Phi, \nexists r_{t''}^{a_{rec}} \in rs(R^{a_{rec}}, K_i) \setminus \Phi \text{ such that } |crit(r_{t''}^{a_{rec}}) \cap crit(r_t^{a_{init}})| \geq |crit(r_{t'}^{a_{rec}}) \cap crit(r_t^{a_{init}})|; \text{ and}$$

$$-\forall r_{t'}^{a_{rec}}, r_{t''}^{a_{rec}} \in \Phi, |crit(r_{t''}^{a_{rec}}) \cap crit(r_t^{a_{init}})| = |crit(r_{t'}^{a_{rec}}) \cap crit(r_t^{a_{init}})|.$$

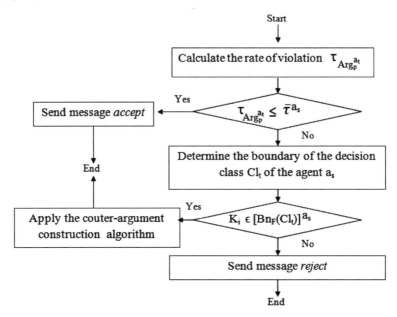

Figure 4.8. *Argument evaluation process*

If $|\Phi|>1$, go to the second step, else (if $|\Phi| = 1$), this unique rule is chosen for the counter-argument construction and the algorithm stops.

– Step ∂_2 once the cardinality of Φ is greater than 1, the receiving agent selects among rules contained in Φ that (or those) with the maximal strength. The new set is called Φ'. If a rule $r_{t'}^{a_{rec}}$ is selected in Φ', then there are no more rules in Φ of greater or equal force to that of $r_{t'}^{a_{rec}}$:

$$-\forall r_{t'}^{a_{rec}} \in \Phi', \nexists r_{t''}^{a_{rec}} \in \Phi \setminus \Phi' \text{ such that } force(r_{t''}^{a_{rec}}) \geq force(r_{t'}^{a_{rec}});$$
and

$$-\forall r_{t'}^{a_{rec}}, r_{t''}^{a_{rec}} \in \Phi', force(r_{t'}^{a_{rec}}) = force(r_{t''}^{a_{rec}}).$$

If $|\Phi'|>1$, the receiving agent performs the third selection criterion in step ∂_3. Else, the unique rule in Φ' is selected and the process stops.

– Step ∂_3: receiving agent builds from the set Φ', a set Φ'' of rules with maximum number of criteria in common with its criteria core:

$$-\forall r_{t'}^{a_{rec}} \in \Phi'', \nexists r_{t''}^{a_{rec}} \in \Phi' \setminus \Phi'' \text{ such that } |crit(r_{t'}^{a_{rec}}) \cap CORE(a_{rec})| \geq |crit(r_{t''}^{a_{rec}}) \cap CORE(a_{rec})|; \text{ and}$$

$$-\forall r_{t'}^{a_{rec}}, r_{t''}^{a_{rec}} \in \Phi'', |crit(r_{t'}^{a_{rec}}) \cap CORE(a_{rec})| = |crit(r_{t''}^{a_{rec}}) \cap CORE(a_{rec})|.$$ If multiple rules are identified ($|\Phi''|> 1$), the agent selects a rule randomly among Φ'', else the unique rule is chosen and the algorithm stops.

4.5. Example

To explain the multiagent argumentative approach, we have illustrated an example of two DMs: an initiator agent a_1 and a receiving agent a_2. Let K = $\{K_1...K_{24}\}$ be the 24 knowledge set and F = $\{g_1..g_{15}\}$ be a 15 criteria set on the basis of which knowledge is evaluated. Consider that DMs a_1 and a_2 have conflicting opinions concerning the classification of knowledge K_{11} of K. In fact, agent a_1 classified, with certainty, knowledge K_{11} in the class Cl_2 of crucial knowledge. By contrast, agent a_2 classified, as possible, the same knowledge in the class Cl_1 of non-crucial knowledge, i.e. $K_{11} \in [Bn_F(Cl_1)]^{a_2}$. We suppose that agent a_1 is the last agent who stated his/her classification of the knowledge K_{11}. Agent a_1 is, thus, called, via a message $call\_for\_argument$, which is transmitted by the mediator agent, to initiate an argumentative process with the agent a_2. Agent initiator, a_1, is committed, so, to build its first argument using the strategy of an argument construction (see Figure 4.7). We suppose that the individual rules base of the agent a_1 is formed of 17 rules and that of agent a_2 contains 12 rules. The core criteria of a_1 are $CORE(a_1) = \{g_1, g_3, g_7, g_9, g_{14}, g_{15}\}$ and those of a_2 are $CORE(a_2) = \{g_3, g_4, g_6, g_9\}$ (see Table 4.3).

Initiator agent a_1 starts by selecting rules supporting the classification $\alpha(a_1, K_{11}, Cl_2)$ among its individual rules base, returned by the function rs (see Table 4.4):

R^{a_s}	a_1	a_2
R^{a_s}	$\{r_i^{a_1}, i \in \{1..17\}\}$	$\{r_i^{a_2}, i \in \{1..12\}\}$
CORE	$g_1, g_3, g_7, g_9, g_{14}, g_{15}$	g_3, g_4, g_6, g_9
$[Bn_F(Cl_t)]^{a_s}$	K_{19}, K_{20}	K_{11}
τ^{a_s}	0.2	0.2
α	(a_1, K_{11}, Cl_2)	(a_2, K_{11}, Cl_1)

Table 4.3. *Illustrative table*

Rules	Strength%
$r_4^{a_1}, r_{11}^{a_1}$	46.15
$r_8^{a_1}, r_9^{a_1}$	38
$r_3^{a_1}$	30.76
$r_1^{a_1}, r_6^{a_1}$	23
$r_5^{a_1}, r_{10}^{a_1}$	15

Table 4.4. *Agent a_1 rules supporting the classification $\alpha(a_1, K_{11}, Cl_2)$*

$rs(R^{a_1}, K_{11}) = \{r_1^{a_1}, r_3^{a_1}, r_4^{a_1}, r_5^{a_1}, r_6^{a_1}, r_8^{a_1}, r_9^{a_1}, r_{10}^{a_1}, r_{11}^{a_1}\}$. We apply strategy:

– Step ∂_1:   The initiator agent a_1 selects one or several rules of maximum force, called Φ, among rules supporting the defended classification $\alpha(a_1, K_{11}, Cl_2)$, returned by the function rs. So, $\Phi = \{r_4^{a_1}, r_{11}^{a_1}\}$(see Table 4.4). $|\Phi|>1$, agent a_1 executes, then, the second stage .

– Step ∂_2: among rules contained in Φ, agent initiator a_1 selects that (or those) containing the maximum number of a_1 core criteria. Knowing that $r_4^{a_1}$ and $r_{11}^{a_1}$ are as follows:

$-r_4^{a_1} = $ if $f(x, g_1) \geq 2 \wedge f(x, g_4) \geq 3 \wedge f(x, g_5) \geq 1 \wedge f(x, g_7) \geq 2$, then x $\in Cl_2$.

$-r_{11}^{a_1} = $ if $f(x, g_{11}) \geq 1 \wedge f(x, g_{13}) \geq 2 \wedge f(x, g_{14}) \geq 3 \wedge f(x, g_{15}) \geq 3$, then x $\in Cl_2$.

We have $|crit(r_4^{a_1}) \cap CORE(a_1) = \{g_1, g_7\}| = |crit(r_{11}^{a_1}) \cap CORE(a_1) = \{g_{14}, g_{15}\}|$.

$|\Phi'| = \{r_4^{a_1}, r_{11}^{a_1}\}| = 2 > 1$, agent a_1 executes, then, the third stage to construct Φ''.

– Step ∂_3: among the set rules contained in Φ', a_1 selects that (or those) with the maximum number of premise criteria. We have:

$$|crit(r_4^{a_1})| = |crit(r_{11}^{a_1})| = 4$$

The most selective set Φ'' retains the same content of Φ'. Agent a_1 selects, then, randomly a rule from Φ''. Suppose that a_1 selected the rule $r_{11}^{a_1}$ and constructed its first argument as follows:

$$Arg_1^{a_1} = \langle\{f(K_{11}, g_{11}) = 2 \wedge f(K_{11}, g_{13}) = 2 \wedge f(K_{11}, g_{14}) = 3 \wedge f(K_{11}, g_{15}) = 4;\ \text{if}$$
$$f(x, g_{11}) \geq 1 \wedge f(x, g_{13}) \geq 2 \wedge f(x, g_{14}) \geq 3 \wedge f(x, g_{15}) \geq 3, \text{then}$$
$$K_{11} \in Cl_2\}, K_{11} \in Cl_2\rangle.$$

Receiving agent a_2, upon receipt of the argument $Arg_1^{a_1}$, triggers the evaluation phase to reason about what action to take: reject, accept or counter-argue. Let Ω be the set, returned by the function rv, of all rules belonging to the individual rules base of the agent a_2 and that are violated by the argument $Arg_1^{a_1}$:

$$\Omega = rv(R^{a_2}, Arg_1^{a_1}) = \{r_7^{a_2}, r_8^{a_2}, r_9^{a_2}, r_{10}^{a_2}, r_{12}^{a_2}\}$$

The violation rate calculated by the receiving agent is:

$$\tau_{Arg_1^{a_1}} = \frac{|rv(R^{a_2}, Arg_1^{a_1})|}{|R^{a_2}|} = \frac{5}{12} = 0.41$$

The violation rate calculated is greater than the acceptable violation rate already fixed by a_2 (0.2). The receiving agent cannot, thus, accept this argument. It should reason about its boundary to decide whether it will be a rejection or a counter-argumentation. Knowledge K_{11} belongs to the boundary of the receiving agent (see Table 3), it was classified with uncertainty in the class of non-crucial knowledge Cl_1. Thus, agent a_2 decides to counter-argue and executes the counter argument construction process.

4.6. Conclusion

In this chapter, we propose an argumentative approach that fits into the platform Agent-KC. This approach aims to minimize the recourse to the mediator agent to build a model of agents' preferences from assignment examples. Our literature review allowed us to identify the characteristics of the methods previously proposed. Some of them offer the intervention of an intermediary to make an objective decision in a case of disagreement between the DMs. However, these methods do not allow us to resolve the conflict between DMs, or eliminate the repetitive recourse to the intermediary. Through this work, we propose an argumentative approach based on a communication protocol and characterized by strategies allowing agents to exchange arguments and counter arguments in order to reach an agreement. Thus, our contribution compared to the related work lies in the adoption of an argumentative method whose objectives are to:

– reach a unanimous agreement, which would allow us to eliminate the recourse to the mediator agent favoring thus an important group consultation;

– ameliorate the quality of the objective decision of the mediator agent by refining its meta-rules on the basis of the argumentative process result.

In this chapter, we have not conducted an experimental approach that would allow us to test our argumentative approach and to assess its contribution. Agents' strategies that we have developed are to be tested in different contexts (heterogeneous agents, altruistic agents, etc). that would permit us to characterize each strategy of construction and evaluation of arguments with respect to agents' profiles. Thus, our short-term outlook is to develop a Java module that would fit into the platform Agent-KC. This module will also characterize their impact on the success of an argumentative approach.

4.7. Bibliography

[AMG 04] AMGOUD L., PRADE H., "Using arguments for making decisions", *Proceedings of the 20th Conference on Uncertainty in Artificial Intelligence*, pp. 10–17, 2004.

[AMG 06] AMGOUD L., PRADE H., "Explaining qualitative decision under uncertainty by argumentation", *21st National Conference on Artificial Intelligence (AAAI-06)*, pp. 219–224, 2006.

[AMG 12] AMGOUD L., VESIC S., "A formal analysis of the role of argumentation in negotiation dialogues", *Journal of Logic and Computation*, vol. 5, pp. 957–978, 2012.

[BEL 97] BELTON V., PICTET J., "A framework for group decision using a MCDA model: sharing, aggregation or comparing individual information", *Revue des Systèmes de Décision*, vol. 6, pp. 283–303, 1997.

[BEL 07] BELABBES S., "Contribution aux systèmes de délibération multi-agent: une approche argumentative", PhD Thesis, University of Toulouse, 2007.

[BON 97] BONDARENKO A., DUNG P.M., KOWALSKI R.A., *et al.*, "An abstract, argumentation-theoretic approach to default reasoning", *Artificial Intelligence*, vol. 93, pp. 1–2, 1997.

[BRA 96] BRACKER H., "Utilisation de la théorie de Dempster-Shafer pour la classification d'images satellitaires à l'aide de données multi-sources et multi-temporelles", PhD thesis, Ecole Nationale des Télécommunications de Bretagne, 1996.

[BRI 11] BRIGUI-CHTIOUI I., SAAD I., "A multi-agent approach for collective decision making in knowledge management", *Group Decision and Negotiation*, vol. 20, pp. 19–37, 2011.

[CAC 08] CACCIATORI E., "Memory objects in project environments: storing, retrieving and adapting learning in projects-based firms", *Research Policy*, vol. 37, no. 9, pp. 1591–1601, 2008.

[CAS 94] CASTELFRANCHI C., "Guarantees for autonomy in cognitive agent architecture", *Proceedings of the 1994 Workshop on Agent Theories*, Architectures and Languages, 1994.

[CAY 05] CAYROL C., LAGASQUIE-SCHIEX M., "On the acceptability of arguments in bipolar argumentation framework", *Proceedings of 8th European Conference on Symbolic and Quantitative Approache to Reasoning with Uncertainty (ECSQARU 2005)*, Barcelona, Spain, pp. 378–389, 2005.

[CHA 12] CHAKHAR S., SAAD I., "DRSA-based methodology for group multicriteria classification problems", *Decision Support Systems*, vol. 54, no. 1, pp. 372–380, 2012.

[CHE 04] CHESNEVAR C., MAGUITMAN I., ARGUENET A., "An argument-based recommender system for solving web search queries", *Proceedings of the 1st International Workshop on Argumentation in Multiagent Systems*, (ArgMAS 2004), vol. 3366, pp. 95–110 2004.

[DAV 98] DAVENPORT T., PRUSAK L., *Working Knowledge: How Organizations Manage What They Know*, Harvard Business School Press, Boston, MA, 1998.

[DUN 95] DUNG P., "On the acceptability of arguments and its fundamental role in non monotonic reasoning, logic programming and n-person games", *Artificial Intelligence*, vol. 77, no. 2, pp. 321–358, 1995.

[EEM 96] EEMEREN F., GROOTENDORST R., SNOECK HENKEMANS F., *Fundamentals of Argumentation Theory: A Handbook of Historical Backgrounds and Contemporary Applications*, Lawrence Erlbaum Associates, Hillsdale, NJ, 1996.

[ELV 93] ELVANG-GORANSSON M, FOX J., KRAUSE P., "Acceptability of arguments as logical uncertainty", *Proceedings of the European Conference on Symbolic and Quantitative Approaches to Reasoning under Uncertainty*, pp. 85–90, 1993.

[GRE 01] GRECO S., MATARAZZO S., SLOWINSKI R., "Rough sets theory for multicriteria decision analysis", *European Journal of Operational Research*, pp. 1–47, 2001.

[GRU 04] GRUNDSTEIN M., ROSENTHALL-SABROUX C., "GAMETH: A decision support approach to identify and locate potential crucial knowledge", *Actes de: 5th Conference on Knowledge Management (ECKM), Paris, France.*, 2004.

[JAU 94] JAULENT P., *Génie logiciel les méthodes*, Armand Colin, Paris, 1994.

[KRA 98] KRAUS S., SYCARA K., EVENCHIK A., "Reaching agreements through argumentation: a logical model and implementation", *Artificial Intelligence*, vol. 104, pp. 1–69, 1998.

[LIN 89] LIN F., SHOHAM Y., "Argument systems - a uniform basis for non-monotonic reasoning", *Proceedings of the 1st International Conference on Principles of Knowledge Representation and Reasoning (KR)*, San Francisco, CA, pp. 245–255, 1989.

[LOR 92] LORINO P., *Le Contrôle de Gestion Stratégique, la gestion par les activités*, Dunod Entreprise, Paris, 1992.

[PAR 98] PARSONS S., JENNINGS N., "Argumentation and multi-agent decision making", *In Proceedings of the AAAI Spring Symposium on Interactive and Mixed-Initiative Decision Making*, Stanford, CA, pp. 89–91, 1998.

[PAW 92] PAWLAK Z., "Rough sets", *International Journal & Computer Sciences*, vol. 11, pp. 341–356, 1992.

[POL 74] POLLOCK J.L., *Knowledge and Justification*, Princeton University Press, NJ, 1974.

[POL 96] POLANYI M., *The Tacit Dimension*, Routledge & Kegan Paul Ltd, London, 1996.

[RAO 93] RAO A., GEORGEFF M., "Modelling rational agents within a bdi-architecture", *Proceedings of the 2nd International Conference on Principles of Knowledge Representation and Reasoning*, pp. 473–484, 1993.

[ROY 85] ROY B., *Méthodologie Multicritère d'Aide la Décision*, Economica, Paris, pp. 141–174, 1985.

[ROY 96] ROY B., *Multicriteria Methodology for Decision Aiding*, Kluwer Academic Publishers, Dordrecht, 1996.

[ROY 00] ROY B., "L'aide à la décision aujourd'hui: que devrait-on en attendre", in DAVID A., HATCHUEL A., LAUFER R., (eds), *Les nouvelles fondations des sciences de gestion*, Vuibert, pp. 141–174, 2000.

[SAA 03] SAAD I., GRUNDSTEIN M., ROSENTHAL-SABROUX C., "Locating the company's crucial knowledge to specify corporate memory: a case study in automotive company", IJCAI 03, Acapulco, 2003.

[SAA 05] SAAD I., ROSENTHAL-SABROUX C., GRUNDSTEIN M., "Improving the decision making process in the design project by capitalizing on company's crucial knowledge", *Group Decision and Negotiation*, vol. 14, pp. 131–145, 2005.

[SAA 09] SAAD I., CHAKHAR S., "A decision support for identifying crucial knowledge requiring capitalizing operation", *European Journal of Operational Research*, vol. 195, no. 3, pp. 889–904, 2009.

[SHO 93] SHOHAM Y., "Agent-oriented programming", *Artificial Intelligence*, vol. 60, no. 1, pp. 51–70, 1993.

[SIM 77] SIMON H., *The New Science of Management Decision*, Prentice Hall, Englewood-Cliffs, NJ, 1977.

[VER 96] VERHEIJ B., Rules, reasons, arguments: formal studies of argumentation and defeat, PhD. Thesis, Maastricht University, Holland, 1996.

[VRE 97] VREESWIJK G., "Abstract argumentation systems", *Artificial Intelligence*, vol. 90, 1997, pp. 225–279.

[WOO 95] WOOLRIDGE M., JENNINGS N.R., *Intelligent Agents: Theories, Architectures, and Languages*, Springer-Verlag, Heidelberg, Germany, vol. 890, pp. 56–70, 1995.

[WOO 01] WOOLRIDGE M., *Introduction to Multiagent Systems*, John Wiley and Sons, 2001.

[WOO 02] WOOLRIDGE M., *An Introduction to Multiagent Systems*, John Wiley and Sons, New York, 2002.

[ZHA 08] ZHA X., SRIRAM R., FERNANDEZ M., MISTREE F., "Knowledge-intensive collaborative decision support for design processes: a hybrid decision support model and agent", *Computers in Industry*, vol. 59, pp. 905–922, 2008.

Chapter 5

Considering Tacit Knowledge When Bridging Knowledge Management and Information Systems for Collaborative Decision-Making

This chapter introduces an approach aiming to evaluate the level of tacit knowledge consideration during collaborative decision-making processes within information systems. The presented approach relies on original theories in the area of collaborative decision-making and information systems such as ethnographic workplace studies and the incommensurability of interpretative frameworks seen as the source of communication breakdown. This approach was inspired by the measurement framework from the international standard ISO/IEC 15504.

The link between knowledge management and information systems for collaborative decision-making can now be considered as an accepted source of improvements by the organizations. Collaborative tools or ontologies are examples of initiatives implemented to promote collaborative decision-making through knowledge management and information systems.

However, knowledge management is not limited to its technological approach, which rests on the codification of explicit knowledge and neglects its tacit dimension. Our research has shown that considering tacit knowledge

Chapter written by Pierre-Emmanuel ARDUIN, Camille ROSENTHAL-SABROUX and Michel GRUNDSTEIN.

within information systems improves collaborative decision-making. This leads us to think that evaluating the level of tacit knowledge consideration during collaborative decision-making processes within information systems could improve these processes.

The approach proposed in this chapter does not only rely on background theories, but also on fieldwork studies. We illustrate this approach with a case study, which has currently been tested within several large companies, and which could be improved in future studies, discussed at the end of this chapter.

5.1. Introduction

Since the 1970s, economic investment in computer science, information technologies and collaborative tools has been considerable. Over the last 20 years, as remarked by Landauer [LAN 95], productivity in the targeted services has been stagnating everywhere in the world.

At the same time, several authors warned the organizations about the possible loss of knowledge when neglecting tacit knowledge within them. Authors such as Tsuchiya [TSU 93] proposed to improve the knowledge creation, while others such as Liebowitz [LIE 08] proposed methodologies to retain it.

We consider that knowledge management should be an indispensable part of collaborative decision-making as it enables knowledge creation, knowledge sharing and knowledge retention. Collaborative decision-making is a process always followed by decision engendering actions. During this process, knowledge is created. We have to prevent the loss of this knowledge and improve its sharing. When knowledge is shared, decisions are more easily accepted, and collaborative decision-making improves. This has been discussed by Arduin et al. [ARD 13], who emphasized the impact of the consideration of tacit knowledge on collaborative decision-making.

In this chapter, we highlight the importance of tacit knowledge when bridging knowledge management and information systems for collaborative decision-making and propose an approach to evaluate the level of tacit knowledge consideration for this process. Being immaterial, tacit knowledge is often (not to say always) neglected. After remembering a vision of knowledge within the organization, we present the original background theories in the area of collaborative decision-making and information systems: the ethnographic workplace study introduced by Jordan [JOR 96] and the concept of incommensurability through the study of communication breakdown introduced by Kuhn [KUH 70]. These background theories consolidated our own research and fieldwork, and lead us to highlight some key points when considering tacit knowledge. Relying on the international standard ISO/IEC 15504 [ISO 03, ISO 04, we propose a manageable and justified approach to evaluate how much tacit knowledge is considered within collaborative decision-making processes and discuss it through a case study.

5.2. Background theory

The work presented in this chapter relies on the assertion that knowledge is not an object but the result of a piece of information interpreted by an individual. After having presented our vision of knowledge within the organization in section 5.2.1, we introduce the ethnographic workplace study and the concept of incommensurability in sections 5.2.2 and 5.2.3.

5.2.1. *A vision of knowledge within the organization*

Our vision of knowledge within the organization is greatly influenced by several piece of research, which are presented in this section.

When Polanyi [POL 67] introduced the concepts of *sense-giving* and *sense-reading*, we simply observed that we continuously appropriate information which is not ours. He defined them as follows: "Both the way we endow our own utterance with meaning and our attribution of meaning to the utterances of others are acts of tacit knowing. They represent sense-giving and sense-reading within the structure of tacit knowing" [POL 67, p. 301]. As the authors of this chapter, we have tacit knowledge that we have structured into information during a process of sense-giving. As the readers of this chapter, you have to interpret this information perceiving forms and colors, integrated words and data during a process of sense-reading, possibly creating new tacit knowledge for yourself (see Figure 5.1).

When a person P_1 structures his/her tacit knowledge and transmits it, he/she creates information. A person P_2 perceiving some data from this information and absorbing it, possibly creates new tacit knowledge. Thus, knowledge is the result of the interpretation of information by someone. This interpretation is acquired through an interpretative framework that filters data contained in the information and makes use of previous tacit knowledge, as presented by Tsuchiya [TSU 93] and Grundstein [GRU 11].

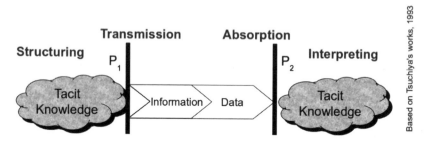

Figure 5.1. *Tacit knowledge transfer*

If the probability that two people will give the same meaning to the same information is high, it is said that their interpretative frameworks have a strong commensurability or are commensurable. On the contrary, if this probability is low, it is said that their interpretative frameworks have a low commensurability or are incommensurable. Many of our studies aim at setting a mean to measure this commensurability. We will see in section 5.2.3 how Kuhn [KUH 70] introduces the concept of incommensurability relying on the observation of communication breakdown between individuals. Is the observation of individuals, stakeholders and a collaborative decision-making process a way to estimate this commensurability and to prevent the risk of communication breakdown? What kind of observation should it be?

5.2.2. *Ethnographic workplace study: participation as a means to observe*

Historically, collaborative tools like the computer-supported cooperative work (CSCW) were the result of information technologies whose design was focused on the individual user [SCH 92]. Individuals are users and as such they are all individually connected to a system.

According to Stockdale and Standing [STO 06, p. 1091], neglecting social activity leads to "meaningless conclusions". AS such, we cannot be satisfied with a technological approach alone. This is confirmed by Jordan [JOR 96] who insists that knowledge is also tacit, embodied in individual minds: "We believe that there is yet another dimension that needs to be explored and that is the knowledge that is not only group-based but also tacit, implicit, embodied, and not articulated" [JOR 96, p. 18]. Therefore, knowledge can be of the following types:

1) Explicit knowledge: it is socially constructed and then can be supported by CSCW or similar technologies. Individuals, as well as computers, can be considered as "information processing systems" [HOR 03, p. 9].

2) Tacit knowledge: it is not always articulated, as expressed by [POL 58] "we can know more than we can tell".

The term "explicit knowledge" is often used (by Nonaka and Takeuchi [NON 95] and Nonaka and Konno [NON 98] notably), whereas it does not reflect the existence of an explicitation process of tacit knowledge. That is the reason why we talk of "explicited knowledge" instead of "explicit knowledge" when we identify knowledge resulting from an explicitation process of tacit knowledge. It is "what we know and can tell" that has been formalized and codified, answering to [POL 58] quoted above.

The creation and use of explicited knowledge within a group have been studied by Lave and Wenger [LAV 91] (Chapter 4). The transfer of knowledge has been characterized by Davenport and Prusak [DAV 98, p. 101] notably: "Transfer = Transmission + Absorption (and Use)". However, there are very few studies known about tacit knowledge and its use within a group, when bridging knowledge management and information systems for collaborative decision-making for example. The immaterial nature of tacit knowledge often leads people to neglect it or to take it into consideration only from a local point of view. Using and sharing tacit knowledge is rarely a part of organizational strategy. Jordan [JOR 96], with this in mind and relying on her anthropologist background, presents ethnographic field methods in order to highlight tacit knowledge within a group.

Early in the 20th Century, anthropologists studied exotic tribes and communities. They were away from civilization and from its rules, even the spoken language was unknown in many cases. As written by Jordan [JOR 96]: "Anthropologists learned to learn not by explicit instruction but by participating in the routine activities of people's daily lives and by immersing themselves in the events of the community [...]". They learned to see the world from the point of view of "the natives". This was the creation of ethnography: a methodology to understand complex functioning systems.

Every ethnographic fieldwork involves what Jordan calls "participant observation" [JOR 96, JOR 13]. A "participant observer" is not only the novice who tries to fit well into a community, but also the observer who needs to maintain a distance, record his/her observations and reflect his/her evolving understanding of the situations he/she encounters. Bardram [BAR 00] and Paoletti [PAO 09] notably presented how this kind of approach can improve collaborative work. Jordan [JOR 13] insists on the difference between an insider (employee) and an outsider (employer) to the studied process when carrying out ethnographic fieldwork. Lave and Wenger [LAV 91] present the apprentice as the "legitimate peripheral participant": he/she can ask questions, "get into interesting situations" and is thus in a powerful position to assimilate tacit knowledge within organizations.

Participant observation can thus be a means to consider tacit knowledge when bridging knowledge management and collaborative decision-making. The participant observer learns to become a part of the community and by doing so, he/she assimilates the tacit knowledge that was only known by "the natives". Here we can refer to [ROY 85] who introduces the "analyst" as the person who makes the problem explicit for the decision maker. At the same time, the analyst is an observer and a participant in the processes, he is a participant-observer in the sense of Jordan [JOR 96], as presented more precisely her fieldwork with the use of cameras, *in situ* question asking, etc. Her work consolidates the idea that doing together is a way to share tacit knowledge. We agree with this idea; nevertheless, doing together is not always sufficient to ensure tacit knowledge sharing. Particularly, when communication breaks down.

5.2.3. *Incommensurability: when communication breaks down*

As a philosopher of science, Kuhn [KUH 70] introduced the term "incommensurable" to characterize two theories whose transition "change their meanings or conditions of applicability in subtle ways" [KUH 70, p. 266]. Such theories are, he said, incommensurable. Kuhn was the first to tackle the problem of "partial communication", which will become "communication   breakdown".   He   identified   the   source   of   this communication breakdown as being a problem of incommensurable points of view.

In collaborative decision-making, or more generally within information systems, individuals share information. They learned a language that attaches terms to nature, the external word. This language is a constructed imprint of their own view of the world. It is the same mechanism that enables specialists to interpret Newton's second law $f = ma$, for example, as $mg = \frac{md^2s}{dt^2}$ for a free-fall or $mg \sin \theta = -ml\frac{d^2\theta}{dt^2}$ for a pendulum. So even this physical law has different interpretations. Language, whether natural or scientific, can be interpreted differently. Depending on what?

Kuhn [KUH 70] proposes to study the sources of communication breakdown, which are "extraordinarily difficult to isolate and by-pass" [KUH 70, p. 276]. Differences are not only in the terms or the language, but also and inseparably in nature. Two men, even if they see the same thing, and hold the same data, can interpret it differently. The differences between what is in nature and what they perceive as being in nature correlate to the corresponding differences in the language–nature interaction. The two men are processing the same data differently. They see the same thing differently. For Kuhn [KUH 70], their general "neural apparatus" is programmed differently.

According to him, this programming should be the same if the stakeholders share a history (except the immediate past), a language, an everyday world and science. Given what they share, they can highlight more about how they differ. They can discover the area where communication breakdown occurs. Often the root of the problem is that terms such as "element" or "compound" are used by both men but attached to nature in different ways (see Figure 5.2). For every identified term, they can found another in a basic vocabulary, whose sense in an intra-group use will cause no discussion, no request for explication, no disagreement. With time, these men will become good predictors of each other's behavior. They have learned to talk each other's language and also learned to see the world from each other's point of view.

We obtain a consideration for tacit knowledge through these efforts to understand each other by transcending ourself. It is a way to avoid communication breakdown, which is one of the difficulties encountered within information systems and collaborative decision-making.

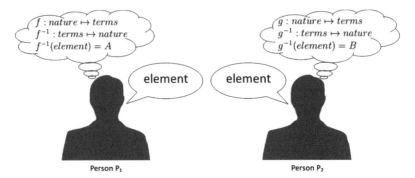

Figure 5.2. *Communication breakdown: when terms are attached to nature in different ways, for example when here $A \neq B$*

5.3. Proposition

In the section 5.3.1, we present research that we conducted within several large companies. Relying on the background theories presented and on our own convictions, we highlight diverse key points showing that tacit knowledge is considered within the collaborative decision-making process. This has already been discussed in the first part of this section and has already been discussed by Arduin *et al.* [ARD 12]. At this stage, a major weakness of our study was that although we knew how to identify relevant points showing that tacit knowledge was considered (or not) within collaborative decision-making processes, we were unable to characterize, compare and assess the collected data through a manageable and justified approach.

The international standard ISO/IEC 15504 [ISO 03, ISO 04] provides a clear and rigorous framework for process assessment. In the sections 5.3.2 and 5.3.3, relying on the background theories presented, the evidence highlighted in the field through participant observation (in the sense of Jordan [JOR 96]) and the measurement framework from ISO/IEC 15504, we propose to structure an approach to evaluate how much tacit knowledge is considered within collaborative decision-making processes. This approach is currently and continuously tested within industrial environments and will be, of course, improved and refined in future studies.

5.3.1. *Fieldwork through participant observation*

Taking into consideration the background theories discussed before, we point out the importance of tacit knowledge in information systems during collaborative decision-making processes. Regarding the human being as a component of a collaborative initiative and not only as a user of a system, we present several essential points for considering tacit knowledge and suggest some features of analysis.

The most recurrent observations in the field are the following:

1) even when collaborative decision-making implied knowledge management activities (document management system, ontologies, etc.);

2) it sometimes neglects tacit knowledge held by individuals;

3) however, collaborative decision-making processes are not always aware of the conditions and limits of enabling explicited knowledge, formalized and codified, to be correctly interpreted by all the stakeholders.

For us, relying on these statements, tacit knowledge is considered within collaborative decision-making processes when:

1) activities enabling the use and retention of knowledge created during the collaborative decision-making process are implemented;

2) the stakeholders are aware of the fact that knowledge is not an object (it results from the interpretation of information by someone, see section 5.2.1);

3) the conditions and limits, so that codified and formalized knowledge will have the same meaning regardless of who is receiving it, are known.

These three key points can be observed through organizational and individual behaviors. We present some of them below, which we have met in industrial fields.

5.3.1.1. *Activities that enable the use and retention of knowledge created during the collaborative decision-making process are implemented*

Knowledge has to be considered as a resource for every process, including a collaborative decision-making process. Although obvious, this is still not admitted for all the initiatives of collaborative decision-making met. Moreover, knowledge being created in the action, it is created within collaborative decision-making processes. They imply actions and create knowledge. We should maintain, retain and use the knowledge created through collaborative decision-making processes. One should manage this resource.

First, the stakeholders of collaborative decision-making processes should be aware that activities retaining or using knowledge are necessary. These activities can then be introduced in a local, informal and nonhierarchical way. Notably, we think about the SECI model of Nonaka and Takeuchi [NON 95] or the concept of Ba of Nonaka and Konno [NON 98]. Those are examples of activities managing not only explicited knowledge but also tacit knowledge. At best, knowledge management activities should be integrating parts of every collaborative decision-making initiative.

5.3.1.2. *The stakeholders are aware of the fact that knowledge is not an object*

Knowledge resulting from individual interpretation [TSU 93] can diverge from one person to another. That is the reason why knowledge management is not only the management of an "object knowledge", but also the management of the activities creating, retaining and using knowledge (see above). Then, we are sure that we are not losing the tacit dimension, which is often neglected when knowledge is regarded as an object.

First, the stakeholders of collaborative decision-making processes should not use the terms "information" and "knowledge" equally. Neglecting the fact that these words have different meanings shows that the stakeholders are not aware of the fact that knowledge is not an object. Once this distinction has been made, they can implement some activities aiming at highlighting and sharing tacit knowledge, in the sense of Davenport and Prusak [DAV 98, p. 101]. At best, collaborative decision-making processes should consider knowledge as resulting from the interpretation of information by someone and should integrate individual and collective learning and tacit knowledge transfer. We consider the apprenticeship among other things, where the master-apprentice model can be regarded similarly to the participant-observer model from [JOR 96] and considered as a way to ensure tacit knowledge transfer.

5.3.1.3. The conditions and limits, so that codified and formalized knowledge will have the same meaning regardless of who is receiving it, are known

The last point showing that tacit knowledge is considered when bridging knowledge management and information systems for collaborative decision-making has been led by the statement that collaborative decision-making processes can integrate knowledge management activities (first point), they can consider that knowledge is not an object (second point); nevertheless, it is possible that they do not know the conditions allowing an individual to be able to correctly interpret information disseminated within the information system or the collaborative decision-making process, able to interpret the pieces of information as sources of knowledge.

First, individuals should not simply be users of digital information systems or collaborative decision-making technologies. They should be actors of collaborative decision-making and part of an information system: this means that they should create their own knowledge by interpreting information and validate these interpretations through interactions with other individuals. These interactions can be limited, rare, user maintained, or hierarchically imposed. At best, every interpretation should be validated through interactions with other individuals without any hierarchical intervention, the validity of the interpretations then being ensured.

So our approach is a constructed imprint of these practical points that have been observed through ethnographic workplace studies as defined by Jordan [JOR 96] within industrial environments. The international standard ISO/IEC 15504 provides a methodological and manageable assessment framework, which allowed us to refine and characterize more precisely these practical points. They can be regarded as objective evidences: "data supporting the existence or verity of something" [ISO 04]. Our approach relies on the characterization of collaborative decision-making processes and information systems through the rating of organizational and individual behavioral attributes.

5.3.2. *Highlighting evidences and levels with ISO/IEC 15504*

The aim of the measurement framework from ISO/IEC 15504 is to assess process capability, which means to define a six-point ordinal scale depicting "the ability of a process to meet current or projected business goals" [ISO 04, p. 4], from "not achieving the process purpose" to "meeting current and projected business goals" [ISO 03, p. 6]. The measure is based on sets of process attributes, which represent particular aspects of the process capability. The extent of each attribute achievement is characterized on a defined scale and will allow us to determine the process capability level.

We propose to use, adapt and instantiate the manageable measurement framework from ISO/IEC 15504 in order to determine the level of tacit knowledge consideration within collaborative decision-making processes. Regarding these processes, we suggest a refined definition of the levels and a practical scan of their organizational and individual attributes. The proposed approach will thus allow people to evaluate how much information systems and the collaborative decision-making processes in which they are involved consider tacit knowledge. This will then enable them to identify ways of improving this consideration.

5.3.2.1. *Level 0: incomplete*

The collaborative decision-making process does not consider tacit knowledge or fails to achieve tacit knowledge consideration. There is little or no evidence that tacit knowledge is a preoccupation for the stakeholders of the collaborative decision-making process.

5.3.2.2. *Level 1: performed*

All the stakeholders of the collaborative decision-making process are aware of the existence of tacit knowledge. The following attribute of the collaborative decision-making process demonstrates the achievement of this level:

– Attribute 1.1: awareness that knowledge is not an object. This attribute measures the extent to which the stakeholders of the collaborative decision-making process are aware of the fact that knowledge is not an object. As a result of the full achievement of this attribute:

- Evidence 1.1.a: knowledge is not only regarded as an object, but all stakeholders are also convinced of the existence of tacit knowledge.

5.3.2.3. *Level 2: managed*

The collaborative decision-making process is now observed as described above, however, tacit knowledge consideration seems to be done in a managed fashion. The following attributes of the collaborative decision-making process, together with the previously defined attributes, demonstrate the achievement of this level:

– Attribute 2.1: knowledge management activities are implemented. This attribute measures the extent to which activities enabling us to retain and to use knowledge created during the collaborative decision-making process are implemented. As a result of the full achievement of this attribute:

- Evidence 2.1.a: technical tools are implemented in order to support the initiative of knowledge management (document management system for example). These tools are not necessarily completely used by all the stakeholders; however, they are implemented by order of the top management for example.

- Evidence 2.1.b: individual behaviors support the initiative of knowledge management (the stakeholders interact during the collaborative decision-making process without any hierarchical intervention for example).

– Attribute 2.2: knowledge management activities are managed. This attribute measures the extent to which activities enabling us to retain and to use knowledge created during the collaborative decision-making process are managed. As a result of the full achievement of this attribute:

- Evidence 2.2.a: objectives for knowledge management activities are identified.

- Evidence 2.2.b: organizational behavior supports the initiative of knowledge management (stakeholders' calendars include meetings on knowledge management for example).

5.3.2.4. *Level 3: established*

The collaborative decision-making process is now observed as described above, however, consideration of tacit knowledge seems to be an established part of this process. The following attributes of the collaborative decision-making process, together with the previously defined attributes, demonstrate the achievement of this level:

– Attribute 3.1: knowledge management theories are known and accepted. This attribute measures the extent to which the stakeholders of the collaborative decision-making process know and accept knowledge management theories. As a result of full achievement of this attribute:

- Evidence 3.1.a: the terms "knowledge" and "information" are not confused when stakeholders express themselves. Knowledge is considered as the result of the interpretation of information by someone.

- Evidence 3.1.b: the validity of interpretations is ensured through interactions between stakeholders.

- Evidence 3.1.c: the conditions and limits, so that codified and formalized knowledge will have the same meaning regardless of who is receiving it, are identified (same department and same activity for example).

– Attribute 3.2: knowledge is considered as a resource. This attribute measures the extent to which the stakeholders of the collaborative decision-making process consider that knowledge is a resource for their process. As a result of full achievement of this attribute:

- Evidence 3.2.a: there is a collective will to use the technical tools implemented in order to support the initiative of knowledge management.

- Evidence 3.2.b: knowledge retention is a problem already highlighted and knowledge is shared as in of Davenport and Prusak [DAV 98, p. 101].

- Evidence 3.2.c: knowledge creation is promoted.

– Attribute 3.3: there is an experienced knowledge manager. This attribute measures the extent to which a stakeholder of the collaborative decision-making process can be considered as an experienced reference in terms of knowledge management for the other stakeholders. He/she is not necessarily hierarchically superior to the other stakeholders. As a result of the full achievement of this attribute:

- Evidence 3.3.a: a stakeholder can unanimously be identified as the experienced knowledge manager.

- Evidence 3.3.b: required competencies for the knowledge manager are identified.

5.3.2.5. *Level 4: predictable*

The collaborative decision-making process is now observed as described above, however, tacit knowledge consideration seems to operate within defined limits to achieve its outcomes. The following attributes of the collaborative decision-making process, together with the previously defined attributes, demonstrate the achievement of this level:

– Attribute 4.1: knowledge management initiatives are applied. This attribute measures the extent to which all the stakeholders of the collaborative decision-making process accept and use the knowledge management activities implemented within this process. As a result of the full achievement of this attribute:

- Evidence 4.1.a: knowledge management activities are not only implemented, but also accepted and fully used by all the stakeholders (particularly technological tools).

– Attribute 4.2: measures are used. This attribute measures the extent to which assessments are made in order to ensure that tacit knowledge consideration supports collaborative decision-making process improvement. As a result of the full achievement of this attribute:

- Evidence 4.2.a: suitable methods for monitoring the effectiveness of the collaborative decision-making process are determined.

- Evidence 4.2.b: measures and frequency of measurement are defined.

- Evidence 4.2.c: tacit knowledge consideration measurement results are compared with collaborative decision-making process effectiveness and ways of improvements are studied.

5.3.2.6. *Level 5: optimized*

The collaborative decision-making process is now observed as described above, however, tacit knowledge consideration is continuously improved to ensure that the collaborative decision-making process will achieve current and projected business goals. The following attributes of the collaborative decision-making process, together with the previously defined attributes, demonstrate the achievement of this level:

– Attribute 5.1: performance is analyzed. This attribute measures the extent to which changes to the way of considering tacit knowledge are identified as causes of variation in collaborative decision-making process performance. As a result of the full achievement of this attribute:

- Evidence 5.1.a: data are analyzed to identify causes of variation in collaborative decision-making process performance.

- Evidence 5.1.b: data are analyzed to identify best practice and innovation.

- Evidence 5.1.c: improvement opportunities derived from new technologies are identified.

– Attribute 5.2: change is managed. This attribute measures the extent to which changes in the way of considering tacit knowledge are managed in order to minimize the disruptions on collaborative decision-making process performance. As a result of the full achievement of this attribute:

- Evidence 5.2.a: impact of all proposed changes is assessed against the objectives of the collaborative decision-making process.

- Evidence 5.2.b: implementation of all agreed changes is managed to ensure that any disruption to the collaborative decision-making process is understood and acted upon.

So our approach relies on the assessment framework from ISO/IEC 15504. We define six levels of tacit knowledge consideration within collaborative decision-making processes. Each level is composed of attributes characterizing assessed collaborative decision-making processes and information systems. These attributes are rated through ethnographic fieldwork [JOR 96], which allows the observation of evidence. Figure 5.3 shows our approach in an intuitive way: the levels, the attributes and the evidences.

5.3.3. *Rating the attributes and assessing tacit knowledge consideration*

According to ISO/IEC 15504, the extent to which the attributes are achieved is measured using the ordinal scale as defined below [ISO 03, p. 10]:

– N: not achieved (0–15% achievement): there is little or no evidence of achievement of the defined attribute in the assessed process.

– P: partially achieved (>15–50% achievement): there is some evidence of an approach to, and some achievement of, the defined attribute in the assessed process. Some aspects of achievement of the attribute may be unpredictable.

– L: largely achieved (>50–85% achievement): there is evidence of a systematic approach to, and significant achievement of, the defined attribute in the assessed process. Some weakness related to this attribute may exist in the assessed process.

– F: fully achieved (>85–100% achievement): there is evidence of a complete and systematic approach to, and full achievement of, the defined attribute in the assessed process. No significant weaknesses related to this attribute exist in the assessed process.

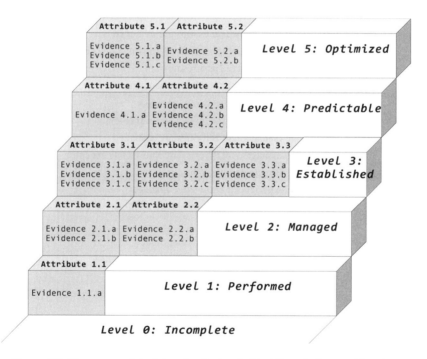

Figure 5.3. *Our approach to determine the level of tacit knowledge consideration*

An output of an assessment is the set of attribute ratings for the considered collaborative decision-making process. This set is called the process profile by ISO/IEC 15504-2 [ISO 03, p. 11]. Based on [ISO 03], in

Table 5.1, we propose the process profile to determine the level of tacit knowledge consideration within a collaborative decision-making process. Every level adds new attributes for the collaborative decision-making process. To achieve a level, these attributes are regarded together with the previously defined attributes as defined by ISO/IEC 15504-2 [ISO 03] and ISO/IEC 15504-1 [ISO 04].

Scale	Attributes	Rating
Level 0		
Level 1	Awareness that knowledge is not an object	L or F
Level 2	Awareness that knowledge is not an object	F
	Knowledge management activities are implemented	L or F
	Knowledge management activities are managed	L or F
Level 3	Awareness that knowledge is not an object	F
	Knowledge management activities are implemented	F
	Knowledge management activities are managed	F
	Knowledge management theories are known and accepted	L or F
	Knowledge is considered as a resource	L or F
	There is an experienced knowledge manager	L or F
Level 4	Awareness that knowledge is not an object	F
	Knowledge management activities are implemented	F
	Knowledge management activities are managed	F
	Knowledge management theories are known and accepted	F
	Knowledge is considered as a resource	F
	There is an experienced knowledge manager	F
	Knowledge management initiatives are applied	L or F
	Measures are used	L or F
Level 5	Awareness that knowledge is not an object	F
	Knowledge management activities are implemented	F
	Knowledge management activities are managed	F
	Knowledge management theories are known and accepted	F
	Knowledge is considered as a resource	F
	There is an experienced knowledge manager	F
	Knowledge management initiatives are applied	F
	Measures are used	F
	Performance is analyzed	L or F
	Change is managed	L or F

Table 5.1. *Tacit knowledge consideration levels and attribute ratings (based on [ISO 03])*

5.4. Case study

According to Jordan [JOR 96], we suggest ethnographic fieldwork is carried out when applying our approach. The participant-observer has to be aware of the distinction between what is said and what is done. Indeed, we have often observed in the field that people sometimes take tacit knowledge into account where the entire tacit dimension should be ignored; or, they do not take it into account where knowledge management activities are inherent in collaborative decision-making processes. When it comes to tacit knowledge, every investigation should be carried out as closely as possible with the stakeholders, who hold tacit knowledge.

The field considered here has been studied through ethnographic fieldwork [JOR 96]: we were not only observers but also participants in the collaborative decision-making processes and actors within information system. This was the best way to observe and collect evidence in the field. Let us present now how much the collaborative decision-making processes and the information system studied within this field, a large insurance company, consider tacit knowledge.

5.4.1. *Describing the field*

In 2010, a large insurance company asked as to implement a knowledge management initiative within a team of four in order to improve knowledge retention and collaborative decision-making. People were doing the same work but separately. The decisions were not shared and not always accepted. Six months after the beginning of our work, knowledge sharing improved not only knowledge retention, but also collaborative decision-making: the decisions collectively taken were shared and accepted by all the stakeholders. The full version of this case study can be found in [ARD 13].

When we began working in this field, the stakeholders agreed with the idea that knowledge is not an object (evidence 1.1.a). Indeed, they were doing service work. At this point, we can thus say that their level of tacit knowledge consideration is at least the level 1: performed.

Technical tools were already implemented (evidence 2.1.a), although they were not very well used. Furthermore, one stakeholder was particularly against the knowledge management initiative. This was then resolved and the individual behaviors of all the stakeholders supported the knowledge management initiative (evidence 2.1.b). We identified the objectives for the knowledge management initiative (evidence 2.2.a) to retain the knowledge acquired by the team and to improve collaborative decision-making. As it was requested by senior management, this initiative was supported by the behavior of the organization (evidence 2.2.b). At this point, we can thus say that their level of tacit knowledge consideration is at least at level 2: managed.

The distinction between the terms "knowledge" and "information" was of course not clear at the beginning. Nevertheless, the stakeholders became more and more precise when they expressed themselves and there was evidence that these terms were not confused at the end of the fieldwork (evidence 3.1.a). Because the behavior of the organization and its individuals supported the knowledge management initiative, the stakeholders ensured the validity of their interpretations through interactions between themselves (evidence 3.1.b), they interacted a lot at the end of the fieldwork and continue today to organize joint events to improve interaction. A major weakness of their collaborative decision-making processes and information system was that they did not know the conditions and limits, so that codified and formalized knowledge has the same meaning regardless of who is receiving it. Evidence 3.1.c is thus not achieved. Although the problem of knowledge retention has already been highlighted (evidence 3.2.b), there was no collective will to use the technical tools implemented to support the initiative of knowledge management, and knowledge creation was not actually promoted. Evidences 3.2.a and 3.2.c are thus not achieved, so that attribute 3.2 is partially achieved (>15–50% achievement). Their collaborative decision-making processes cannot be characterized as considering tacit knowledge up to level 3: established, which requires attribute 3.2 largely or fully achieved (see Tables 5.1 5.2). The achieved level is level 2: managed. Table 5.2 presents this assessment.

More than 3 years after our work, the team considers knowledge management as a key aspect to its activities, and the knowledge retention process continues to provide a space where people can efficiently discuss and improve collaborative decision-making. This space is notably reflected by weekly planned meetings, which are unanimously desired by the stakeholders. However, it is hard to say whether they are now all ready to use the implemented technological tools and to study the conditions and limits so that codified and formalized knowledge will have the same meaning regardless of who is receiving it. The level of tacit knowledge consideration seems thus to remain at level 2: managed.

5.4.2. *Discussing the collected data and the results*

Table 5.2 presents how our approach worked to determine the level of tacit knowledge consideration within the studied field. Attributes are rated due to the observation (or not) of evidence, and this is done until an attribute rating prevents the achievement of an upper level. In Table 5.2, for example, attribute 3.2 is rated P while a rating L or F is needed to achieve the level 3 (see Table 5.1). This is the reason why the evaluation stops, the remaining attributes are not rated and the assessed collaborative decision-making process achieves the level 2 of tacit knowledge consideration.

The evidence defined in section 5.3.2 are the data of our study. This kind of data can be hard to collect within industrial fields, notably because it refers to intangible elements that are located "between two ears, and only between two ears" according to Drucker [DRU 69]. These intangible elements are tacit knowledge. We worked as participant-observers [JOR 96], assimilated explicited and tacit knowledge, and then were able to observe the field from the point of view of the stakeholders. We collected evidence, rated attributes and finally evaluated the level of tacit knowledge consideration according to our assessment framework inspired from ISO/IEC 15504.

One of the strengths of the representation proposed in Table 5.2 is that the weaknesses of the considered field are clearly highlighted: it should consider more knowledge as a resource to increase its tacit knowledge consideration. So, this is a real strength of our approach: to provide information regarding whether or not actions have been taken. It shows ways of improving collaborative decision making processes and information systems, in terms of tacit knowledge consideration.

Scale	Attributes and evidence	Rating
Level 0		
Level 1	1.1: awareness that knowledge is not an object	F
	1.1.a: knowledge is not only regarded as an object	✔
Level 2	2.1: knowledge management activities are implemented	F
	2.1.a: technical tools are implemented	✔

	2.1.b: individual behavior supports the initiative of KM	✔
	2.2: knowledge management activities are managed	F
	2.2.a: objectives for the KM activities are identified	✔
	2.2.b: organizational behavior supports the initiative of KM	✔
Level 3	3.1: knowledge management theories are known and accepted	L
	3.1.a: the terms "knowledge" and "information" are not confused	✔
	3.1.b: the validity of interpretations is ensured through interactions between stakeholders	✔
	3.1.c: the conditions and limits (so that codified and formalized knowledge will have the same meaning regardless of who is receiving it) are identified	✖
	3.2: knowledge is considered as a resource	P
	3.2.a: there is a collective will to use the technical tools implemented in order to support the initiative of KM	✖
	3.2.b: knowledge retention is a problem already highlighted and knowledge is shared in the sense of [DAV 98, p.101]	✔
	3.2.c: knowledge creation is promoted	✖
	3.3: there is an experienced knowledge manager	
	3.3.a: a stakeholder can unanimously be identified as the experienced knowledge manager	
	3.3.b: required competencies for the knowledge manager are identified	
Level 4	4.1: knowledge management initiatives are applied	
	4.1.a: knowledge management activities are not only implemented, but also accepted and fully used by all the stakeholders (particularly technological tools)	
	4.2: measures are used	
	4.2.a: suitable methods for monitoring the effectiveness of the collaborative decision-making process are determined	
	4.2.b: measures and frequency of measurement are defined	
Level 5	5.1: performance is analyzed	
	5.1.a: data are analyzed to identify causes of variation in collaborative decision-making process performance	
	5.1.b: data are analyzed to identify best practice and innovation	
	5.1.c: improvement opportunities derived from new technologies are identified	
	5.2: change is managed	
	5.2.a: impact of all proposed changes is assessed against the objectives of the collaborative decision-making process	
	5.2.b: implementation of all agreed changes is managed to ensure that any disruption to the collaborative decision-making process is understood and acted upon	

Table 5.2. *Evidence, attributes and level of tacit knowledge consideration for the studied field*

A major weakness of our study is that we could not present a comparative study between the tacit knowledge consideration level and the efficiency of the considered collaborative decision-making processes. Relying notably on the studies of the American Productivity and Quality Center (APQC) [YOK 11], which compares knowledge management maturity and organizational performance, we should try to do this comparison. Indeed, our approach focuses not only on tacit knowledge, but also on collaborative decision-making and information system.

As presented in section 5.2.1, if the probability that two people will give the same meaning to the same information is high, it is said that their interpretative frameworks have a strong commensurability or are commensurable. On the contrary, if this probability is low, it is said that their interpretative frameworks have a low commensurability or are incommensurable. With regard to the presented case study, we observed that at the beginning, the interpretative frameworks of the stakeholders were incommensurable: the probability that the same information had the same meaning for every stakeholder was low. Tacit knowledge was poorly considered: when sharing information, people did not share tacit knowledge. Increasing the commensurability of their interpretative frameworks allowed them to share tacit knowledge rapidly (information having the same meaning) which then catalyzes collaborative decision-making. Through our initiative of knowledge management within collaborative decision-making and information systems, we gave stakeholders the opportunity to consider tacit knowledge, showing them ways to increase the commensurability of their interpretative frameworks. Our study is now focusing on finding ways to measure the commensurability of interpretative frameworks.

The use of the international standard ISO/IEC 15504 also needs to be discussed: we do not know today to what extent we can use quality standards to study knowledge management initiatives. The deterministic view of these frameworks goes against the constructivist ambition of our vision of knowledge management [ROY 85]. The idea of evaluating something that is constructing itself during the evaluation has its own limits, and requires further study.

5.5. Conclusions

In this chapter, we presented several background theories unexpected in the classical area of collaborative decision-making such as knowledge seen as an individual interpretation, ethnographic workplace study and incommensurability through communication breakdown study. We finally explain the approach we have developed in the field relying on these theories and on the structure of the measurement framework from the international standard ISO/IEC 15504. This approach evaluates the consideration devoted to tacit knowledge when bridging knowledge management and information systems for collaborative decision-making.

During our study, we observed that time information systems and collaborative technologies often have the same weakness: the collaborative group is only viewed as a network of individual users without considering that each single user creates, shares and assimilates tacit knowledge. Arduin *et al.* [ARD 13], who emphasized the impact of considering tacit knowledge on collaborative decision-making, have led us to think that evaluating tacit knowledge consideration within information systems and during collaborative decision-making processes could improve these processes. Then, we proposed to focus on tacit knowledge, which is our richer resource, the most effective, the most singular and the hardest to disseminate. So, we relied on the theories of Jordan [JOR 96] who explains how tacit knowledge can be handled in practice, and on the concept of incommensurability introduced by Kuhn [KUH 70] in order to study how and when communication breaks down.

The anthropologists were the first to learn, in spite of themselves, without "explicit instruction but by participating in the routine activities" as observed by Jordan [JOR 96]. Doing so, they create a kind of methodology in order to assimilate tacit knowledge and to understand complex systems. They learned to see the world from the point of view of "the natives".

Knowledge resulting from the interpretation of information by someone, [KUH 70] introduced the concept of incommensurability, which is encountered when communication breaks down, when stakeholders' language attaches terms to nature in different ways. They see the same thing but interpret it differently. To bypass communication breakdown, individuals should be able to see the world from each other's point of view and understand how each other's language attaches terms to nature. This can be done using ethnographic fieldwork study as introduced by Jordan [JOR 96] and presented in section 5.2.2.

These theories converge to the idea of transcending individual's points of view, sustaining our research on increasing interpretative frameworks' commensurability. Beyond the theories, our approach has been influenced by three points observed within industrial environments which are: (1) activities that enable us to retain and to use knowledge created during the collaborative decision-making process are implemented, (2) awareness of stakeholders that knowledge is not an object, and, (3) conditions and limits, so that codified and formalized knowledge which will have the same meaning regardless of who is receiving it, are known. On the basis of this, we constructed a manageable and justified measurement framework in order to evaluate tacit knowledge consideration within collaborative decision-making processes.

Our approach is currently being tested by several large companies. To enhance this study, it will be interesting to estimate the impact of tacit knowledge consideration on the efficiency of collaborative decision-making processes or information systems. We should also study the link between the level of tacit knowledge consideration presented in this chapter and the commensurability of stakeholders' interpretative frameworks in order to prevent the risks of communication breakdown within collaborative decision-making processes or information systems.

Knowledge management offers an interesting background in order to improve collaborative decision-making and information systems. Moreover, it gives methodological answers today to old technological weaknesses: beginning to see the human being not only as the user of a system, but also as someone who creates knowledge, shares knowledge and uses knowledge.

5.6. Acknowledgments

The authors would like to express their gratitude to Káthia Oliveira who sincerely devoted her time and knowledge on assessment models. She has been tremendously helpful in the achievement of this study. They would also like to thank the members of every company visited who provided invaluable study material.

5.7. Bibliography

[ARD 12] ARDUIN P-E., ROSENTHAL-SABROUX C., GRUNDSTEIN M., "Considering tacit knowledge when bridging knowledge management and collaborative decision making", *Proceedings of the EWG-DSS Liverpool-2012 Workshop on Decision Systems*, Liverpool, UK, 12–13 April 2012.

[ARD 13] ARDUIN P-E., GRUNDSTEIN M., ROSENTHAL-SABROUX C., "From knowledge sharing to collaborative decision making", *International Journal of Information and Decision Sciences*, vol. 5, no. 3, pp. 295–311, 2013.

[BAR 00] BARDRAM J., "Scenario-based design of cooperative systems", *Group Decision and Negotiation*, vol. 9, no. 3, pp. 237–250, 2000.

[DAV 98] DAVENPORT T., PRUSAK L., *Working Knowledge: How Organizations Manage What They Know*, Harvard University Press, 1998.

[DRU 69] DRUCKER P.F., *The Age of Discontinuity: Guidelines to Our Changing Society*, Harper & Row, 1969.

[GRU 11] GRUNDSTEIN M., "Towards a technological, managerial, and socio-technical well-balanced KM initiative strategy within organizations", *Proceedings of the 8th International Conference on Intellectual Capital, Knowledge Management and Organisational Learning*, vol. 1, The Institute for Knowledge and Innovation Southeast Asia of Bangkok University, Thailand, pp. 200–210, 2011.

[HOR 03] HORNUNG B.R., "Constructing sociology from first order cybernetics: basic concepts for a sociocybernetic analysis of information society", *4th International Conference of Sociocybernetics*, Corfu, Greece, 2003. Available at: http://www.unizar.es/sociocybernetics/congresos/CORFU/papers/hornung.html.

[ISO 03] ISO/IEC 15504-2, Software engineering – process assessment – part 2: performing an assessment, 2003.

[ISO 04] ISO/IEC 15504-1, Information technology – process assessment – part 1: concepts and vocabulary, 2004.

[JOR 96] JORDAN B., "Ethnographic workplace studies and computer supported cooperative work", in SHAPIRO D., TAUBER M., TRAUNMÜLLER R. (eds), *The Design of Computer-Supported Cooperative Work and Groupware Systems*, North Holland/Elsevier Science, Amsterdam, The Netherlands, pp. 17–42, 1996.

[JOR 09] JORDAN B., "Working in corporate jungles: reflections on ethnographic praxis in industry", in CEFKIN M. (ed.), *Ethnography and the Corporate Encounter: Reflections on Research in and of Corporations*, Berghahn Books, New York, 2009.

[JOR 13] JORDAN B., "Introduction", in JORDAN B. (ed.), *Advancing Ethnography in Corporate Environments: Challenges and Emerging Opportunities*, Left Coast Press, Walnut Creek, CA, pp. 7–22, 2013.

[KUH 70] KUHN T., "Reflections on my critics", in LAKATOS I., MUSGRAVE A. (eds), *Criticism and the Growth of Knowledge*, Cambridge University Press, New York, pp. 231–278, 1970.

[LAN 95] LANDAUER T., *The Trouble With Computers: Usefulness, Usability, and Productivity*, MIT Press, 1995.

[LAV 91] LAVE J., WENGER E., *Situated Learning: Legitimate Peripheral Participation*, Cambridge University Press, 1991.

[LIE 08] LIEBOWITZ J., *Knowledge Retention: Strategies and Solutions*, CRC Press, 2008.

[NON 95] NONAKA I., TAKEUCHI H., *The Knowledge-Creating Company: How Japanese Companies Create the Dynamics of Innovation*, Oxford University Press, New York, 1995.

[NON 98] NONAKA I., KONNO N., "The concept of 'Ba': building a foundation for knowledge creation", *California Management Review*, vol. 40, no. 3, pp. 40–54, 1998.

[PAO 09] PAOLETTI I., "Communication and diagnostic work in medical emergency calls in Italy", *Computer Supported Cooperative Work (CSCW)*, vol. 18, nos. 2–3, pp. 229–250, 2009.

[POL 58] POLANYI M., *Personal Knowledge: Towards a Post Critical Philosophy*, Routledge, London, 1958.

[POL 67] POLANYI M., "Sense-giving and sense-reading", *Philosophy: Journal of the Royal Institute of Philosophy*, vol. 42, no. 162, pp. 301–323, 1967.

[ROY 85] ROY B., *Méthodologie Multicritère d'aide à la Décision* (*Multicriteria Methodology for Decision Aiding*), Économica, 1985.

[SCH 92] SCHMIDT K., BANNON L., "Taking CSCW seriously: supporting articulation work", *Computer Supported Cooperative Work (CSCW)*, vol. 1, no. 1, pp. 7–40, 1992.

[STO 06] STOCKDALE R., STANDING C., "An interpretive approach to evaluating information systems: a content, context, process framework", *European Journal of Operational Research*, vol. 173, no. 3, pp. 1090–1102, 2006.

[TSU 93] TSUCHIYA S., "Improving knowledge creation ability through organizational learning", *Proceedings of the International Symposium on the Management of Industrial and Corporate Knowledge (ISMICK 1993)*, UTC, Compiègne, France, 1993.

[YOK 11] YOKELL M., MARTIN L., PENALOZA P., How mature is your KM program? Using APQC's KM capability asssessment tool, Report, American Productivity and Quality Center, 2011.

Chapter 6

Relevant Information
Management in Microblogs

Modern information retrieval (IR) has come to terms with numerous new media in efforts to help people find information in increasingly diverse settings. Among these new media are the so-called microblogs. Twitter, the most popular microblogging service to date, has *seen* an exponential growth. The colossal size of data and user demand poses a challenge to the scientific community to be able to offer effective tools for IR and knowledge management (KM). Several works have proposed tools for searching tweets, but this area is still not well exploited. This gave us the idea to offer a new more developed tool that uses new features such as audience and RetweetRank for ranking relevant tweets. We investigate the impact of these criteria on the search results for relevant information. Finally, we propose a new metric to improve the results of the searches in microblogs. More accurately, we propose a research model that combines content relevance, tweet relevance and author relevance. Each type of relevance is characterized by a set of criteria such as audience to assess the relevance of the author, out of vocabulary (OOV) to measure the relevance of content and others. To evaluate our model, we built a KM system. We used a collection of subjective tweets talking about Tunisian current affairs in 2012.

Chapter written by Soumaya CHERICHI and Rim FAIZ.

6.1. Introduction

Business organizations and the media produce and use today phenomenal amounts of information of all kinds. The problem that we face is how to find this information and transform data collections into new knowledge, which is understandable, useful and interesting in the context where it is located. IR systems solve one of the biggest problems of KM: quickly finding useful information within massive data stores and ranking the results by relevance.

Recent years have revealed the accession of interactive media, which has given birth to a huge volume of data in blogs and microblogs more precisely. These microblogs attract more and more users due to the ease and speed of information sharing, especially in real time.

Peoples' motivations for microblogging are diverse [JAN 09, JAV 07, KRI 08, ZHA 09], ranging from offering autobiographical updates to reporting on current news events [DIA 10, SHA 09] or crisis situations [LON 09, SAK 10, VIE 10]. Peoples' use of Twitter to communicate during political unrest (e.g. the disputed 2009 election in Iran) brought increased attention to microblogs as a communication medium [EVG 09, GRO 09]. Twitter has played a role in important events, but the service also allows people to communicate among a relatively small social circle, and a sizeable part of Twitter's success is because of this function.

Indeed, a microblog is a stream of text that is written by an author. It is composed of regular and short updates that are presented to readers in reverse chronological order called a time-line.

Today, the service called Twitter is the most popular microblogging platform. While microblogging services are becoming more famous, the methods for organizing and providing access to data are also improving. Microbloggers as well as sending tweets are looking for the latest updates according to their interests. Finding the most relevant tweets on a topic depends on the criteria of microblogs.

Unlike other microblogging services, Twitter is positioned by the social relationship of subscription. And since the association is led, it allows users to express their interest in the items of other microbloggers. The social network of Twitter is not only limited to bloggers and subscription relationships, it also includes all the contributors and data that interact in both contexts of use and publication of articles. We have analyzed the microblogging service Twitter and identified the main criteria of Twitter.

But the question arises, what is the impact of each feature on the quality of results?

Our work consists of searching a new metric of the impact of features on the search result quality. Several criteria have been proposed in the literature [BEN 11, CHA 10], but there are still other criteria that have not been exploited as audience, which could be the size of the potential audience for a message: what is the maximum number of people who could have been exposed to a message?

We gathered the features on three groups: those related to the content, those related to the tweet and those related to the author. We used the coefficient of correlation with human judgment to define our score.

Our experimental result uses a corpus of a thousand subjective tweets that are neither answers nor retweets, and we also collected a corpus of human judgments to find the correlation coefficient.

The remainder of this chapter is organized as follows. In section 6.2, we describe the task Twitter IR. In section 6.3, we present all the features that we have used to calculate our score. In section 6.4, we discuss experiments and obtained results. Finally, section 6.5 concludes this chapter and outlines future work.

6.2. Twitter IR

Recent years have witnessed the advent of interactive media and especially Web 2.0. This has led to a huge volume of data from blogs, discussion forums and commercial sites. Indeed, blogs, being the figurehead of Web 2.0, are characterized by their evaluative usage, in the sense that users are using them to express themselves freely and share their opinions on their interests.

A microblogging service is at once a means of communication and a collaboration system that allows the sharing and disseminating text messages. In comparison with other social networks on the Web (for example Facebook, Myspace, LinkedIn and FourSquare), the microblogs articles are particularly short and submitted in real time to report a recent event. At the time of writing this chapter, several microblogging services exist. In this chapter, we will focus on the microblogging service Twitter, which is the most popular and widely used. Twitter is characterized from similar sites by certain features and functionalities. An important characteristic is the presence of social relationship subscription. This directional relationship allows users to express their interest on the publications of a particular blogger. Twitter is distinguished from similar Websites by some key features [BEN 11]. The main feature consists of the following social relationship. This directed association enables users to express their interest in other microbloggers' posts, called tweets, which do not exceed 140 characters. Moreover, Twitter is marked by the retweet feature that gives users the ability to forward an interesting tweet to their followers. A blogger, also called a twitterer, can annotate his/her tweets using hashtags (#) or send it to a specific user through the user @ mentions. Finally, a tweet can also share a web resource referenced by a URL.

Given the specificity of microblogs, looking for tweets faces several challenges such as indexing the flow of items [SAN 09], spam detection, diversification of results and evaluating the quality of tweets [NAG 10]. We find that most approaches for IR in microblogs do not take into account all the features to narrow the search. In fact, each feature has a unique impact on the other features. On the basis of this observation and to improve the results of the search, we will try to overcome these limitations by measuring the impact of these criteria. We will propose a measurement metric impact criteria for improving outcome research. The search for tweets is an *ad hoc* IR task whose objective is to select the relevant microblog itmes in response to a query. The definition of relevance in the search for tweets is not only limited to textual similarity but also takes account of social interactions in the network. In this context, the relevance of the items also depends on the tweets' technical specificities and the importance of the author.

Regarding the relevance of content, several studies have used the Okapi BM25 algorithm [ROB 98], while other studies, like the work of Duan *et al.* [DUA 10], have added new features such as tweet quality, i.e. the tweet that contains the least amount of OOV is considered as the most informative tweet. Also, Duan *et al.* consider that the longer the tweet, the better amount of information it contains.

The Merriam-Webster dictionary defines influence "as the power or capacity of causing an effect in indirect or intangible ways". Although there is a large number of theories of influence in sociology, there is no tangible way to measure such a force or a concrete definition of what influence means, for instance, in the spread of news [CHA 10]. With the aim to measure the importance or influence of a blogger, many studies have suggested to study the quality of bloggers as a first step to estimate the relevance of their articles. We note that an article published by a major blogger is more relevant in this context than the article written by an "unknown". With the aim to measure the importance of a blogger, Balog *et al.* [BAL 08] propose to assess its expertise about the application based on a language model. Language modeling IR relies on generative models to rank documents against queries. Under this approach, we assume that the terms in a document d_i were generated by a particular probability distribution M_i.

To avoid numeric underflow, we typically use log probabilities, replacing the product in equation [6.2] with a summation of logarithms. In either case, in the language modeling approach, documents whose corresponding language models have a high probability of generating q are ranked higher than those with low probability.

Other approaches [ZHA 07, NOL 09] consider that the domain experts are connected by social relations and propose to explore the topology of the social network to identify them.

We introduce, in this chapter, our approach for tweet search that integrates different criteria, namely the *social authority* of microbloggers, the *content relevance*, the *tweeting features* as well as the *hashtag presence*. In section 6.3, we present the main features of our criteria.

6.3. Features for tweet ranking

Among the most important tasks for a tweet ranking system is the selection of features set. We propose three types of features to rank tweets:

1) Content features refer to those features that describe the content relevance between queries and tweets.

2) Tweet features refer to those features that represent the particular characteristics of tweets, such as OOV and hashtags in tweet.

3) Author features refer to those features that represent the authority of authors of the tweets in Twitter.

6.3.1. *Feature set*

6.3.1.1. *Content relevance features*

The criterion "content" refers to the thematic relevance traditionally calculated by IR system standards. The thematic relevance is generally measured by one of the several IR models. One of the reference IR models is the probabilistic model [JON 00] with the weighting scheme BM25 as a matching request document function. For this reason, we have adopted this model for the calculation of the thematic relevance. Of course, it is possible to calculate using any other IR model. BM25 is a search function based on the "bag of words", which allows us to organize all documents based on the occurrences of the query terms given in the documents (see section 6.2).

We used four content relevance features:

1) *Relevance(T,Q)*: we used the OKAPI BM25 score that measures the content relevance between the query Q and the tweet T.

$$TF - IDF(w,Ti) = TF(w,Ti).IDF(w,Ti) = TFw,Ti((\log_2 * \frac{N}{DF_w}) + 1) \qquad [6.1]$$

where w is a term in the query Q and Ti is the tweet i.

2) *Popularity(Ti,Tj,Q)*; with i and j belong to n and *j≠i,* it is used to calculate the popularity of a tweet from the corpus. It measures the similarity between the tweets in the context of the tweet's topic. We used cosine similarity; according to a study done by Sarwar *et al.* [SAR 01], cosine similarity is the most efficient similarity measure, in addition it is not sensitive to the size of each tweet:

$$Cosine(Ti,Tj) = \frac{\sum_{w \in (Ti \cap Tj)} TFIDF_{w,Ti} * TFIDF_{w,Tj}}{\sqrt{\sum_{w \in i}(TFIDF_{w,Ti})^2 * \sum_{w \in Tj}(TFIDF_{w,Tj})^2}} \qquad [6.2]$$

where w is a term in the query Q, Ti is the tweet i, Tj is the tweet j, and j belongs to n and *j≠i.*

3) *Length of tweet (Lg(Ti,Q))*: length is measured by the number of characters that a tweet contains. It is said that longer the tweet, the more information it contains.

$$Lg(Ti,Q) = \frac{Lg(Ti) - MinLg(T)}{MaxLg(T)}$$ [6.3]

4) *Out of vocabulary (OOV(Ti))*: this feature is used to roughly approximate the language quality of tweets. Words OOV in Twitter include spelling errors and named entities. This feature aims to measure the language quality of a tweet as follows:

$$Quality(T) = 1 - \frac{NumberofOOV(Ti)}{Lg(Ti)}$$ [6.4]

where the number of *OOV(Ti)* is calculated as follows:

String tweet[] = tweet.split(" ");

int count = 0;

for (int i = 1; i<tweet.length; i++)

if (checker.isNotCorrect(tweet[i]))

{

Number of oov ++;

}

The smaller the OOV, the better the quality of the tweet.

6.3.1.2. *Tweet relevance features*

We note that the thematic relevance depends solely on the item and query. Each tweet has many technical features, and each feature forms selection criteria that we have exploited.

1) *Retweet(Ti,Q)*: this is defined as the number of times a tweet is retweeted. In a rational manner, the more retweeted tweets are more

relevant. Retweets are forwards of corresponding original tweets, sometimes with comments by retweeters. According to Duan *et al.* [DUA 10], they are supposed to contain no more information than the original tweets.

Figure 6.1. *Tweet retweeted*

$$Retweet(Ti,Q) = \frac{Retweet(Ti) - MinRetweet(T)}{MaxRetweet(T)}$$ [6.5]

2) *Reply(Ti)*: an @reply is any update posted by clicking the "reply" button on a tweet, it will always begin with @username. This feature aims to calculate the number of replies to a tweet. Ultimately tweets that have received the most responses are more relevant.

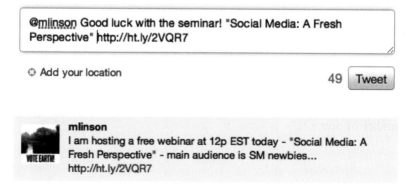

Figure 6.2. *Tweet as reply*

$$Reply(Ti,Q) = \frac{Retweet(Ti) - MinReply(T)}{MaxReply(T)}$$ [6.6]

3) *Favor(Ti)*: this feature aims to calculate the number of times a tweet is classified as a favorite. If a message is considered by many followers as a favorite, it means that it is relevant.

Figure 6.3. *Tweet selected as favorite*

$$Favor(Ti,Q) = \frac{Favor(Ti) - MinFavor(T)}{MaxFavor(T)} \qquad [6.7]$$

4) *Hashtag count(Ti)*: the # symbol, called a hashtag, is used to mark keywords or topics in a Tweet. It was created organically by Twitter users as a way to categorize messages. This feature aims to calculate the number of hashtags in a tweet.

$$HashtagCount(Ti) = \sum \text{of occurrences of hastag} \qquad [6.8]$$

Loren Ridinger @lorenridinger   1 h
#DIY pampering this weekend! :) #happysunday ow.ly/qFxcK
Ouvrir   ← Répondre ↥ Retweeter ★ Favori ••• Plus

Figure 6.4. *Tweet contains hashtag*

5) *Urlcount(Ti)*: Twitter allows users to include URLs as a supplement in their tweets. This feature aims to estimate the number of times the URL appears in the tweet corpus. According to Damak *et al*. [DAM 12], tweets containing URLs are more informative.

Figure 6.5. *Tweet contains URL*

$$URLCount(Ti) = \sum \text{of occurrences of URL} \qquad [6.9]$$

6.3.1.3. Author relevance features

Each blogger has specific characteristics such as the number of followers and the number of mentions. We said that users who have more followers and have been mentioned in more tweets, listed in more lists and retweeted by more important users are thought to be more authoritative.

1) *Tweet count(a)*: this feature represents the number of tweets posted by the author.

2) *Mention count(author)*: a mention is any Twitter update that contains "@username" anywhere in the body of the tweet, this means that @replies are also considered mentions. This feature aims to calculate the number of times an author is mentioned.

3) *Follower(author)*: this feature represents the number of followers of the author.

4) *Following(a)*: this feature represents the number of subscriptions of the author (a) to other authors.

5) *Expertise(a)*: this feature was found by conducting a survey that asks people to rate the expertise of the blogger from 0 to 10.

6) *RetweetRank(a)*: RetweetRank looks up all recent retweets, the number of followers, friends and lists of a user. It then compares these numbers with those of other users and assigns a rank. RetweetRank tracks both ReTweets (RTs) posted using the Retweet button and other *RTs* (e.g. *RT @username*). This feature is an indicator of how a blogger is influential on Twitter.

TwitterPageRank(a): this feature represents the rank of the author of the total Twitter users using PageRank algorithm.

Audience(a): it is the size of the potential audience for a message. What is the maximum number of people who could have been exposed to a message?

6.3.2. Metric measure of the impact of criteria to improve search results

We introduce a research model that combines relevant tweet content, the specificities of tweets and the authority of bloggers. This model considers the specificities of tweets and the authority of bloggers as important factors, which contribute to the relevance of the results.

As shown in Figure 6.6, we present the architecture of our approach to search for relevant tweets that consists of three steps.

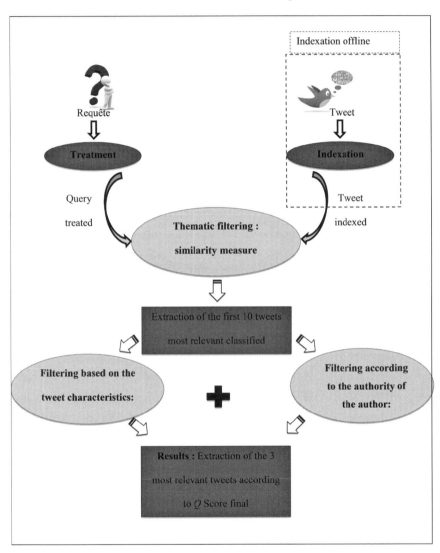

Figure 6.6. *General architecture of our process*

A general algorithm called "extraction of the most relevant tweets" describes the steps of our proposed approach

---

Algorithm 6.1. *Extraction of the most relevant tweets*

Input:

Q: User query

C: Tweets' collection

Begin

Pretreatment $(C; Q)$: (1)

    Indexation(C): $T \longleftarrow$ Indexed Tweet

    Treatment(Q): $Q \longleftarrow$ Query treatment

Thematic filtering: (2)

1. Calculate the standard score of the content relevance

    For Each Indexed Tweet Ti in C:

        Calculate Scorecontent (Ti, Q)

    End

2. Sort Tweets by Scorecontent

    Vector $C_{10} \longleftarrow$ Extraction of the first 10 tweets most relevant classified for Q

    Filtering based on the tweet characteristics: (3)

3. Calculate the standard score of the specificity of tweet Ti

    For Each Tweet T in C_{10}:

        Calculate ScoreTweet (Ti, Q)

    End

4. Sort Tweets by ScoreTweet

Filtering according to the authority of the author:

5. Calculate the standard score of the importance of the author who published A tweet Ti

For each Tweet T in C_{10}:

Calculate ScoreAuthor (A,Ti)

End

6. Sort Tweets by ScoreAuthor

Filtering by final score:

7. Calculate final score:

Score = Scorecontent+ ScoreTweet + ScoreAuthor

8. Sort tweets by their final scores

Vector C_3 ⟵ Extraction of the first three tweets most relevant classified for Q

End Extraction of the three most relevant tweets according to Q Score final

Output: three most relevant tweets for Q

The search for tweets is a task of IR whose goal is to select the relevant sections in response to a user's request. To present an accurate list of articles, our model combines a score of the content's relevance, a score of the author's authority and a score of the tweets' specificities. The objective of this combination is to provide a list of tweets that cover the subject of the request and are posted by major bloggers. After normalizing the feature scores, these three scores are combined linearly using the following formula:

$$Score(Ti,Q) = scoreContent(Ti,Q)$$
$$+\beta * scoreTweet(Ti,Q) \qquad [6.10]$$
$$+\gamma + scoreAuthor(Ti,Q)$$

with score (Ti,Q) on [0, 2] and $\beta + \gamma = 1$,

where Ti and Q represent tweet and request, respectively. β and γ on [0,1] are a weighting parameter [AKE 12]. Scorecontent(Ti, Q) is the normalized score of the relevance of content. ScoreTweet is the normalized score of the specificity of the tweet Ti and scoreAuthor(a, Ti) is the normalized score of the importance of the author, where a corresponds to the blogger who published the tweet Ti.

We note that:

1) -Scorecontent(Ti,Q)=Relevance(T,Q) + Lg(Ti) + Popularity(Ti,Tj,Q) + Quality(Ti);

2) -ScoreTweet(Ti,Q)= Url count(Ti)+ Hashtag Count(Ti) + Retweet(Ti) + Reply(Ti) + Favor(Ti);

3) -ScoreAuthor(a,Q)= TwitterPageRank(a) + Audience(a) + Tweet Count(a) + Mention Count(a) + Expertise(a) + RetweetRank(a) + Follower(a) + Following(a).

6.4. Experimental evaluation

We conducted a series of preliminary experiments on a collection of articles from Twitter in order to evaluate the performance of our model.

6.4.1. *Description of the collection*

In the absence of a standard framework for evaluating IR in microblogs, we collected a set of articles and queries. Our concern is that the database size is small. In the following, we describe a collection of articles and the approach for collecting relevance judgments.

6.4.1.1. *Search engine TWEETRIM*

We built a search engine called "TWEETRIM", which allows us to calculate all scores and display the most relevant tweets according to these scores. It has as input a query composed of three keywords and as output a set of relevant tweets relative to the query.

6.4.1.2. *Tweet set*

We built a collection of articles, metadata about relationships subscription and reply. This corpus was collected manually, i.e. a thousand blogs and thousands of tweets have been browsed. This collection contained a total of 3,000 tweets published by 50 active Tunisian bloggers who are interested in the Tunisian news (we chose the period of March 4, 2012 until June 4, 2012).

6.4.1.3. *Queries and relevance judgments*

To perform queries and to collect the human judgement of relevance, we followed the following steps:

1) We collected 500 queries on current affaires in Tunisia from users.

2) Then, we used the system that we have built, which allows us to view the 10 results that are especially relevant according to the score of the content.

3) Finally, we asked 300 users to judge the first 10 results of each query.

We assumed that the content relevance already exists and we will improve our search result by varying our two other scores ScoreTweet and ScoreAuthor. We calculated the correlation coefficient between our scores and the corpus, which allowed us to find our weighting coefficients β and γ.

6.4.2. Results

6.4.2.1. *Comparing the relevancy factors*

In this experiment, we evaluated the factors relevant to know the specifics of tweets and blogger authorities, and then we compared their performance independently. Figure 6.7 shows the values of correlation coefficients obtained by the different configurations of our metric measure.

We emphasize that the content relevance already exists and we will improve our search result by varying our two other scores ScoreTweet and ScoreAuthor.

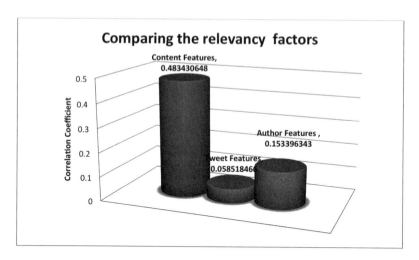

Figure 6.7. *Comparing the relevancy factors*

6.4.2.2. *Estimation of weights*

We made a comparison within the values of correlation coefficients and from these results, we observed that the best correlation coefficient between βScoreTweet+γScoreAuthor with human judgment score = 0.161456763 when β = 0.4 and thus γ = 0.6.

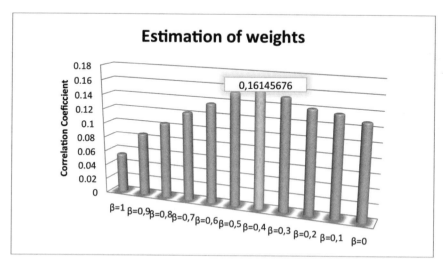

Figure 6.8. *Estimation of weights*

6.4.2.3. *Evaluation of our model*

We compare, in Figure 6.2, the values of correlation coefficients obtained by Tweet Features and Author Features with the parameters β and γ values, respectively, (1.0) and (0.1) obtained by experiments and the third configuration with $\beta = 0.4$ and $\gamma = 0.6$.

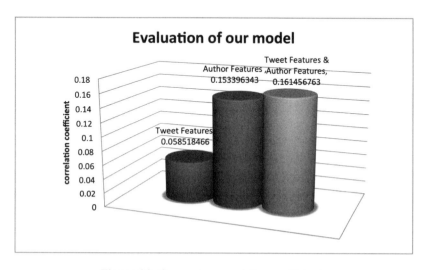

Figure 6.9. *Comparing correlation coefficients*

We note that the performances of the last two configurations are very close with a slight advantage for the combination "Tweet Features & Author Features" on the model based only on the specificities of the tweet and the importance of the author. We conclude that Author Features have more impact on the search results than Tweet Features.

The reference model combines only the features linearly with out weighting. This model gave us the correlation coefficient equal to 0.10 and our model gave us the correlation coefficient of 0.16. An improvement of 35% can be clearly seen in the satisfaction of our human judgment.

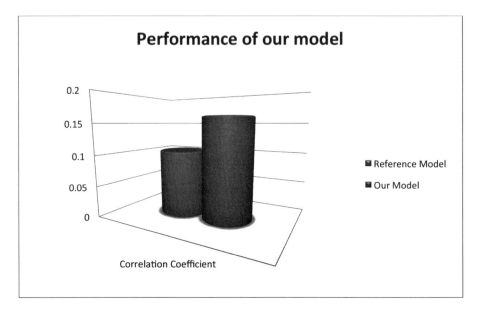

Figure 6.10. *Comparing our model with the reference model*

6.5. Conclusion

Research conducted under the auspices of KM varies greatly in direction and scope. There are several approaches that have been proposed that are based on the features. Therefore, the choice of characteristics is important to obtain a satisfactory result and one close to the human judgment. We have proposed in this chapter a new metric for Social Research on Twitter. This has to integrate relevance of the content, the specificities of tweets and the author's importance where we incorporate new features such as the audience. The primary experimental evaluation that we conducted on a collection of articles of Twitter shows that the measurement that we propose allows a better assessment of the impact of bloggers and tweets' technical specificities.

Looking ahead, we plan to conduct experiments under the microblog text retrieval conference (TREC) evaluation framework that will include a larger collection of articles and queries and whose relevance judgments are social. We also need to evaluate the influence of each feature independently. We plan to compare the performance of our model with other models for the social searching of tweets.

6.6. Bibliography

[AGA 08] AGARWAL N., LIU H., TANG L., *et al.*, "Identifying the influential bloggers in a community", *Proceedings of the International Conference on Web Search and Web Data Mining (WSDM '08)*, ACM, New York, pp. 207–218, 2008.

[AKE 12] AKERMI I., FAIZ R., "Hybrid method for computing word-pair similarity based on web content", *Proceedings of the International Conference on Web Intelligence, Mining and Semantics (WIMS '12)*, ACM, New York, 2012.

[AME 07] AMER-YAHIA S., BENEDIKT M., BOHANNON P., "Challenges in searching online communities", *IEEE Data Engineering Bulletin*, vol. 30, no. 2, pp. 23–31, 2007.

[BAL 08] BALOG K., DERIJKE M., WEERKAMP W., "Bloggers as experts: feed distillation using expert retrieval models", *Proceedings of the 31st Annual International ACM SIGIR Conference on Research and Development in Information Retrieval (SIGIR '08)*, ACM, New York, pp. 753–754, 2008.

[BAR 11] BARRY S., "Web search: social & collaborative" *in Conférence en Recherche d'Infomations et Applications CORIA 2011*, 8th French Information Retrieval Conference CORIA : Conférence en Recherche d'Information et Applications Avignon, France, Proceedings CORIA, Editions Universitaires d'Avignon, March 16–18 2011.

[BAZ 05] BAZIZ M., BOUGHANEM M., AUSSENAC-GILLES N., "Evaluating a conceptual indexing method by utilizing wordnet", *CLEF, 2005, p238-246 proceedings Accessing Multilingual Information Repositories, 6th Workshop of the Cross-Language Evalution Forum*, CLEF 2005, Vienna, Austria, 21–23 September, 2005, Revised Selected Papers, Springer, 2006

[BEN 10] BEN JABEUR L., "Vers un modèle de recherche d'information sociale pour l'accès aux ressources bibliographiques", *Conférence francophone en Recherche d'Information et Applications (CORIA 2010),* Centre de Publications Universitaires, Sousse, Tunisia, pp. 325–336, 18–20 March 2010.

[BEN 11] BEN JABEUR L., TAMINE L., BOUGHANEM M., "Un modèle de recherche d'information sociale dans les microblogs: cas de Twitter", Conférence sur les Modèles et l'Analyse des Réseaux: Approches Mathématiques et Informatique (MARAMI), Grenoble, 2011.

[BEN 12] BEN JABEUR L., TAMINE L., BOUGHANEM M., "Intégration des facteurs temps et autorité sociale dans un modèle bayésien de recherche de tweets", *Conférence en Recherche d'Information et Applications (CORIA)*, Bordeaux, France, Proceedings, pp. 301–316, March 21–23 2012.

[BRI 05] BRINI H., Un modèle de recherche d'information basé sur les réseaux possibilistes, Thesis, 2005.

[CHA 10] CHA M., HADDADI H., BENEVENUTOKRISHNA F., *et al.*, "Measuring user influence in twitter: the million follower fallacy", *Proceedings of the 4th International AAAI Conference on Weblogs and Social Media*, (ICWSM '10), 2010.

[CHE 12] CHERICHI S., FAIZ R., "Recherche d'information pertinente dans les microblogs: mesure métrique de l'impact des critères pour améliorer les résultats de la recherche", *Conférence Internationale sur l'Extraction et la Gestion des Connaissances – Maghreb, (EGC-M)*, Hammamet, Tunisia, 2012.

[CHE 13a] CHERICHI S., FAIZ R., "Relevant information discovery in microblogs – combining post's features and author's features to improve search results", *The International Joint Conference on Knowledge Discovery, Knowledge Engineering and Knowledge Management* (IC3K), KDIR, 2013.

[CHE 13b] CHERICHI S., FAIZ R., "Relevant information management in microblogs", *In International Conference on Knowledge Management, Information and Knowledge Systems (KMIKS 2013)*, Hammamet, Tunisia, April 2013.

[CHE 13c] CHERICHI S., FAIZ R., "New metric measure for the improvement of search results in microblogs", *Proc. of the International Conference on Web Intelligence, Mining and Semantics (WIMS 2013),* New York, NY, USA, ACM, 2013.

[DIA 10] DIAKOPOULOS, N.A., SHAMMA D.A., "Characterizing debate performance via aggregated twitter sentiment", *In Proceedings of the 28th International Conference on Human Factors in Computing Systems,* Atlanta, Georgia, USA, ACM, pp. 1195–1198, 2010. Doi:10.1145/1753326.1753504.

[DAM 12] DAMAK F., PINEL-SAUVAGNAT K., CABANAC G., "Recherche de microblogs: quels critères pour raffiner les résultats des moteurs usuels de RI?", *Conférence en Recherche d'Information et Applications (CORIA '12)*, Bordeaux, pp. 371–328, 2012.

[DON 10] DONG A., ZHANG R., KOLARI P., *et al.*, "Time is of the essence: improving recency ranking using Twitter data", *Proceedings of the 19th International Conference on World Wide Web (WWW '10)*, ACM, New York, NY, pp. 331–340, 2010.

[DUA 10] DUAN Y., JIANG L., QIN T., *et al.*, "An empirical study on learning torank of tweets", *COLING Proceedings of the 23rd International Conference on Computational Linguistics Proceedings of the Conference*, 23-27 August 2010, Beijing, China, Tsinghua University Press, pp. 295–303, 2010.

[EFR 10] EFRON M., "Hashtag retrieval in a microblogging environment", *Proceeding of the 33rd International ACM SIGIR Conference on Research and Development in Information Retrieval, (SIGIR '10)*, ACM, New York, NY, pp. 787–788, 2010.

[EVG 09] EVGENY M., Iran: Downside to the "Twitter revolution", *Dissent*, vol. 56, no. 4, pp. 10–14, 2009.

[GRO 09] GROSSMAN L., (2009, June 17) "Iran Protests: twitter, the medium of the Movement", *Time.com*. Retrieved August 24, 2010, http://www.time.com/time/world/article/0,8599,1905125,00.html.

[HIE 01] HIEMSTRA D., Using language models for information retrieval, Univ. Twente, 200, I-VIII, 1-163

[ING 94] INGWERSEN P., "Polyrepresentation of information needs and semantic entities: elements of a cognitive theory for information retrieval interaction", *Proceedings of the 17th Annual International ACM SIGIR Conference on Research and Development in Information Retrieval*, ACM/Springer, pp. 101–110, 1994.

[JAN 09] JANSEN B. J., ZHANG M., SOBEL K., *et al.*, "Twitter power: tweets as electronic word of mouth", *J. Am. Soc. Inf. Sci. Technol.*, vol. 60, no. 11, pp. 2169–2188, 2009.

[JAV 07] JAVA A., SONG X., FININ T., *et al.*, "Why we twitter: understanding microblogging usage and communities", *In Proceedings of the 9th WebKDD and 1st SNA-KDD 2007 workshop on Web mining and social network analysis*, San Jose, California, ACM, pp. 56–65, 2007. Doi:10.1145/1348549.1348556.

[JON 00] JONES S., WALKER K., ROBERTSON S., "A probabilistic model of information retrieval: development and comparative experiments", *Information Processing & Management*, vol. 36, no. 6, pp. 779–808, 2000.

[KIR 06] KIRSCH M., GNASA M., CREMERS A.B., "Beyond the web: retrieval in social information spaces", *Proceedings of the 28th European Conference on Information Retrieval, (ECIR '06)*, Springer, 2006.

[KOM 08] KOMPAORÉ N.D.Y., Fusion de systèmes et analyse des caractéristiques linguistiques des requêtes: vers un processus de RI adaptatif, PhD Thesis, Paul Sabatier University of Toulouse, 2008.

[KRI 08] KRISHNAMURTHY B., GILL P., *et al.*, "A few chirps about twitter", *In Proceedings of the first Workshop on Online Social Networks,* Seattle, WA USA, ACM, pp. 19–24, 2008. Doi:10.1145/1397735.1397741.

[KWA 10] KWAK H., LEE C., PARK H., *et al.*, "What is Twitter, a social network or a news media?" *Proceedings of the 19th International Conference on World Wide Web (WWW '10)*, ACM, New York, pp. 591–600, 2010.

[LON 09] LONGUEVILLE B.D., SMITH R.S., LURASCHI G., "OMG, from here, I can see the flames! a use case of mining location based social networks to acquire spatio-temporal data on forest fires", *Proceedings of the International Workshop on Location Based Social Networks*, Seattle, Washington, ACM, pp. 73–80, 2009 Doi:10.1145/1629890.1629907

[MAR 60] MARON M.E., KUHNS J.L., "On relevance, probabilistic indexing and information retrieval", *Journal of the ACM*, vol. 7, no. 3, pp. 216–244, 1960.

[MAS 11] MASSOUDI K., TSAGKIAS E., DE RIJKE M., *et al.*, "Incorporating query expansion and quality indicators in searching microblog posts", *33rd European Conference on Information Retrieval (ECIR '11)*, Springer, Dublin, pp. 362–367, 2011.

[MOR 06] MORNEAU M., Recherche d'information sémantique et extraction automatique d'ontologie du domaine, Thesis, 2006.

[MUT 01] MUTSCHKE P., "Enhancing information retrieval in federated bibliographic data sources using author network based stratagems", *Research and Advanced Technology for Digital Libraries: 5th European Conference (ECDL '01)*, Darmstadt, Germany, 4–9 September 2001.

[NAG 10] NAGMOTI R., TEREDESAI A., "Ranking approaches for microblog search", *Proceedings of the 2010 IEEE/WIC/ACM International Conference on Web Intelligence and Intelligent Agent Technology (WI-IAT '10)*, vol. 1, pp. 153–157, 2010.

[NOL 09] NOLL G., AU YEUNG C.-M., GIBBINS N., *et al.*, "Telling experts from spammers: expertise ranking in folksonomies", *Proceedings of the 32nd International ACM SIGIR Conference on Research and Development in Information Retrieval (SIGIR '09)*, ACM, New York, pp. 612–619, 2009.

[OUN 10] OUNIS I., MACDONALD C., LIN J., *et al.*, "TREC 2011 MicroblogTrack", *Text Retrieval Conference TREC*, November 2010.

[OUR 11] OURDIA R., Accès contextuel à l'information dans un environnement mobile: approche basée sur l'utilisation d'un profil situationnel de l'utilisateur et d'un profil de localisation des requêtes, Thesis, 2011.

[RAM 10] RAMAGE D., DUMAIS S.T., LIEBLING D.J., "Characterizing microblogs with topic models", ICWSM'10, *Proceedings of the Fourth International Conference on Weblogsand Social Media, ICWSM 2010*, Washington, DC, USA, pp. 1–1, May 23–26 2010.

[RAM 11] RAMAGE D., MORRIS M.R., "#TwitterSearch: a comparison of microblog search and web search", *Proceedings of the 4th ACM International Conference on Web Search and Data Mining (WSDM '11)*, ACM, New York, NY, pp. 35–44, 2011.

[ROB 76] ROBERTSON S., SPARCK J.K., "Relevance weighting for search terms", *Journal of the American Society for Information Science,* vol. 27, no. 3, pp. 129–146, 1976.

[ROB 98] ROBERTSON S., WALKER S., HANCOCK-BEAULIEU M., "Okapi at TREC-7: automatic ad hoc, filtering, VLC and interactive", text retrieval conference *(TREC)*, pp. 199–210, 1998.

[SAK 10] SAKAKI T., OKAZAKI M., MATSUO Y., "Earthquake shakes twitter users: real-time event detection by social sensors", *Proceedings of the 19th International Conference on World Wide Web (WWW '10)*, ACM, New York, NY, pp. 851–860, 2010.

[SAL 71] SALTON G., "A comparison between manual and automatic indexing methods", *Journal of American Documentation*, vol. 20, no. 1, pp. 61–71, 1971.

[SAL 83] SALTON G., MCGILL M., *Introduction to Modern Information Retrieval*, McGraw-Hill, New York, 1983.

[SAN 09] SANKARANARAYANAN J., SAMET H., TEITLER B.E., *et al.*, "TwitterStand: news in tweets", *Proceedings of the 17th ACM SIGSPATIAL International Conference on Advances in Geographic Information Systems (GIS '09)*, ACM, New York, NY pp. 42–51, 2009.

[SAR 01] SARWAR B., KARYPIS G., KONSTAN J., *et al.*, "Item-based collaborative filtering recommendation algorithms", *Proceedings of the 10th International Conference on World Wide Web (WWW '01)*, ACM, New York, NY, pp. 285–295, 2001.

[SHA 09] SHAMMA D.A., KENNEDY L., CHURCHILL E.F., "Tweet the debates: understanding community annotation of uncollected sources", *Proceedings of the first SIGMM Workshop on Social media* Beijing, China, ACM, pp. 3–10 2009.

[SON 10] SONG S., LI Q., ZHENG N., "A spatio-temporal framework for related topic search in microblogging", *Proceedings of the 6th International Conference on Active Media Technology (AMT '10)*, Springer-Verlag, Berlin/Heidelberg, pp. 63–73, 2010.

[VIE 10] VIEWEG S., HUGHES A.L., STARBIRD K., *et al.*, "Microblogging during two natural hazards events: what twitter may contribute to situational awareness", *Proceedings of the 28th International Conference on Human factors in computing systems,* Atlanta, Georgia, USA, ACM, pp. 1079–1088, 2010. Doi:10.1145/1753326.1753486.

[WEN 10] WENG J., LIM E.-P., JIANG J., *et al.*, "TwitterRank: finding topic-sensitive influential twitterers", *Proceedings of the 3rd ACM International Conference on Web Search and Data Mining (WSDM '10)*, ACM, New York, NY, pp. 261–270, 2010.

[YAN 10] YANG Z., GUO J., CAI K., *et al.*, "Understanding retweeting behaviors in social networks", *Proceedings of the 19th ACM International Conference on Information and Knowledge Management (CIKM '10)*, ACM, New York, NY pp. 1633–1636, 2010.

[ZAI 10] ZAIHAN Y., HONG L., DAVISON B.D., "Topic-driven multi-type citation network analysis", *9th International Conference on Adaptivity, Personalization and Fusion of Heterogeneous Information*, RIAO, Paris, France, 28–30 April 2010.

[ZHA 07] ZHANG J., TANG J., LI J., "Expert finding in a social network", in KOTAGIRI R., KRISHNA P., MOHANIA M., NANTAJEEWARAWAT E. (eds), *Advances in Databases: Concepts, Systems and Applications,* vol. 4443, Lecture Notes in Computer Science, Springer, Berlin/Heidelberg, pp. 1066–1069, 2007.

[ZHA 09] ZHAO D., ROSSON M.B., "How and why people twitter: the role that micro-blogging plays in informal communication at work", *In Proceedings of the ACM 2009 International Conference on Supporting Group Work,* Sanibel Island, Florida, USA, ACM, pp. 243–252, 2009. Doi:10.1145/1531674.1531710.

Chapter 7

A Legal Knowledge Management System Based on Core Ontology

7.1. Introduction

Knowledge management (KM) has been one of the pillars of basic research in different areas for many years. It promises that if the best knowledge is captured, shared and reused, then efficiency will be created, time will be saved and costs of production will drop as quality improves.

Schreiber and Akkermans [SCH 00] define KM as "a framework and tool set for improving the organization's knowledge infrastructure, aimed at getting the right knowledge to the right people in the right form at the right time".

Law practice is paying more and more attention to the deployment of KM. Lawyers have to abandon their personal working habits and technology innovations must fit into the pattern of their work by using KM tools.

The purpose of KM tools is to profit from expertise and provide an ever increasing work quality. Among the needs of lawyers for these tools, we can mention the following:

Chapter written by Karima Dhouib and Faïez Gargouri.

– Knowledge conservation and preservation of intellectual capital. This is essential to compensate for the loss of knowledge due to the departure of lawyers.

– Linking lawyers in a particular domain by competency identification.

– Sharing knowledge and information whenever there are regulatory changes.

– Legal documentation management, which facilitates the access to the "know-how" from corpuses of documents.

We focus our research on the last area that aims at extraction and information retrieval in legal databases and the development and use of thesauri and legal ontologies. In fact, the norm inflation and the multiplication of jurisprudence decisions make the control of legal information more difficult. The main goal of lawyers is to find from this large documentation the useful norm or jurisprudence and in some cases provide added value.

We are mainly interested in the jurisprudence corpuses. In the case of Tunisia, two sources of jurisprudence are available: journals and collections, which are periodically updated. The Tunisian jurisprudence database, set up in 2009, consists of 12,000 decisions of the Court of Cassation since 1959. This database is accessible via the Tunisian portal of justice and human rights[1]. According to lawyers, checking journals is very time consuming. Searching the jurisprudence database does not guarantee the recovery of useful documents because it is usually based on simple search criteria.

We propose to develop a search system of Tunisian jurisprudence taking into account the advances in the field of information retrieval including the use of semantic resources such as a legal ontology in the Arabic language. This system provides time-saving and more relevant results for Tunisian lawyers. The construction of the system consists of following three phases: 1) decision structuring, 2) new legal problem description and 3) research process.

In this chapter, we mainly focus on describing the legal ontology construction approach that we have adopted and presenting our methodology for decision structuring.

---

1 http://www.e-justice.tn/.

We begin by giving an insight into technologies that can be considered as part of the KM resources in the legal field. Then, the functional architecture of our system is presented. We also describe the legal ontology construction approach by detailing the domain concept extraction step, the reference ontological framework, our building blocks and our contribution over the existing legal ontologies.

In the second part of this chapter, the jurisprudence decision structuring methodology is presented. First, we provide an overview of related works of the thematic document structuring. Then, we detail the linguistic analysis and the linguistic marker extraction steps. Next, we describe the extraction pattern construction and, finally, we show how the legal ontology and the extraction patterns are used to structure the jurisprudence decisions.

7.2. Legal KM

Apistola and Oskamp [API 02] identify some problems in the legal practices:

– Legal knowledge is not shared: solutions for legal problems are not reused but developed over and over again.

– Legal knowledge is not up to date: legal problems are sometimes solved on the basis of old legal knowledge.

– There is less awareness of legal job descriptions: not all employees know who deals with a certain legal problem within a legal organization.

– Legal expert systems are not used because of their cost and complexity.

For these reasons, law practice is paying more and more attention to the deployment of KM. Lawyers are having to abandon their personal working habits and technology innovations must fit into the pattern of their work by using KM tools.

Traditionally, the most important meeting points between law and computer science have been legal information search and retrieval, legal knowledge representation and management, legal reasoning, legal argumentation and expert and knowledge-based system (KBS) design [CAS 11].

Knowledge sources can be humans (e.g. experts or end users), writings (e.g. jurisprudence) or information technology (e.g. databases containing cases or legislation) [API 02]. All of the following technologies can be considered part of the KM resources in the legal field.

7.2.1. *Legal portals*

Portals now play a significant role across the KM spectrum. Besides the ability to serve as the single entry point to multiple sites on the web, portals provide features for managing [STA 03]:

– the knowledge content: captured information and knowledge residing in the databases;

– communities: a place for experts or project workers to collaborate and share information and manage in progress work documents in real time;

– information aggregation: the ability to mine different databases for specific records or content, then combine information to create new information or knowledge.

In law, the corpuses of documents are mainly composed of text. The outcomes of the private publishing (via portals) are quite widely enriched with keywords and abstracts. Currently, documentary research tools facilitate these enhancements and make information retrieval more reliable. However, due to their cost, these documentary collections are only accessible to a limited number of users. Available and free texts are still largely lacking these enrichments. In the following, we mention some examples of legal portals:

E-justice: the Tunisian portal of justice and human rights provides lawyers the possibility to access and monitor cases reported at the Court of Cassation, the appellate courts and courts of first instance.

Legifrance[2]: the official portal of the French government for the diffusion of laws and regulations and Supreme Court decisions. This portal is free, open and refers to all relevant institutions and administrations and all texts still in effect since 1539. It also provides a jurisprudence base that holds the most relevant decisions since 1875.

---

2 http://www.legifrance.gouv.fr/.

Dalloz[3]: this constitutes a business area for lawyers. It provides documentary collections for different types of law, a jurisprudence base and permanent online dictionaries of legislative editions. The Dalloz community is still limited because of the high cost of access.

7.2.2. *Legal decision support systems and legal expert systems*

Expert systems emulate the decision-making ability of a human expert. They contain on the one hand, the knowledge base which represents knowledge of the domain and rules. On the other hand, an inference engine applies the rules to the knowledge to deduce new knowledge. In the legal field, expert systems can be used for many purposes:

– Classification, which aims at identifying a legal situation from facts supplied by the user.

– Assistance for the design and drafting of legislative texts and acts.

– Prediction and simulation, particularly in the area of jurisprudence decisions, which is a tool for decision support for lawyers.

7.2.3. *Legal case-based reasoning*

Case-based reasoning (CBR) is an important model from artificial intelligence that assists the decision-making process. It is a way to solve new problems by simulating human analogical reasoning, memory-based technology and past experiences based on the degree of similarity through a deductive inference form. Typically, a case contains two parts: a description of a situation representing a "problem" and "solution" used to remedy this situation.

Textual CBR approaches are relatively new and are mainly based on the techniques of information retrieval, machine learning and automatic natural language processing. This approach is necessary for some fields such as legal jurisprudence or medical diagnosis, whose reasoning is based on reports [LAM 02b]. Most of the CBR systems are used for information retrieval tasks [LAM 02b] such as DRAMA [LEA 99], FAQ Finder [BUR 97], CBR-Answers [LEN 99], SPIRE [DAN 96] and PRUDENCIA

---

3 http://www.dalloz.fr/.

[WEB 98]. Take the case of PRUDENCIA, which is a system that facilitates information retrieval in legal jurisprudence. It makes it possible to search for situations described in text documents, which are similar to a new legal cause.

7.2.4. *Legal ontology*

[GRU 93] defines ontology as a formal, explicit specification of a shared conceptualization.

The use of ontologies has been regarded as key to implementing the semantics for human–machine communication. Although initially ontologies were mainly exploited to enable knowledge sharing and reuse in the construction of KBS, nowadays ontologies are powerful tools to also implement the semantic web vision [CAS 11].

Several foundational ontologies have been built in order to conceptualize general domain-independent concepts such as SUMO[4], PROTON[5] and DOLCE[6].

Most domains are of interest for ontology modeling; however, the legal domain offers a perfect domain for conceptual modeling and for ontology use in different types of intelligent applications and legal reasoning systems, not only for its complexity as a knowledge intensive domain, but also for the large amount of data that it generates. In this sense, during the last decade, the use of legal ontologies as a technique to represent legal knowledge has increased [CAS 11].

Among existing legal ontologies, we can mention: core legal ontology (CLO) [GAN 05], legal knowledge interchange format (LKIF) [HOE 09], LRI-CORE [BRE 04] and functional ontology of law (FOLaw) [VAL 96].

7.3. Functional architecture of the system

As shown in Figure 7.1, four components are integrated in to our system [DHO 12a]: a corpus of jurisprudence decision, an Arabic legal ontology

---

4 SUMO: http://suo.ieee.org.
5 PROTON: http://proton.semanticweb.org.
6 DOLCE: http://www.loa.istc.cnr.it/dolce.html

(ALO, used to describe the semantic content of the corpus), a pattern base (used to delimit the beginning of each part of a decision) and finally a structured decision base, which is the result of the decision structuring step. The construction of the system consists of the following three phases [DHO 12b]:

– Decision structuring: during this phase, a decision analysis is performed to identify a common organizational structure, and to build patterns that can define the different parts of the chosen structure. Then, the decisions are structured, based on the patterns as well as the legal ontology.

– New legal problem description: the new legal problem is described using the legal ontology.

– Search process: this is based on the ontology and will be developed to provide decisions that are most similar to the new problem.

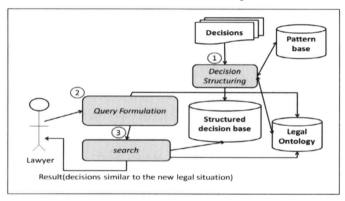

Figure 7.1. *Functional architecture of the system*

7.4. Legal ontology construction approach

The following are the five main uses or roles of ontologies for the legal domain [BRE 04]:

– *Organize and structure information* by describing things or phenomena in the domain of interest. The ontology thus plays the role of vocabulary by taking into account the lexical and the semantic aspects.

– *Reasoning and problem solving* by representing the knowledge of the domain so that an automated reasoner can represent problems and generate solutions for these problems.

– *Semantic indexing and search* by giving the possibility to represent and search the content of documents semantically.

– *Semantics integration and interoperation* by supporting applications to exchange information electronically.

– *Understanding the domain* by providing a view of what a domain is about and trying to make sense of the variety of knowledge in that domain.

In our research context, we have built an ALO that constitutes a repository of semantically rich concepts and establishes a consensus among legal experts and resolves the ambiguity of the term variability.

The ontology describing the semantic content of the textual jurisprudence decisions can be deployed at several levels: improve the results of decision structuring, facilitate the formulation of queries when accessing the system and finally optimize the search of decisions.

In this section, we will begin by giving an overview of existing ontology construction methodologies. Then, we detail steps that we have followed to extract domain concepts from jurisprudence decisions and present our reference ontological framework and our building blocks. We conclude with juxtaposing our ontology with existing legal ontologies.

7.4.1. *Existing ontology construction methodologies*

Existing ontology construction methodologies follow different approaches: top-down, bottom-up and middle-out. In a top-down approach, we start by modeling concepts and relationships at a very generic level; these elements are subsequently refined. This approach is usually performed manually, leading to high-quality ontologies which can be reused and are typically used as a starting point to develop new ontologies.

Regarding the middle-out approach, it is necessary to identify the most important concepts that are then used for the generalization and specialization hierarchy. However, with support for automatic analysis of documents, the bottom-up approach can be applied. The relevant concepts are extracted semi-automatically from the available documents, which may help the automatic construction of ontologies [SUR 03].

The choice of one of these approaches depends on the specified needs of the studied field, the knowledge resource availability, etc.

In the following, we present some of the ontology construction methodologies.

7.4.1.1. *Methontology*

This is a structured method for building ontologies. It is based on experiences gained in the development of ontologies in the chemistry field. It is based on seven steps [FER 97, FER 99]:

Specification: the objective of this phase is to produce an informal, semi-formal or formal specification for the ontology written in a natural language. It is necessary to define the ontology, its use cases and its potential future users.

Knowledge acquisition: it is a step that can be performed in parallel with the specification phase. Structured and unstructured interviews with the domain expert are used to acquire knowledge, in addition to formal and informal text analysis.

Conceptualization: domain knowledge is structured in the form of a conceptual model that describes the problem and its solution in terms of the domain vocabulary identified in the specification stage. A terminological base is then built and provides a basis for defining the concepts and relations between them.

Implementation: the ontology is codified with a formal language.

Evaluation: the evaluation should lead to a technical judgment of the ontology, its software environment and its documentation with respect to a reference framework during each phase and between phases of its lifecycle.

Documentation: methontology requires documentation of all activities throughout the ontology construction lifecycle.

7.4.1.2. *Building ontology from text method*

The particularity of the proposed method [LAM 02] is to rely mainly on the corpus. It combines two ways for knowledge acquisition from texts:

extraction of domain terms contained in the documents and the development of explicit knowledge models brought by documents.

The first step toward the ontology development is linguistic analysis, which leads to the creation of a terminological knowledge base containing candidate terms and their lexical relations. Several techniques are used to filter term extraction step results. Once the list of domain concepts is drawn up and validated by experts, relations must be identified and a taxonomy is elaborated.

7.4.1.3. ON-TO-methodology

This methodology [SUR 03] consists of five steps:

Feasibility study: this phase is used to study the economic and technical feasibility and identify problems and possible solutions.

Kickoff: this step begins by writing an ontology requirements specification document (ORSD), in which we describe the need for ontology, knowledge sources and potential users. The ORSD must guide an ontology engineer to decide on the inclusion and exclusion of concepts and relationships and the hierarchical structure of the ontology. Then, a semi-formal description of the ontology should be performed.

Refinement: to formalize the initial semi-formal description of the ontology, the engineer forms a taxonomy and adds relationships other than a "is a" relationship. Changes can be made after discussions with experts.

Evaluation: this includes three aspects: checking consistency and conformity of used languages, checking the specified requirements satisfaction and finally formal analysis and hierarchy ontology verification based on the ON-TO clean approach.

Application and evolution: this is to deploy the ontology in an ontology-based system and to specify who is responsible for the ontology evolution and how it is done and at which time intervals the ontology is maintained.

7.4.1.4. DOGMA

This method [JAR 07] provides a methodological framework for ontology engineering which aims to guide ontology builders toward building ontologies that are highly reusable and usable, easier to build and maintain. The main steps of this method are [SPY 08]:

Preparatory stage: this is to define ontology needs and a feasibility study and to identify knowledge sources, users and domain experts.

Conceptualization: based on domain knowledge acquisition.

Specification: this is based mainly on semantic constraints definition.

7.4.1.5. *TERMINAE*

This method was proposed by the Terminology and Artificial Intelligence (TIA) group; it guides the knowledge engineer in ontology building from text [AUS 08].

Since its definition, the methodology has been supported by a specific tool, the TERMINAE platform that provides guidelines for the conceptualization activities and includes functions for linguistic analysis and conceptual modeling.

The method covers only the conceptualization phase and consists of four steps:

Corpus constitution: allows the collection of domain knowledge sources;

Linguistic analysis: based mainly on the automatic extraction of textual units and manual or semi-automatic filtering and grouping of these units;

Normalization: consists of a terminological analysis and a termino-conceptual network building;

Formalization: enables the concept and conceptual relation creation from the termino-conceptual network.

7.4.2. *Our approach*

For building our legal ontology, we adopted a multilayer approach by structuring this ontology into subontologies at different levels of abstraction.

At the most abstract level, we have reused some concepts of the foundational DOLCE ontology [MAS 03], which provides a set of abstract concepts and relations for structuring (by specialization) any domain.

At an intermediate level, "core" domain ontologies [GAN 04] which define, for each domain concerned, a minimal set of generic and central concepts (e.g. in the legal domain, legal fact, legal agent and legal artifact) have been consulted to have an insight for the legal concepts. Then, we have defined our own generic concepts, which will be detailed later. Moreover, we have reused the proposed concepts in [KAS 12], which are collective, organization, action of collective and action of organization.

At the most specific level, core domain ontologies are in their turn refined to introduce, by specialization, domain-specific concepts (e.g. in the legal domain, contact of sale, lawyer and decision). To extract the legal domain concepts from jurisprudence decisions, we were inspired by the TERMINAE method [AUS 08] and by works of [LAM 02].

7.4.2.1. *Domain ontology extraction*

To extract the legal domain concepts from jurisprudence decisions, we were inspired by the TERMINAE method [AUS 08] and by works of [LAM 02]. We have mainly followed four steps: corpus constitution, linguistic analysis of the corpus, candidate-term extraction and conceptualization.

The corpus of study is initially composed of 600 decisions issued by the Court of Cassation, available on the Tunisian portal of justice and human rights. A sample of 50 decisions was analyzed in close collaboration with legal experts to identify the organizational structure of a decision, which facilitates the decision structuring step. These decisions are considered as a support of stabilized knowledge for legal concepts. A linguistic analysis of the corpus should then be made to build our terminological knowledge base and extract candidate terms in the field. This step must be performed based on the automatic language processing tools of natural language processing (NLP). These tools, called linguistic terms extractors, carry out a linguistic study of the documents submitted to them and allow the acquisition of terminological knowledge corpus. Their results are validated by human expertise [LAM 03]. In the case of Latin languages, several tools are available such as Lexter and TERMINAE.

For the Arabic language, similar tools have been developed for extracting terms from a corpus of Arab documents. Among these tools, we mention AraFreq that can scan the text and carry out a morphological analysis of all words entered and also offers an interactive component of verification and validation of morphological analyses. The output of this tool is a frequency file for each text examined, the frequency list is in the form of a text file containing for each word, its analysis information as well as the number of occurrences [ABB 02]. Acabit is another tool for building semi-automatic terminology banks, it helps experts by offering them potential candidates as well as morpho-syntactic formats for each term [BOU 05].

Since these tools are unfortunately not available, we developed a module that allows us to extract candidate terms from our corpus. This extractor is mainly based on statistical methods. For morphological analysis, we used the tool morph2. It is a morphological analyzer of Arabic in order to recognize the composition of words and provide specific morphological information to words [CHA 10].

Next, we have retained composed lexical units in the form of noun-noun (for example cassation court), noun-adjective (for example criticized judgment) or noun-preposition-noun (for example appeal). To filter the result obtained from the extractor, we have grouped the lexical units that have the same head or have the same expansion. In the following, we present an excerpt of the results of this filter.

طعن بالإبطال	مطلب تعقيب	وكيل الجمهورية	قرار إستعجالي	محكمة إبتدائية	حكم غيابي
طعن بالتعقيب	مطلب النفاذ	وكيل عام	قرار إحداث	محكمة ناحية	حكم منتقد
طعن في حكم	مطلب إستئناف	وكيل مأجور	قرار التحجير	محكمة تعقيب	حكم مطعون
طعن بالإستئناف	مطلب التعديل	وكيل معين	قرار الحماية	محكمة جنائية	حكم إبتدائي
	مطلب كتابي	وكيل مفوّض	قرار قضائي	محكمة عقارية	حكم جناحي
	مطلب جزئي	وكيل الرئيس الأول	قرار الهيئة	محكمة زجرية	حكم أصلي
		وكيل الدولة العام	قرار المصادقة	محكمة مختصّة	حكم المحكمة
			قرار تحفظي	محكمة إدارية	حكم بالإدراج

Figure 7.2. *Extract from the lexical units list*

This collection of lexical units led us to define hierarchical relations between concepts. For example, the following lexical units محكمة , محكمة إبتدائية

محكمة إدارية, محكمة مختصّة, محكمة زجرية, محكمة عقارية, محكمة ناحية, محكمة إدارية, تعقيب
(appeal court, cassation court, administrative court, etc.) will specialize the concept محكمة (Court). The concept "Court" will specialize, in the second level, the juridical organization concept, which is linked to the organization concept.

7.4.3. *Our reference ontological framework*

The multilevel abstraction approach that we have adopted amounts to applying the same set of generic principles for the conceptualization of the various domains covered by the application ontology. The main motivation is to facilitate the development and maintenance of the domain ontologies and to ensure a high degree of cross-domain consistency [KAS 10].

After the selection of the candidate concepts of our ontology, we have classified them according to three classes:

– Legal agents: these are actors who may interact in a legal context.

– Legal actions: these are actions performed by actors in a legal context.

– Legal artifacts: used to model legal documents and their contents.

In the following, we describe the reference ontological framework we are based on for modeling legal agent and legal action.

7.4.3.1. *Particulars (DOLCE)*

DOLCE's domain is that of particulars, that is to say entities that cannot be instantiated rather than universals. Some subdomains of particulars are distinguished:

Endurants are entities "enduring in time". Within endurants, physical objects are distinguished from non-physical objects, this distinction corresponding to a difference between two realities or modes of existence for the entities. Basically, non-physical objects exist insofar as agents conceive them and communicate about them. The domain of non-physical objects covers entities whose existence depends on either a single agent or a community of agents.

Perdurants are entities "occurring in time" in which endurants temporarily participate. Among perdurants, statives and events are distinguished according to a cumulativity principle. An important complementary dimension of perdurants is the fact of being (or not) intentionally performed. Following [TRY 08], actions are perdurants controlled by an intention. They contrast with happenings that lack an intentional cause. Among actions, deliberate actions are premeditated actions.

Endurants and perdurants have qualities that we perceive and/or measure. Qualities take "values" or "magnitudes", called Qualia within value spaces named regions.

7.4.3.2. Action

We have reused a set of basic concepts for the action notion already defined by means of concepts of DOLCE. A synthesis of these concepts is presented in [PAC 00].

Actions are perdurants controlled by at least one intention. They contrast with happenings, which lack an intentional cause.

Among actions, deliberate actions are premeditated actions. They are controlled by a prior intention, which consists of planning the action (before its initiation) and then in controlling it in a rational way.

Various entities participate in these actions in various ways playing different roles. The agentive entity concept classifies these entities precisely with the ability to perform actions (or, equivalently, to implement intentions).

Kassel *et al.* [KAS 12] introduced the notion of collective action and defined it as a combination of several individual actions combining their effects. They also introduced the concept of action of organization, which is a collective action whose agent is an organization.

7.4.3.3. Organization

To conceptualize the notion of organization, we rely on the formal ontology of organizations defined by [BOT 09]. An essential characterization of the organizations that we adopt is the fact that they have a strong structuring. This structuring allows them to perform all kinds of actions, including those that are deliberate. Further characterization of organizations is that they are social constructs, in other words intentionally built entities to which a function (mission) is socially attributed. It is therefore a social artifact [KAS 10].

Organization is a collective intentionally created and whose structure is largely formal: the members of an organization are formally affiliated and play roles formally recognized by the organization [BOT 09].

Kassel *et al.* [KAS 12] introduced the concept of the collective and defined it as a group of humans unified by a joined intention to form a group that can act. They classify the concept of organization as a collective, which can perform an action of organization.

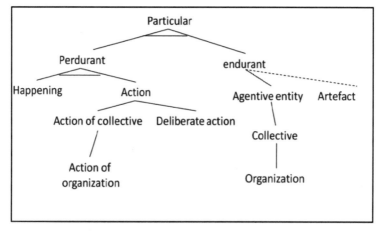

Figure 7.3. *Reference ontological framework*

7.4.4. *Our building blocks*

The core ontologies for the legal domain have been consulted to have an idea for legal concepts already studied. We provide, as follows, the list of concepts that we define as well as the two taxonomies for ontological modules for legal action and legal agents.

Legal fact is an event likely to produce legal effects. It may be an *intentional fact*, such as murder, theft, but also a *non-intentional fact*, such as a death or an accident. A legal fact is a desired or not desired event whose legal effects are not granted by individuals but by the law.

A legal act is an intentional expression of will in order to achieve specific legal effects. The will is what distinguishes legal fact from legal act. A legal act is the manifestation of will intended to produce legal effects. In our context, the legal act concept can be further enriched by defining its different types: unilateral legal act, which depends on a will of a single actor such as testament or acknowledgment of debt. It can be also a bilateral legal fact, which is defined as a voluntary agreement between two or more actors, for example a contract of sale or contract of lease.

A unilateral legal act is a legal act in which its creator, acting alone, intends to produce an effect of law.

A bilateral legal act is a legal act that is created by at least or more than two actors.

A legal task is a legal action defined by a legal description.

We consider three main types of legal agent:

Legal organizations are legal agents (e.g. court and tribunal) that perform legal acts based on powers conferred upon them. They are created by the standards of behavior that justify their existence and validity.

Legal agent: agents who are part of the legal professionals such as judge and lawyer.

Social legal agent: agents that may interact in the legal context but that are not part of the world of legal professionals such as witness, heir and party.

In the following, we present the proposed taxonomy for the legal action ontological module.

We have classified a non-intentional legal fact as a happening because as was shown in the definition previously presented, it is not guided or caused by the intention of an agent. We can give an example here: an accident is an undesirable result, which appears occasionally in the space and time, due to one or more causes, and resulting damages to persons (agent), or property.

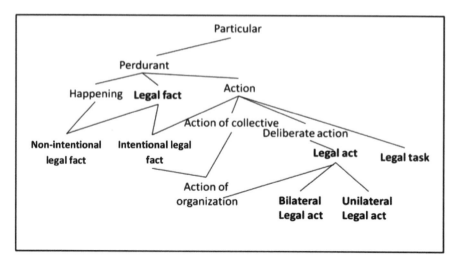

Figure 7.4. *Ontological module for legal action*

In addition, we have classified intentional legal fact, legal act and legal task as actions based on the proposed definition of action, which is also previously presented. We define in the following some examples of legal actions:

– The sales contract is a bilateral legal act by which one of the parties, the seller (agent), is obliged to deliver one thing and the other party, the buyer (agent), has to pay.

– Murder is an intentional legal fact that voluntarily gives (agent) death to a person (agent).

– Testament is a unilateral legal act through which a person (agent) indicates the persons to whom he/she wishes to convey his/her property after his/her death.

– Pleading is a legal task that can be performed by an advocate (agent) to defend a case.

In the following, we present the proposed taxonomy for the legal agent ontological module.

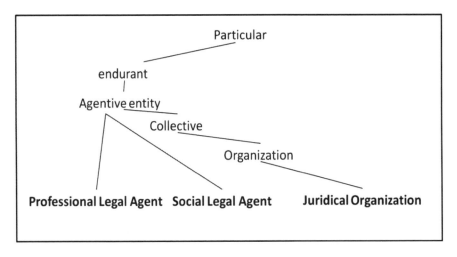

Figure 7.5. *Ontological module for legal agent*

7.4.5. *Discussion*

We have studied the existing works on legal core ontologies. We have identified two references works:

CLO [GAN 05]: this is currently used to support the definition of domain ontologies, the definition of a juridical Wordnet, and the design of legal decision support systems. CLO is a so-called constructive ontology, since it allows us to reason over the contextual constraints that can be intentionally adopted by a cognitive agent when recognizing or classifying a state of affairs. Three kinds of legal task in the civil law countries are supposed to be supported by CLO: conformity checking, legal advice and norm comparison. CLO organizes legal concepts and relations on the basis of formal properties defined in DOLCE.

LKIF [HOE 09]: this was developed in the Estrella project. LKIF has two main roles: first, it enables the translation between legal knowledge bases written in different representation formats and formalisms and second as a knowledge representation formalism that is part of a larger architecture for developing legal knowledge systems. The LKIF core ontology consists of 15 modules, each of which describes a set of closely related concepts from both legal and common sense domains.

In the following, we present some criticisms that we have identified for these two works:

For LKIF, the only concept that defines legal action is an act of law defined as a public act by a legislative body that creates an expression with legal status. Contrary to CLO, it has a more extensive classification of legal action such as legal fact, legal act and human legal fact.

Certainly, the semantics are richer for CLO, but here we criticize, first, the classification of these actions as situations and, second, the hierarchy presented to the concepts. In fact, a legal act cannot be, from legal point of view, considered as a subclass of legal fact because a legal fact is an event likely to produce legal effects. In contrast, a legal act is an intentional expression of will in order to achieve specific legal effects. The will is what distinguishes the act of legal fact. A legal act is the manifestation of wills intended to produce legal effects. We note also that there is no distinction between individual and organizational actions.

In our ontology, we estimate that we have defined concepts for all types of legal agent and legal action, and we have emphasized the distinction between intentional actions and non-intentional legal actions. In addition, we have proposed taxonomies based on the concepts defined in reference and recent works, which treat the notions of action, organization and agentive entity.

These taxonomies also take into account the legal classification of concepts proposed by legal experts.

7.5. Jurisprudence decision structuring methodology (JDSM)

A jurisprudence decision is presented as a textual document of two to five pages. Decisions share a regularity of content. When a lawyer reads a decision, he/she takes quite a long time to define its parts and determine the subparts or parts that are most interesting and can help him/her to solve the new problem. Unlike the case law retrieval systems that currently exist, the methodology we suggest henceforth will present decisions not in their original text states but rather in a structured format. The structuring of decisions can be justified by the following arguments:

– Facilitate, to lawyers, decision reading.

– Take advantage of the structuring to index content portions of the decisions.

– When searching, the lawyer can then use in his/her query both structural and content criteria.

In this section, we begin by presenting some related works of thematic document structuring. Then, we will detail our JDSM.

7.5.1. *Thematic document structuring: some related works*

Automatic document structuring is to provide a cutting of document thematically homogeneous fragments. This task is particularly useful for information retrieval applications. In this field of research, it is sometimes preferable to index and present to users portions of a document rather than the whole document, especially if it is long [MIS 10]. Some other works use it for automatic summarization of texts [FAR 04]. Several research works have been carried out, in the past few decades, concerning thematic document structuring, mainly for English and French languages [HAR 09]. This is not the case for the Arabic language for which few works have studied this technique [ELS 07, HAS 96]. The problem of thematic document structuring is traditionally approached by distributional or statistics methods. These methods are based explicitly on the notion of lexical cohesion [HAR 09]. They are not based (or rarely) on linguistic analysis, but rather on statistical methods for the segmentation, using some similarity calculations based on word frequency [CON 08].

Several algorithms are proposed for thematic document structuring such as C99 and TextTiling. The TextTiling algorithm [HEA 94] uses the cosine similarity measure between the vectors of terms to measure the density of cohesion between adjacent blocks. The C99 algorithm [CHO 00] also uses the cosine similarity measure to determine similarities among the sentences of the text, and then it projects them graphically [HAR 09]. Concerning the Arabic language, globally the algorithm TextTiling seems to be more adapted than that of C99 [HAR 09].

The nature of thematic segments delimiting the statistical methods remains unclear, since the notion of lexical cohesion is not sufficient to linguistically characterize a hypothetical textual object as a "thematic segment". However, it is also clear that the reality of the thematic organization of a text involves many other criteria, which motivate other approaches that emphasize the linguistic modeling of the textual objects studied. It is important then to exploit markers or signs holders of indications of textual thematic structure [WID 06]. Knowledge-based techniques thus require the manual effort of knowledge engineering to create a knowledge base (semantic network and/or frames). This is only achievable in a few limited areas [HAS 96]. As a result, linguistics systems are often built specifically for a given corpus, and in this case, it is difficult to transpose them to another collection [PES 04].

7.5.2. *Our methodology*

As shown in Figure 7.6, JDSM aims to structure decisions by following these steps: linguistic analysis of the corpus, linguistic marker extraction, pattern construction and finally decision structuring based on the pattern base and on the legal ontology.

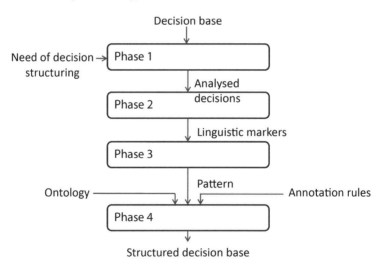

Figure 7.6. *Jurisprudence decision structuring methodology*

7.5.2.1. *Linguistic analysis of the corpus and linguistic marker extraction*

The analysis stage was carried out in close collaboration with legal experts to determine how to structure a decision. Reading a decision is not always clear. Fluency is acquired with experience. When reading a decision, the lawyer reviews it in a comprehensive manner, and attempts to recognize the descriptive and reasoning blocks. Descriptive blocks describe facts and legal actions. Reasoning blocks are the step in which the judge uses the facts to reach a decision in law. Our initial corpus is composed by 50 decisions of different types (civil, administrative, criminal, etc.). This corpus was analyzed in order to identify regularities in decision contents and to establish a common organizational structure, which is composed of general information, the principle, introduction, facts, the appeal means, legal reasoning and a conclusion [DHO 12b].

A linguistic analysis was carried out in order to extract linguistic markers. By reviewing some decision extracts, we identified some problems. For example, phrases, which mark the beginning of the part "facts", have the same meaning "according to the judgment and facts", but their formulations are different:

حيثتفيدالوقائعالمثبتةبالحكمالمنتقد

(According to the facts proven in the criticized judgment)

حيثيستفادمنالقرارالمطعونفيهومنالأبحاثالمجراةفيالقضية

(As concluded from the impugned decision and from research conducted in the case)

حيثأنتجتالأبحاثفيالقضيةأن

(Research of the case produced)

By examining these extracts, several problems can be introduced:

– The term is designated by its synonyms in different texts. For example, to describe the expression "it seems that", several synonymous terms can be used: تبين, تفيد, إتضح.

– The same word appears in different morphological forms. For example, the phrase "it seems that" can be designated with the term in different forms أفاد, تفيد, يستفاد.

– We can find words with the same legal meaning and different cities but which are not necessarily synonyms such as الوقائع (the facts) and الأبحاث في القضية (research of the case).

As a result, and to solve the problems mentioned below, we propose, on the one hand, to build a database of patterns that will be used to identify the different parts of the decisions and, on the other hand, to use our legal ontology that establishes a consensus among legal experts and resolves the ambiguity of a term's variability.

7.5.2.2. *Pattern construction*

To construct patterns, we started by making a linguistic analysis of the corpus and extract the field markers. Hereafter in Figure 7.7, we present a first list of markers that may be present in different parts of a decision.

Part	Markers	Equivalent of markers in English
General information	قرار، عدد، مؤرخ في، صدر برئاسة، نشرية، مادة، مفاتيح	decision, number, published on, published under the presidency, volume, reference, key-words
The principle	المبدأ	The principle
Introduction	أصدرت محكمة التعقيب القرار الآتي، بعد الإطلاع على مطلب التعقيب ، بتاريخ، من طرف، في حق، ضد، طعنا في، و بعد الإطلاع على/على ملحوظات المدعي العام/على أوراق القضية/ على الحكم المنتقد/..وبعد المفاوضة القانونية صرح بما يلي، من حيث الشكل	The Court of Cassation delivered the following Judgment, since the contested judgment, at the date, from, for, against, given the General Attorney notes / seen the documents of the case / seen the judgment / and after the legal negotiation /was stated the following/ form viewpoint
Facts	من حيث الأصل،حيث إتضح من الحكم المنتقد و من الوقائع التي إبنى عليها / حيث تفيد وقائع القضية حيث أن	On basic point of view, whereas according to the judgment and the facts of the case, whereas the facts of the case, whereas..
Appeal means	أولا،ثانيا،ثالثا، المطعن الأول،المطعن الثاني،المطعن الثالث،ضعف التعليل، تحريف الوقائع،ضعف التعليل،خطأ في تطبيق القانون	First, second, third, first appeal mean, second appeal mean, third appeal mean, poor reasoning, distortion of facts, weak reasoning, an error in the application of the law
Legal reasonning	المحكمة، عن المطعن الأول، عن المطعن الثاني،عن المطعن الثاني،عن المطعن الثالث،عن المطعنين معا،عن المطعن الوحيد، حيث أنه من القوعد الثابتة، حيث تبين تعليل الأحكام وتسبيبها، حيث تبين ..من القرار المنتقد، حيث أن	The court, on the first appeal mean, on the second appeal mean, on the third appeal mean, on the single mean, on the both appeal means,...
Conclusion	ولهذه الأسباب	For these reasons

Figure 7.7. *Examples of a field's markers of different part of a decision*

The big syntactic and lexical variability of the markers of the same segment have obliged us to think about building extraction patterns for each segment. There is sometimes a necessity to define several patterns for the same segment. An extraction pattern is a structure allowing the identification of information that we want to extract. It also establishes relationships between these pieces of information. It is characterized by syntactic constraints (position of arguments in a related subject-verb-object) and semantic constraints (semantic type classes) for filtering a subset of statements that contain information relevant to the application field [BOU 05].

We have manually built our extraction patterns and then classified them according to the parts to which they belong (introduction, facts, appeal means, legal reasoning and conclusion).

The definition of patterns was done on two levels: syntactic and semantic. The syntactic level allows us to define the syntactic structure of a given pattern. The semantic level gives the nature of lexical terms composing a given pattern.

Let us consider the following example, where we started with some excerpts from the introductory part of the decision:

أصدرتمحكمةالتعقيببتونسالقرارالتالي

(The cassation court in Tunis issued the following decision)

أصدرتمحكمةالتعقيبالقرارالآتي

(The cassation court issued the following decision)

أصدرتالدائرةالرابعةبمحكمةالتعقيببصفاقسالحكمالتالي

(The fourth district of the cassation court in Sfax issued the following judgment)

The first level of definition of the pattern is as follows:

P =   فعل(غير ناسخ)+إسم(مكان/زمان)+إسم+إسم علم(بلاد)+إسم(مصدر)+إسم(إسم فاعل

P = Verb + [Noun] + Noun+ [Noun] + Noun + Noun

A second definition of the same pattern is then proposed:

P =   فعل مقدّمة+إسم دائرة+إسم محكمة+إسم مدينة+إسم+إسم تعداد

P = Verb_introduction + [noun of a district] + Noun of the court + [town] + Noun + Noun_listing

The use of these patterns in the structuring step will be explained in the following section.

7.5.2.3. *Decision structuring based on the pattern database and the legal ontology*

To structure the decision, we have relied on the pattern base and the legal ontology.

Pattern localization in decisions is made at two levels by the use of annotation rules. In the first level, we check whether the terms of a given sentence have the same syntactic form with the elements of a given pattern. The second level aims to verify the existence of each term among those in the ontology and belonging to the class of terms of the annotated part (Figure 7.8). Annotation rules are, therefore, applied to a select sentence which marks the beginning of the corresponding part of the decision and tags this part. Two types of rule are then defined to check the syntactic and lexical correspondence of a sentence's terms with those of the pattern. The general form of the rules is as follows:

We consider a pattern $P = e_1 + e_2 + ... + e_n$ and a sentence $S = t_1 + t_2 + ... + t_n$

R1 (first level): *for* each term t_i of the sentence S and for each element e_i of the pattern, if category (t_i) = category (e_i), *then* S is considered as candidate sentence and the second level rule R2 is run.

R2 (second level): *if* each term t_i of the candidate sentence is among the list of synonymous terms of a concept belonging to the ontology and whose class (t_i) = class (e_i), *then* assign the corresponding tag of the part starting from this same sentence.

We have developed a prototype that implements the method proposed for the decision structuring. The input for the prototype is a textual document containing a decision; the output is a structured XML document whose tags are the parts of a decision. The results of this prototype were assessed and validated by the legal experts [DHO 12a].

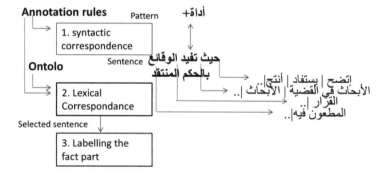

Figure 7.8. *Presence control of patterns in a decision
in order to tag the fact part*

Figure 7.9. *Decision structuring result interface*

7.6. Conclusion

Lawyers deplore more and more the complexity of the legal documentation they use and require better management of their knowledge. The recourse to legal ontologies can be, in this case, very useful especially in extraction and information retrieval from legal textual corpuses. As to the case of Tunisia, lawyers, for example, find it difficult to use and manage the different sources of jurisprudence.

The context of our research is the development of a system of search of Tunisian jurisprudence in the Arabic language based on a legal ontology.

In this chapter, we have presented an insight into technologies that can be considered as part of the KM resources in the legal field such as legal portals, legal expert systems, legal CBR and legal ontologies.

We have also given an overview of the conceptualization step of this ontology by showing the formal approach, based on foundational ontology DOLCE and a CLO.

We have also focused on the description of the methodology we have proposed for the decision structuring and which is based on extraction patterns and on legal ontology. The definition of the extraction patterns was carried out on two levels: syntactic and semantic. Annotation rules are then applied to carry out pattern localization in decisions and select each sentence, which may mark the beginning of the corresponding part of the decision and tag this part.

We have developed a prototype that implements the proposed method for decision structuring. The results of this prototype were assessed and validated by the legal experts.

We envision in our future work the enrichment of our ontology by adding an ontological module for the representation of legal artifacts. This ontology will also be used to index decisions, facilitate search processes and query formulations by giving to lawyers the possibility of using both structural and content criteria in their queries.

7.7. Bibliography

[ABB 02] ABBES R., HASSOUN M., "AraFreq: un outil pour le calcul de fréquences de mots arabes", *Proceedings of the International Symposium on the Automatic Processing of the Arabic Language*, Manouba University, pp. 213–225, 18–20 April 2002.

[API 02] APISTOLA M., OSKAMP A., "Knowledge management for law practice: do we really need it?", *Proceedings of the 17th BILETA Annual Conference*, Free University, Amsterdam, 5–6 April 2002.

[AUS 08] AUSSENAC-GILLES G., DESPRES S., SZULMAN S., "The TERMINAE method and platform for ontology engineering from texts", in BUITELAR P., CIMIANO P. (eds), *Bridging the Gap between Text and Knowledge: Selected Contributions to Ontology learning from Text*, IOS Press, pp. 199–223, 2008.

[BOT 09] BOTTAZI E., FERRARIO R., "Preliminaries to a DOLCE ontology of organization", *International Journal of Business Process Integration and Management*, Special Issue on Vocabularies, Ontologies and Business Rules for Enterprise Modeling, vol. 4, no. 4, pp. 225–238, 2009.

[BOU 05] BOUFADEN, N., LAPALME, G., "Apprentissage de relations prédicat-argument pour l'extraction d'information à partir de textes conversationnels", *TAL 2005 (Poster)*, vol. 1, Dourdan, France, pp. 397–402, June 2005.

[BOU 08] BOULAKNADEL S., DAILLE B., DRISS A., "Acabit: un outil d'extraction des termes complexes", *Acte du colloque sur les nouvelles technologies d'information: opportunités pour lamazighe*, IRCAM, 2008.

[BRE 04] BREUKER J., VALENTE A., WINKELS R., "Legal ontologies in knowledge engineering and information management", *Artificial Intelligence and Law*, vol. 12, pp. 241–277, 2004.

[BUR 97] BURKE R., HAMMOND K., KULYUKIN V., *et al.*, "Question Answering from frequently-asked question files: experiences with the FAQ finder system", *AI Magazine*, vol. 18, no. 2, pp. 57–66, 1997.

[CAS 11] CASELLAS N., "Legal ontology engineering, methodologies, modelling trends, and the ontology of professional judicial knowledge", *Law, Governance and Technology Series*, Springer, the Netherlands, vol. 3, 2011.

[CHA 10] CHAÂBEN KAMMOUN N., HADRICH BELGUITH L., BEN HAMADOU A., "The MORPH2 new version: a robust morphological analyzer for Arabic texts", *Actes des 10èmes journées internationales d'analyse statistique des données (JADT '10)*, Rome, Italy, 9–11 June 2010.

[CHO 00] CHOI F., "Advances in domain independent linear text segmentation", *Proceedings of the 1st North American Chapter of the Association for Computational Linguistics (NAACL)*, Seattle, Washington, pp. 26–33, 29 April–4 May 2000.

[CON 08] CONSTANT M., DISTER A., EMIKARIAN L., *et al.*, *Description Linguistique pour le Traitement Automatique du Français*, Presses Universitaires de Louvain, Université catholique de Louvain, p. 210, 2008.

[DAN 96] DANIELS J., Retrieval of Passages for Information Reduction, Phd Thesis, Massachusetts University, Amherst, 1996.

[DHO 12a] DHOUIB K., DESPRES S., GARGOURI F., "Structuration des décisions de jurisprudence basée sur une ontologie juridique en langue arabe", *12th Conférence Internationale Francophone sur l'Extraction et la Gestion de Connaissance (EGC '12)*, Bordeaux, France, 2012.

[DHO 12b] DHOUIB K., GARGOURI F., "Jurisprudence decision-structuring based on a legal ontology in Arabic", *5th World Summit on the Knowledge Society (WSKS'12)*, Rome, Italy, 2012.

[ELS 07] EL-SHAYEB M.A., EL-BELTAGYAND S.R., RAFEA A., "Comparative analysis of different text segmentation algorithms on Arabic news stories", *Proceedings of the IEEE International Conference on Information Reuse and Integration (IRI 07)*, Las Vegas, NV, pp. 441–446, 13 August 2007.

[FAR 04] FARZINDAR A., LAPALME G., DESCLES J., "Résumé de textes juridiques par identification de leur structure thématique", *Traitement automatique de la langue (TAL)*, vol. 45, pp. 39–64, 2004.

[FER 97] FERNÁNDEZ M., GÓMEZ-PÉREZ A., JURISTO N., "Methontology: from ontological art towards ontological engineering", *Proceedings of AAAI97 Spring Symposium Series, Workshop on Ontological Engineering*, pp. 33–40, 1997.

[FER 99] FERNÁNDEZ M., GÓMEZ-PÉREZ A., SIERRA A.P., *et al.*, "Building a chemical ontology using METHONTOLOGY and the ontology design environment", *IEEE Expert (Intelligent Systems and Their Applications)*, vol. 14, no. 1, pp. 37–46, 1999.

[GAN 04] GANGEMI A., BORGO S. (eds), *Proceedings of the 14th International Conference on Knowledge Engineering and Knowledge Management (EKAW'04), Workshop on Core Ontologies in Ontology Engineering*, [online], Northamptonshire, UK, vol. 118, 2004. Available at: http://ceur-ws.org.

[GAN 05] GANGEMI A., SAGRI M., TISCORNIA D., A constructive framework for legal ontologies, BENJAMINS V., CASANOVAS P., BREUKER J., GANGEMI A. (eds), *Law and the Semantic Web*, Springer Verlag, pp. 97–124, 2005.

[GRU 93] GRUBER T.R., "A translation approach to portable ontology specifications", *Knowledge Acquisition*, vol. 5, no. 2, pp. 199–220, 1993.

[HAR 09] HARRAG F., BENMOHAMMED M., Etude comparative des algorithmes de segmentation thématique pour la langue Arabe, *Proceedings of the 2nd Conférence Internationale sur l'Informatique et ses Applications (CIIA '09)*, Saida, Algeria, 3–4 May 2009.

[HAS 96] HASNAH A.M., Full text processing and retrieval: weight ranking text structuring, and passage retrievel for arabic document, PhD Thesis, Illinois Institute of Technology, 1996.

[HEA 94] HEARST M.A., "Multi-paragraph segmentation of expository text", *32nd Meeting of the Association for Computational Linguistics*, Los Cruces, NM, June 1994.

[HOE 09] HOEKSTRA R., BREUKER J., DI BELLO M., *et al.*, "Core: principled ontology development for the legal domain", in BREUKER J., CASANOVAS P., KLEIN M.C.A., FRANCESCONI E. (eds), *Law, Ontologies and the Semantic Web: Channelling the Legal Information Flood (Frontiers in Artificial Intelligence and Applications)*, IOS Press, Amsterdam, vol. 188, pp. 21–52, 2009.

[JAR 07] JARRAR M., MEERSMAN R., "Ontology engineering – the DOGMA approach", *Advances in Web Semantic, A state-of-the Art Semantic Web Advances in Web Semantics IFIP2.12.*, vol. 1, Chapter 3, Springer-sbm, Berlin/Heidelberg, 2007.

[KAS 99] KASSEL G., PERPETTE S., "Co-operative ontology construction needs to carefully articulate terms, notions and objects", *International Workshop on Ontological Engineering on the Global Information Infrastructure*, Dagstuhl Castle, Germany, pp. 57–70, 1999.

[KAS 10] KASSEL G., "A formal ontology of artefacts", *Applied Ontology*, vol. 5, nos. 3–4, pp. 223–246, 2010.

[KAS 12] KASSEL G., TURKI M., SAAD I., *et al.*, "From collective actions to actions of organizations: an ontological analysis", *Symposium on Understanding and Modelling Collective Phenomena (UMoCop'12)*, Birmingham, UK, July 2012.

[LAM 02a] LAME G., Construction d'ontologie à partir de textes: une ontologie du droit dédiée à la recherche d'informations sur le Web, PhD Thesis, center of research in computer science, Higher national school, Mines, Paris., 2002.

[LAM 02b] LAMONTAGNE L., LAPALME G., Raisonnement à base de cas textuel – état de l'art et perspectives futures, *Revue d'intelligence artificielle*, vol. 16, no. 3, pp. 339–366, 2002.

[LAM 03] LAME G., "Using text analysis techniques to identify legal ontologie's components", *Workshop on Legal Ontologies & Web Based Legal Information Management (ICAIL 2003)*, 2003.

[LEA 99] LEAKE D.B., WILSON D.C., "Combining CBR with interactive knowledge acquisition, manipulation and reuse", *Proceedings of ICCBR-99, LNAI 1650*, Springer Verlag, pp. 203–217, 1999.

[LEN 99] LENZ M., GLINTSCHERT A., "On texts, cases, and concepts.",, *Proceedings of XPS-99, LNAI 1570*, Springer Verlag, pp. 148–156.

[MAS 03] MASOLO C., BORGO S., GANGEMI A., *et al.*, WonderWeb Deliverable D18: Ontology Library (final), technical report, LOA-ISTC, CNR, 2003.

[MIS 10] MISRA H., YVON F., "Modèles thématiques pour la segmentation de documents", *Proceedings of the 10th International Conference on Statistical Analysis of Textual Data (JADT 2010)*, Sapienza University of Rome, 9–11 June 2010.

[MON 11] MONDARY T., Construction d'ontologies à partir de textes: L'apport de l'analyse de concepts formels, Doctorate Thesis, University Paris-Nord – Paris XIII, 2011.

[PES 04] PESSIOT J.F., CAILLET M., AMINI M.R., *et al.*, "Apprentissage non-supervisé pour la segmentation automatique de textes", *Proceeding of the 4th Conference Recherche d'Information et Application (CORIA)*, Toulouse, France, pp. 213–228, 2004.

[PAC 00] PACHERIE E., "The content of intentions", *Mind and Language*, vol. 15, no. 4, pp. 400–432, 2000.

[SCH 00] SCHREIBER G., AKKERMANS H., ANJEWIERDEN A., *et al.*,. *Knowledge Engineering and Management, The CommonKADS Methodology*, A Bradford Book, MIT Press, Cambridge, 1999.

[SPY 08] SPYNS P., TANG Y., MEERSMAN R., "An ontology engineering methodology for DOGMA", *Applied Ontology Journal*, vol. 3, nos. 1–2, pp. 13–39, 2008.

[STA 03] STAUDT R., Perspectives on knowledge management in law firms: Lexis Nexis, White Paper, 2003. Available at http://www.Lexisnexis.com.

[SUR 03] SURE Y., STAAB S., STUDER R., "On-to-knowledge methodology (OTKM)", in STAAB S., STUDER R. (eds), *Handbook on Ontologies (International Handbooks on Information Systems)*, Springer, Berlin, pp. 117–132, 2003.

[TRY 08] TRYPUZ R., *Formal Ontology of Action: A Unifying Approach*, Wydawnictwo Kul, Lublin, 2008.

[VAL 96] VALENTE A., BREUKER J., "Towards principled core ontologies", *Proceedings of the 10th Banff Knowledge Acquisition for Knowledge-Based Systems Workshop (KAW '96)*, Banff, 1996.

[WEB 98] WEBER R., MARTINS A., BARCIA R., On legal texts and cases, Textual Case-Based Reasoning: Papers from the AAAI-98 Workshop, Technical Report WS-98-12, AAAI Press, pp. 40–50, 1998.

[WID 06] WIDLÖCHER A., BILHAUT F., HERNANDEZ N., *et al.*, "Une approche hybride de la segmentation thématique: collaboration du traitement automatique des langues et de la fouille de texte", *Acte du Deuxième Défi de Fouille de Textes (DEFT '06), Semaine du Document Numérique (SDN '06)*, France, 2006.

Chapter 8

Foundations for a Core Ontology of an Organization's Processes

New performance requirements to adapt to the changing environment and to maintain a competitive advantage have contributed since the 1980s to the emergence of new types of organizations focused on projects or processes. To facilitate the implementation of this process view of organizations, many theorists and practitioners have proposed analysis and modeling frameworks, ontologies being considered as a relevant tool to conduct a "semantic analysis" of business processes. Approaches in this area are, however, based on *ad hoc*, often implicit, modeling principles and the proposed ontologies remain poor in terms of expressiveness. The objective of this chapter is to analyze the ontological foundations of the processes of organizations following a *formal* approach. We propose a core ontology of an organization's processes (COOPs) specializing the descriptive ontology for linguistic and cognitive engineering (DOLCE) foundational ontology and supplementing Bottazzi and Ferrario's DOLCE-based formal ontology of organizations. This ontology comprises several modules to reflect both the "static" aspects of organizations and their behaviors, including intentional ones. In this chapter, we present the contents of the ontology, the formal ontological tools reused for its design and the various theories to which the ontology is committed.

Chapter written by Mohamed Turki, Gilles Kassel, Inès Saad and Faïez Gargouri.

8.1. Introduction

In a highly competitive environment, organizations have to improve the performance of their activities. Therefore, it is crucial for them to create and design novel products (or services) in order to keep or increase their market share. At the same time, the development cycle of the product as well as its cost should be reduced while ensuring an acceptable level of quality. These new performance requirements have contributed, since the late 1980s, to the development of a new type of organizations that are project-centered.

Since projects are unique processes for achieving specific objectives, the process view in the organization becomes more important and several researchers and practitioners have been focusing on the management of these processes by analyzing and modeling them. The goal of the process view is, on the one hand, to better understand the functioning and the properties of these processes to improve them and, on the other hand, to reorganize the structure of the organization while preserving self-determination of the different business divisions.

Several works are being developed by practitioners and researchers in quality management [ISO 00, ISO 03] to master and improve the different types of processes of organization, and consequently to improve their results and performance, while focusing on the needs of the clients. In strategic management, the works [LOR 03] aim at improving the performance of the organizations through the identification of the strategic resources and processes. Other works have been done in the fields of information systems [MEL 00, NUR 05], workflow management [WFM 99], business process management [HAM 93] and business for innovation [DAV 93] in order to improve and optimize the internal processes of the organization and also the processes that are shared with other organizations. In addition, the goal is to underlay the processes by information systems to enhance further their efficiency and efficacy. All these works carried out both by practitioners and theorists in various disciplines lead to a complex understanding of concepts and practices.

In this chapter, we adopt an ontological approach to account for a set of concepts necessary for the analysis of an organization's processes and to improve their modeling. We are in a line of works offering ontological models of enterprises [FOX 92, USC 98, BER 07] and more generally of organizations [BOT 09].

Recent works in this line (e.g. [BOR 04]) use a more rigorous approach that summarizes the term "formal ontology". This term refers to a research field known as "Applied Ontology" (or "Applied Formal Ontology"), at the crossroads of Formal Ontology, Philosophy and Knowledge Representation (a subfield of Artificial Intelligence).

The objective of this chapter is to work within this particular vein and also to further scrutinize the "dynamic" aspects of organizations through their actions and, more particularly, their processes. Progress in this direction is made possible by the conjunction of two facts. On the one hand, in the field of formal ontologies, we have resources such as the foundational ontology DOLCE [MAS 03] widely opened to the analysis of social entities. We also have recent works in the fields of formal ontologies of collections and collectives [BOT 06, WOO 09], formal ontologies of actions [TRY 08] and formal ontologies of processes [GAL 09]. On the other hand, there emerges from the recent work in philosophy of action, particularly in the philosophy of collective social action [TUO 05a, PAC 12] and in the philosophy of the social science [LIS 11], a conceptual coherent framework to analyze social collective actions. These two facts together lead us to propose, in a first step, an original ontological framework facilitating the analysis of the concepts accounting for an organization's processes.

The remaining part of this chapter is organized as follows. In section 8.2, we present our ontological reference framework structured around the foundational ontology DOLCE. In section 8.3, we detail our contribution, namely the COOP ontology. COOP consists of a first set of modules providing sets of basic concepts to analyze collective and organizational phenomena. This ontological framework is then enriched with several concepts of an organization's processes such as the concepts of *process of organization*, *organizational subprocess*, *internal process*, *core process*, *strategic process* and *project*. In section 8.4, we position our contribution with respect to works carried out in the field of formal ontologies of organizations, especially the work conducted in the laboratory for applied ontology (LOA) [BOT 09]. In section 8.5, we talk about two ongoing application projects using the COOP ontology and we identify further opportunities for research.

8.2. Our reference ontological framework

For building our COOP ontology, we adopted a multilayer and multicomponent approach already used to structure the ontological resources of the OntoSpec method [KAS 05]. The set of all these resources constitutes a global and consistent ontology (named with the same name of the method). The OntoSpec ontology is indeed organized into subontologies (modules) with different levels of abstraction. Schematically, three levels are identified: (1) at the most abstract level, the foundational DOLCE[1] ontology [MAS 03] provides a set of abstract concepts (e.g. physical object, event and quality) and relations (e.g. parthood and constitution) for structuring (by specialization) any domain, (2) at an intermediate level, "core" domain ontologies [GAN 04] define generic and central concepts in various domains such as organizations or organization's processes; (3) lastly, at the most specific level, core domain ontologies are in their turn refined to introduce, by specialization, domain-specific concepts (e.g. in the academic domain, university, research laboratory, laboratory permanent member and team head).

This multilevel of abstraction approach amounts to applying the same set of generic principles for the conceptualization of the various domains covered by an application ontology. The main motivation is to facilitate the development and maintenance of the domain ontologies and to ensure a high degree of cross-domain consistency.

The original ontologies presented in this chapter are situated at the intermediate level of core domain ontologies. Therefore, COOP provides a set of generic and central concepts for conceptualizing an organization's processes in various contexts. The new modules composing COOP specialize concepts present in OntoSpec's modules situated at the foundational level. In the following part of this section, we briefly recall the structuring principles of the modules useful for the definition of COOP (see Table 8.1) by introducing some main concepts and relations.

To carry out our analysis, we adopt a basic ontological principle, which can be summarized as follows: the *object* and the *process* are two complementary sides of any reality. According to this principle, corresponding to a view widely shared in formal ontology, this

---

1 http://www.loa-cnr.it/DOLCE.html.

complimentarity of the objects and processes is explained by a strong mutual dependence, as stated by Galton and Mizoguchi [GAL 09, p. 72]: "(a) matter and objects by nature presuppose the participation in processes or events, and (b) processes and events by nature presuppose the existence of matter or objects". This principle is already firmly anchored in most upper-level (foundational) ontologies, including basic formal ontology (BFO) and DOLCE. In DOLCE, which we consider as a framework of reference, the principle corresponds to the distinction between *endurants* and *perdurants*, applied so far to the analysis of individual phenomena. For our work, we make this principle a precept and therefore propose to apply it to the analysis of collective phenomena in distinguishing, on the one hand, objects-groups and, on the other, process-behaviors borne by these groups.

Modules	Domains	Addresses
Particular (DOLCE)	Endurant, physical object, social object, perdurant, event, process, quality, region	*prefix*/Particular-v1.2-OS.pdf
Participation role	Agent, consequent, result, instrument, data	*prefix*/Participation_role-v1.3-OS.pdf
Capacity	Capacity, capacity to perform action, capacity to enable action	*prefix*/Capacity-v1.1-OS.pdf
Agentive entity	Agentive entity, agentive physical object, agentive social object	*prefix*/Agentive_entity-v1.1-OS.pdf
Resource	Resource, material resource, immaterial resource	*prefix*/Resource-v1.0-OS.pdf
Action	Intention, action, deliberate action, successful action	*prefix*/Action-v1.1-OS.pdf
Function & Artefact	Artificial object, functional object, artifact, technical artifact, social artifact	*prefix*/Function_&_Artefact-v1.0-OS.pdf

Table 8.1. *Main generic ontological modules used for the definition of COOP, with the location of their specification in the semi-formal language of the OntoSpec method (prefix = http://www.laria.u-picardie.fr/IC/site/IMG/pdf)*

8.2.1. *DOLCE*

The DOLCE ontology [MAS 03] constitutes the keystone of OntoSpec (hence, also of COOP). DOLCE's domain is that of Particulars[2], that is to say entities that cannot be instantiated (e.g. "my car") rather than universals (e.g. "being a car"). Four subdomains of Particulars are distinguished (see Figure 8.1):

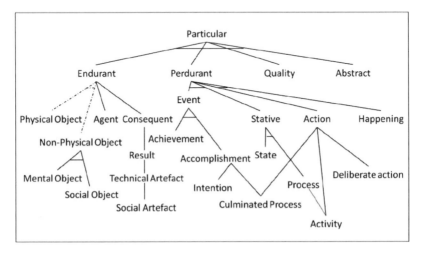

Figure 8.1. *Taxonomy of the main concepts defining our ontological framework. A descending edge between two concepts represents a subsumption link. A dashed line reflects the existence of intermediate concepts. A horizontal line between edges from a father concept indicates that the sibling concepts are incompatible*

– Endurants are entities "enduring in time". Within Endurants, Physical Objects (e.g. a hard copy of this chapter) are distinguished from Non-Physical Objects (e.g. the content of this chapter resulting from your interpretation), this distinction corresponding to a difference between two realities or *modes* of existence for the entities. Basically, Non-Physical Objects exist insofar as agents. The domain of Non-Physical Objects covers entities whose existence depends on either a

---

2 With respect to our notation, the informal labels on DOLCE's categories appear in the text in the Courier new font with First Capital Letters for the concepts and a javaLikeNotation for relations. The same conventions apply for all the ontologies presented in this chapter.

single agent (for `Mental Objects`) or a community of agents (for `Social Objects`).

– `Perdurants` are entities "occurring in time" (e.g. your reading of this chapter) in which `Endurants` temporarily participate (`participatesInDuring`). Among `Perdurants`, `Statives` and `Events` are distinguished according to a cumulativity principle. Within the former class, `States` are distinguished from `Processes` according to a homogeneity principle. Among the latter, `Achievements` are distinguished from `Accomplishments` according to whether they are, or not, atomic (e.g. a birth vs. a life). Among `Perdurants`, the notion of *action* is considered as central for our purposes. Indeed, `Actions` are `Perdurants controlledBy` at least one `Intention`. They contrast with `Happenings` that lack an intentional cause. Among `Actions`, `Deliberate Actions` are premeditated actions. They are `controlledBy` a `Prior Intention` that consists of planning the action (before its initiation) and then in controlling it in a rational way.

– `Endurants` and `Perdurants` have `Qualities` that we perceive and/or measure (e.g. the weight of the printed copy of an article and the time it takes for us to read this article).

– `Qualities` take "values" or "magnitudes", called Qualia (e.g. 25 g and 20 min), within value spaces named `Regions`.

Before presenting other modules of OntoSpec supplementing DOLCE, we wish to make two clarifications. The first concerns the position of DOLCE with respect to Searle's [SEA 95] social ontology about the concept of *social object*. The second is a clarification of the nature of *processes* in connection with recent work on the formal ontology of processes.

As we will see in section 8.3.2, the consideration of a class of `Social Objects` is crucial for our conceptualization of the organizations and their actions. It is important in this regard to note that this stand is in strong opposition to Searle's [SEA 95] social ontology. Indeed, according to Searle, social reality is, above all, constituted of social *facts* dependent on collective intentionalities of humans (or animals capable of collective intentionality). This is the case (for a group of agents) of the fact of considering that such a piece of paper with a special green inscription *counts for* a $1 bill, or the fact that such an individual human *counts for* the President of the French Republic. According to Searle, neither the dollar bill nor the President of the French Republic exist as object: only the piece of paper and the human individual exist. On the contrary, the authors of DOLCE recognize that these social objects, which are *money*, *governments* and *universities*, have an existence analogous to that of material objects and one of their research projects is to define the essence of these social objects [MAS 04, MAS 05]. Our proposal of ontology of an organization's processes is fully within this perspective.

To refer again to the concept of *process*, an important and widely recognized relationship between *events* and *processes* needs to be mentioned (we however adopt it in the characterization of our concepts): an `Event` (e.g. a *street crossing*) is *constituted of* – in the sense of DOLCE's `constitution` relationship – one (or more) `Process(es)` (e.g. *walking* and *running*) on which it depends. Recently, Trypuz [TRY 08] has incorporated this property in its formal ontology of actions (with an extension of DOLCE). A close view can also be found in the work of Galton and Mizoguchi [GAL 09, p. 75], consisting of identifying an event (somehow) to a process bounded in time: "… processes endure, but only once we have assigned bounds to them can we speak of duration, and the act of assigning bounds means that we have switched our attention from the process to an event". On this view, we will define in section 8.3 our organization's processes as (intentional) `Events` constituted of (intentional) `Processes`. Prior to this, we need to be able to consider intentionally performed `Perdurants`, which leads us to introduce a concept of *action*.

8.2.2. *Actions, participation roles and participatory capacities*

– `Actions` are `Perdurants` `controlledBy` at least one `Intention`[3]. They contrast with Happenings that lack an intentional cause[4]. Following a classification of Actions proposed by Trypuz [TRY 08], we

---

3 In the current state of our ontology, the different concepts of *intention* introduced are defined without reference to their content (conceptual or not). The definition of these contents would require to deal with an ontology of mental objects such as the one whose bases have been laid by Ferrario and Oltramari [FER 04] as an extension of DOLCE.

4 In DOLCE-Lite-Plus, a notion of action was informally introduced as "an Accomplishment exemplifying the intention of an agent" [MAS 03]. By more generally defining Actions as arbitrary Perdurants controlled by an Intention, as recently proposed by Trypuz [TRY 08] in an extension of DOLCE to actions, we allow other categories of Perdurants, namely States and Processes, to be intentionally realized.

define the concepts Culminated Process (respectively, Activity) as intentional Accomplishments (respectively, Processes).

– Among Actions, Deliberate Actions are premeditated actions. They are controlledBy a Prior Intention that consists of planning the action (before its initiation) and then controlling it in a rational way[5].

Various entities participate in these Actions in various ways, i.e. playing different roles. As a complement to DOLCE, our participation role-OntoSpec (OS) module specializes the participation relation participatesInDuring to account for specific ways in which Endurants temporarily participate in Actions (e.g. isAgentOfAt, isInstrumentOfAt and isResultOfAt) and such relations, in turn, are used to define *participation roles* specializing the concept Endurant (e.g. Agent, Instrument and Result).

These different roles are played by entities with specific capacities or dispositions. For example, only entities capable of Intentions can play the role of Agent. The Agentive Entity concept classifies precisely those entities with the ability to perform Actions (or, equivalently, to implement Intentions). Similarly, the Resource concept classifies entities with the ability to enable performing Actions. This last concept reflects a general sense of the term "resource" to be entities "available for action". In OntoSpec, we identify these *participatory capacities* (or capacities to play roles in Actions) to States, considering that they may be acquired or lost. Therefore, they are temporarily borne by entities, but their temporal extension is different from that of the roles they can play in Actions. The Agentives Entities (respectively Resources) play the role of Agent (respectively Instrument) only during the performance of particular Actions.

---

5 Though we use a Searlian terminology to designate this intention, the intended concept is somewhat different. Thus, based on Pacherie's [PAC 00] dynamic theory of intentions, we consider that the Prior Intention does not stop at the point where the Action begins. On the contrary, the Prior Intention continues and plays a control role to guide the Action and determine its success.

8.2.3. *Artifacts*

To account for the status of an (intentional) social construct usually ascribed to the organizations, we need a general notion of artifact in the sense of an "entity intentionally made or produced for some reason" [HIL 04]. The ontological module Function & Artefact-OS provides a set of concepts to account for the main properties characterizing these entities. According to this ontology [KAS 10]:

– Artifacts are the result of an intentional production (with the meaning of a Prior Intention) and thus have an Author.

– Artifacts are produced for a certain reason and various types of reasons (hence various types of Artifacts) are considered: (1) conveying an emotion and being of aesthetic interest, for works of art; (2) enabling their author (or another agent) to do something, for "functional" or Technical Artifacts. The latter are Artifacts to which a Function is ascribed, taking a Function to be an "acknowledged capacity to enable the realization of a kind of action" [KAS 10].

– Among Technical Artifacts, Private Artifacts are distinguished from Social Artifacts according to whether their function is ascribed by an individual or a community of agents.

8.3. A core ontology of an organization's processes

In this section, we use and expand the ontological framework that has just been presented for conceptualizing the field of processes of organizations. This extension is mainly done to make space for plural entities – collections of entities – and to account for their collective (including intentional) behavior. To this end, we proceed in two main stages (see Figure 8.2).

In the first step, we focus on works in the social sciences to clarify the concept of a *social group* (or *collective*) that we adopt as a brick base to account for collective actions.

In the second step, we focus on the structured and formal collectives that are *organizations*. To account for the actions of an organization, we rely, respectively, on the ontological work of Bottazzi and Ferrario [BOT 09] on the organizational structures and on works in the philosophy of collective action, including those of Tuomela [TUO 05a], for the behavioral aspects.

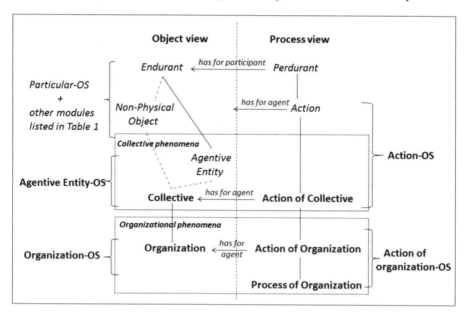

Figure 8.2. *Overview of the ontological modules (in bold)*
and their contribution to the object and process views

It should be noted that the modeling approach adopted to analyze the collective phenomena (section 8.3.1), and more particularly the organizational phenomena (sections 8.3.2 and 8.3.3), is based on an ontological principle that can be summarized as follows: the *object* and the *process* are two complementary faces of any reality (see Figure 8.2)[6]. This principle is already anchored in DOLCE (and most foundational ontologies) with the distinction between Endurants and Perdurants, applied until now to the analysis of individual phenomena. We make this principle a precept and therefore propose to apply it to the analysis of collective phenomena in distinguishing, on the one hand, objects-collections and, on

---

6 The complementarity of the *objects* and *processes* is explained by a strong mutual dependence, as reminded by Galton and Mizoguchi [GAL 09, p. 72]: "(a) matter and objects by nature presuppose the participation in processes or events, and (b) processes and events by nature presuppose the existence of matter or objects". Usually applied to physical objects, our intention in this chapter is to extend the scope of this principle to social objects.

the other, process-behaviors that result in these collections. It is useful to note that by assigning a full existence to collections (then to collectives and organizations), we are not in accordance with the Searlian naturalism and, more generally, with methodological individualists in the philosophy of social science [HEA 11]. This note explains the choice of the works to which we refer in this section to develop our ontological modules. The main argument that we put forward is linguistic. There are many cases in the current language for assigning properties to collections (e.g. the jam "paralyzed the city center", the crowd "dispersed in silence" and the flotilla of boats "filled the bay"), which cannot be attributed to individuals. We consider this argument as sufficient, taking into account the direction of DOLCE of "capturing the ontological stands that shape natural language and human cognition" [MAS 03, p. 7].

8.3.1. *Collective phenomena*

In the domain of applied ontology, the analysis of "collective phenomena" is relatively recent. This term refers to a phenomenon by a plurality of entities. This term encompasses a wide variety of situations such as a *load from a horde of buffalo*, a *process of deforestation of a geographical area* and a *formation of a traffic jam of cars*. As shown, these phenomena relate to a large variety of fields. They have in common to correspond to a global effect resulting from several individual effects. In this chapter, we focus on collective (and more particularly intentional) behaviors that are the fact of individuals, for example an *interpretation by an orchestra of a piece of music*.

Following our precept to distinguish the *object* of the *process*, we postulate the existence of a plural entity to which we attribute the responsibility for such behavior. First, we show that the concept of *collection* that has been defined in formal ontology is not adapted to account for this plural entity and that we should prefer the notion of *collective*, as defined in the social sciences. Then, we give a first characterization of the actions of these collectives.

In the literature on formal ontologies, various formalizations of the notion of *collection* have been proposed [BOT 06, WOO 09]. Beyond the differences, these works agree to consider that an organization is, in a sense, a "complex" collection. Such a posture was, in particular, adopted by

Bottazzi *et al.* [BOT 06]. According to these authors, a `Collection` is a whole to which entities *belong*. The membership relation of an entity to a `Collection` (`isMemberOfAt`) is identified with a relationship connecting content to a container: the member is, somehow, "in" the `Collection`. The criterion for membership of an entity to the `Collection` is a property temporarily classifying the entity (e.g. the property "being a stamp that I keep for its value" for the `Collection` "my collection of stamps"). It follows that: (1) over time, the same `Collection` can see a change in its members, and (2) two `Collections` can be extensionally equivalent (having the same members) while being distinct. Moreover, according to these authors, a `Collection` is a `Non-Physical Object` depending on agents in the sense where one (or more) agent(s) conceive a `Collection`; the latter ceases to exist as soon as it ceases to be conceived by this (or these) agent(s). We adopt this concept for our ontological framework according to this minimal characterization. However, to emphasize the representational nature of a `Collection`, we are not in accordance with the original proposal by constraining a `Collection` to be a `Non-Agentive Object` (see Figure 8.3).

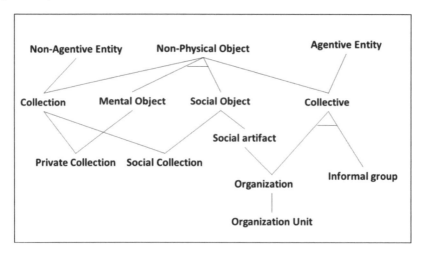

Figure 8.3. `Collection` *and* `Collectives` *are* `Non-Physical Objects`. *A collective is an* `Agentive Object`. *An* `Organization` *is a* `Collective` *and a* `Social Artifact`. *An* `Organization Unit` *is an* `Organization` *(in its own sake) managed by (and dependent on an encompassing* `Organization`*)*

8.3.1.1. *Collections and collectives*

The question now arises is whether such a notion of collection is a good starting point to define what is an organization? To this question, we respond negatively. To figure out the reason, let us consider the example of a physical object such as a wall of bricks in the first place. Given a wall made up of apparent different shades of brick, an agent has every opportunity to conceive the collection of the bricks of the wall of clear shade, the collection of the bricks of dark shade and many other collections, based on his/her imagination. It appears that, according to the definition of the concept Collection, the brick members of the collections are not considered as physical objects but as objects satisfying a property. The forces that bricks exert on themselves and that ensure the integrity of the wall are abstracted. This is also true for their position in the wall, giving the latter its general form. In other words, based on a very general notion of organization implying relationships between constituents, we can say that a Collection does not correspond to any form of organization. Considering this, instead of considering that an organization of individuals is a "complex" Collection of individuals, we prefer to focus on the notion of organization and distinguish, as for the wall, the organization of the entity corresponding to the group of individuals constituting the organization. The same concept has been supported by Slater and Varzy [SLA 07] in their analysis of organizations such as a baseball team. According to these authors, the team should be distinguished from the group of players who constitute it (we can identify this group as a Collection of players).

However, we should note that unlike a brick wall, which is a Physical Object, an organization of individuals is usually characterized as a Non-Physical Object. Intuitively, this seems related to the fact that it is not possible to act physically on an organization of individuals, for example to beat a baseball team with a stick. However, we did take some form of "organization" to the brick wall by suggesting an analogy with an "organization" of individuals. Without prejudging the merits of such an analogy, we will now clarify this last concept.

To define our notion of *organization* (of individuals), we decide to take a different path and start from the notion of a *collective* as set forward in the literature in social science. This concept is based on a way of definition of a plural whole, which is radically different from that of a Collection. The term indeed refers to a minimum form of organization between individuals endowing the plural-*collective* with a capacity to act.

Historically, seeking to define this concept, the sociologist French [FRE 84] proposed a distinction between "aggregate collectivities" and "conglomerate collectivities". According to French, the "aggregate collectivities" see their identity changing during a change of composition and are unable to act. On the contrary, the "conglomerate collectivities" have their own identity, above that of their members, and are capable of actions.

Concerning the changes of identity of these communities, it is clear from the above that we strongly deny the point of view of French. Concerning their capacity to act, returning to the examples cited by French, some sociologists argued then that the "aggregate collectivities" can be considered as able to act, but in a weak sense of the notion of action. Pfeiffer [PFE 90], in particular, has supported the idea that the distinction of French is more a distinction of degrees than types. A similar view is today advocated in the philosophy of action [PAC 00] and collective action [PAC 12], which amounts to distinguishing between different forms of actions controlled by different types of intention. For these reasons, we identify our `Collective` concept to this notion of "collectivity" and we therefore see them as `Agentive Entities` (see Figure 8.3).

8.3.1.2. *Collective action*

The admission that the `Collectives` can act raises the question of what the word "act" means. By analogy with human action, the terms "collective mind" and "collective intention" are also used by some authors and the question of the meaning of these terms is raised.

Beyond the linguistic argument already referred to (the fact that our speeches commonly ascribe actions to collectives), authors like May [MAY 87] (following French), from the viewpoint of social theory, have attempted to explain how groups (our `Collectives`) may legitimately be regarded as agents. According to Smiley [SMI 11]: "May sets down two conditions under which we can legitimately say of an relationally-based action that it is collective rather than individual – which for May means, not trans-individual, but relational. The first condition is that the individuals in question be related to each other so as to enable each to act in ways that could not manage on their own. The second is that some individuals be authorized to represent their own shares as the stock of the group as a whole [MAY 87, p. 55]". The first condition highlights cooperation to achieve cooperative joined actions (such actions have been analyzed in philosophy of action especially by Searle [SEA 90] and Bratman [BRA 92]). The second condition requires a coordination mechanism based on the recognition of a delegation of authority to "represent" the actions of the `Collective`. In the presence of joint actions, we are – in a more general sense [PAC 12] – featuring, according to May, actions "of the group as a whole".

Saying that *an action is collective* and that *a collective is the agent* of an action are two different things. According to the theories of Searle and Bratman, notably, the intentions that they call "collective" are participatory intentions that are only present in the mind of individuals. On the contrary, as seen with French, and May, other authors make the hypothesis of a supra-individual collective agent. The latter is clearly our `Collective`, whose nature we can specify. This agent first has, like an individual agent, a capacity to implement intentions, which implies their own cognitive system, a kind of group mind as defined by Sosa [SOS 09, p. 215]: "The persons that are members of the group have minds, and the group's mind (in whatever sense it has one, its beliefs and desires) is some sort of construct from those minds". The group mind is thus based on a set of representations (consisting of objectives and plans) that are collectively recognized by a set of individuals. These representations allow these groups to control actions, as for individual actions. In this sense, we can talk of *collective intentions*. On the contrary, however, on an individual, a `Collective` does not have (directly) a physical body (this is a `Non-Physical Object`) at its disposal. This does not prevent it from acting, in particular, on the physical world, but its actions are carried out through individuals and their physical bodies. As a result, we identify the `Collective Actions` with these `Actions` having a `Collective` agent. This amounts to conceptually extending the `hasForAgentAt` relationship to integrate these situations of a control of `Actions` by a `Collective` and to admit the ontological existence of `Collective Intentions`. Therefore, we assume that in such situations we have both a collective action and one (or more) individual action(s) constituting the collective action. In the next section, we detail our model of collective action in placing us in an organizational context.

8.3.2. *Organizational phenomena*

As we have seen, our concept `Collective`, defined as an *agentive whole consisting of individuals*, covers a wide reality of groups. It notably covers a part of the "aggregative collectivities" of French [FRE 84], including groups with a short existence that constitute themselves on the occasion of an action, this action being not necessarily deliberate. In this section, we focus on the *organizations* described as groups with a perennial, often formalized, structure, which are able to carry out complex premeditated actions (the equivalent of the "conglomerate collectivities" of French). Following our precept to distinguish between the *object* and the *process*, we first propose a model for organizations refining our model of `Collectives`, and then we present a model of the actions of organization granting organizations a full agent status.

8.3.2.1. *Organization*

A first essential characterization of the organizations that we adopt is the fact that they have a strong structuring. This structuring allows them to perform all kinds of actions, including those (in the strong sense of the term) that are deliberate [LIS 11]. In other words, an organization is able to set goals and develop plans to achieve these goals. It associates with these objectives deadlines and an importance (some objectives are more strategic than others), and has indicators to evaluate the success of its actions. All these elements, *goals*, *plans*, *delays* and *success criteria*, are collectively recognized by members of the organization and are part of what is called, in a broad sense, the *structure* of the organization.

Further characterization of organizations is that they are social constructs, in other words intentionally built entities to which a function (mission) is socially attributed [BOT 07]. According to our definitions, they are `Social artifacts` [KAS 10]. This characterization is important for the definition of the identity of the organizations because it adds to an intrinsic dimension – a disposition to act – an extrinsic dimension – the enjoyment of an external recognition – and we can consider, like Slater and Varzy [SLA 07], that these two dimensions combine in the identity criteria of the organizations. Moreover, to achieve its mission, the organization can define specific missions for subgroups and individuals: these are functions assigned to organizational units and roles specifying the tasks to be performed by individuals. All these elements contribute to the structure of the organization, which is most often hierarchical. This structure is nothing more than a collection of social entities developed by the organization (therefore other `Social artifacts`) to enable it to coordinate its collective behaviors.

The origin of existence of the social group (an intentional construction rather than emergence), the dependence of the social group on external agents (including other organizations) and the formalization of the group structure are usually put forward to distinguish, within `Collectives`, between `Organizations` and `Informal Groups` (see Figure 8.3).

For our conceptualization of organizations, we strongly rely on the formal ontology of organizations of Bottazzi and Ferrario [BOT 09]. For the purpose of this chapter, we list only a few main relations and concepts that structure our ontological framework:

– The relationship `isValidFor` models the social commitment of the `Organization` to `Propositions`. This fundamental relation (on which most of other concepts and relations depend) allows integrating descriptions, or representations, in the structure of the `Organization` (objectives, plans, various norms, roles, etc.).

– The relationship `isAffiliatedToAt` models the fact that an `Agentive Entity` (a `Human` or an `Organization`, in the case of systems of organizations) *formally* temporarily belongs to an `Organization`. This relationship implies that the affiliate satisfies the rules set by the `Organization`.

– An `Organization Unit` is an `Organization` that `isManagedBy` (a subrelation of `isProperPartOf`) the `Organization` upon which it depends. The only parts of an `Organization` that we consider are `Organization Units`.

8.3.2.2. *Action of organization*

According to Tuomela [TUO 05a], in substance, an `Action of Organization`, in the sense of an action that can be attributed to an organization, is an action consisting of joint actions of persons. Given an action X of the organization, in general only a few members (possibly one) of the organization, called "operant agents", realize actions X1, X2,... ,Xn, corresponding to their part of action X. The term "joint action" means that operant agents join their efforts in order to achieve something that conventionally counts, according to social and normative right conditions, for an action of the organization. Ontologically speaking, two categories of actions are therefore to be distinguished: action X, that we call `Action of Organization`, and actions Xi, that we call `Organizational Actions` (see Figure 8.4). To account for the contribution of the latter to the former, we propose to consider the `isProperPartOf` relationship [KAS 12].

`Organizational Actions` entail for their agent a specific action mode, called "we-mode", and the implementation of specific intentions, named "we-intentions". In short, a "we-intention" may paraphrase, in its prior form, as "we will collectively do X". The "us" refers to the `Organization`, and the intention corresponding to the `Action of Organization` is to understand the "we-intention" shared by members of the organization. Acting according to the "we-mode", for a participating agent, is to commit to collectively achieve his/her part of action X, namely X_i. It is important to note that there is no constraint on the way in which the X_i actions are carried out [TUO 05b, p. 67]: "Even if on the group level, so to speak, the members are jointly seeing to it that G, they may act separately or jointly to achieve this goal and use whatever 'tools' (e.g. hiring agents to do something) that are believed to be useful". Note in this connection that an `Action of Organization` X may be composed of a single `Organizational Action` X_1 as in the case where a government announces a decision (X) by the voice of his spokesperson (X_1).

For the purpose of this chapter, we would not discuss the mechanism of formation of the "we-intentions". We would also not discuss their possible contents (on these points, we refer the readers to [TUO 05a]). To establish a link with our model of the organization, we simply note that these `Organizational Actions` may have for an agent either an `Organization Unit` or an individual affiliated to the `Organization`. To distinguish between these two cases, we distinguish explicitly two types of `Organizational Actions` that we call, respectively, `Organizational Unit Action` and `Organizational Individual Action` (see Figure 8.4).

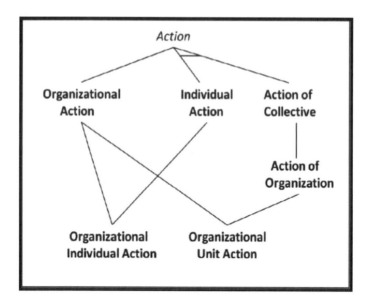

Figure 8.4. *An* `Action of Organization` *is a particular case of* `Action of Collective`*. An* `Organizational Action` *is* `ProperPartOf` *an* `Action of Organization`

8.3.3. *Process of organization*

We now return to the main topic of this chapter, namely the processes of organization. In the literature, a vast majority of works relating to this notion of *process of organization* are carried out in the context of business organizations. In particular, in information system and business process management, there are many researchers who focus on what are called "business processes". For our ontology COOP, we choose to follow this path in conceptualizing the class of the business processes rather than a more general class of process of organization. In this section, we first adopt a definition that seems to us consensual, then we model it in the form of the `Business Process` concept that we introduce in the ontological framework defined until then. In a second step, by exploiting the dimensions commonly put forward in the literature to distinguish different classes of business processes, we propose a taxonomy of these processes.

In the literature emanating from the above-mentioned disciplines, several definitions are given[7] for the notion of *business process*. Hammer and Champy [HAM 93], for instance, define the business process as "... a collection of activities that takes one or more kinds of inputs and creates outputs that is of value for the customer. A business process has a goal and is affected by events occurring in the external world or other processes". For Davenport [DAV 93] "a business process is a set of logically related tasks performed to achieve a defined business outcome".

Taking into account the recurring elements in the definitions, we adopt the following characterization for our notion of *process of organization* (see Figure 8.5):

– A Process of Organization is a Collective Action that hasForAgent an Organization. It is therefore an Action of Organization.

– Each Process of Organization must provide a result that has a value. It is therefore a Culminated Process.

– The Process of Organization meets an Organizational Objective; it is *controlledBy* a distal intention. Then, the Process of organization is a Deliberate Action.

– Each Process of Organization *hasForproperPart* at least one Organizational Action (Organizational Activity), which *hasForAgent* either a Human or an Organization Unit.

– A *business process* is a set of activities that need some coordination to be performed. These activities are possibly more or less ordered according to a predefined order.

Several features of Processes of Organization have been further described in the literature and this leads us to classify them according to some dimensions (see Figure 8.6). In this chapter, we retain the following dimensions: the *granularity* [MOR 07], *affiliation of operant agents* [LAU 06], *perceptible value* [POR 85], *strategic* [LOR 93] and *repetition* dimension [ISO 03].

---

7 The majority of the works proposed in literature concern the improvement of business processes to be supported by information systems within different types of organizations (industrial organization, public sector, etc.).

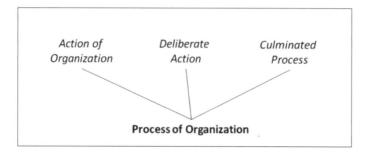

Figure 8.5. *A Process of Organization is an Action of Organization, a Deliberate Action and a Culminated Process*

1) *Granularity*: this dimension is relative to the degree of decomposition of the process. In information systems, researchers and practitioners have used this criterion to analyze the process decomposition and study the business division, which may compromise the effectiveness of the process. We have seen that a Business Process is composed of Organizational Actions. An Organizational Action, in its turn, may haveForAgent either a Human or an Organization Unit. In the first case, this is an Organizational Individual Action. An example is a commercial agent who makes an invoice. In the second case, as the Organizational Action is itself a Business Process, we define it as an Organizational Sub-Process. Let us consider the example of the treatment of a customer order. This Business Process hasForProperPart the following four organizational sub-processes:

i) Checking the availability of the ordered products (made by the service provisioning).

ii) Preparation of a delivery order (made by the sales department).

iii) Preparation of the invoice (made by the sales department).

iv) The invoice payment (managed by the financial department).

2) *Affiliation*: this dimension is relative to the affiliation as well as the transversality (in terms of Organization Units) of the agents operating in the process. Following Lorino [LOR 03], we propose three classes of processes: *internal processes*, *external processes* and *partial external processes*. Using the concepts already present in the ontology, we model these notions as follows:

i) An `Internal` `process` is a `Process` `of` `Organization` all `partsOf` which `haveForAgent` either `Humans` which `areAffiliatedTo` the `Business` `Organization` or `Organization` `Units` which `areAUnitsOf` the `Business` `Organization`.

ii) An `External` `process` is a `Process` `of` `Organization` all `partsOf` which `haveForAgent` `Agentive` `Entities` that are not `AffiliatedTo` or `UnitsOf` the `Business` `Organization`.

iii) A partial external process is a `Process` `of` `Organization` that has at least one `Part` that `hasForAgent` an `Agentive` `Entity` that is not `AffiliatedTo` the `Business` `Organization` and that has at least one `Part` that `hasForAgent` an `Agentive` `entity` that `isAffiliatedTo` the `Business` `Organization`.

Among `Internal` `Processes`, according to a *functional* dimension [LAU 06], a further distinction can be made between *intra-functional processes* and *inter-functional processes*:

i) An `Inter-functional` `Process` is an `Internal` `Process` that `hasForPart` at least two `Organizational` `Sub-Processes` that `haveForAgent` a distinct `Business` `Unit`. Informally, it is a business process that implies more than one function in organization. An example is a process of purchasing products involving the sales department and the finance department. This process crosses the organizational structures, as it mobilizes two departments.

ii) In contrast, an `Intra-functional` `Process` is an `Internal` `Process` all `partsOf` which, which are `Organizational` `Individual` `Actions`, `haveForAgent` `Humans` `AffiliatedTo` the same `Business` `Unit`. Informally, it is a business process that implies only one function and is performed by employees who are affiliated to the same department. Examples, in the field of human resources, are the process of collaborators recruitment, and the process of the collaborators competence development. Both processes involve only members of the Department of Human Resources.

3) *Value*: the value dimension has been defined by researchers in several disciplines. In our research, we adopted the definition proposed in

management [MEL 00, POR 85, ISO 00] that is an appreciation of the utility of a product or a service by a costumer. To identify activities of an organization, which contribute directly to the development of the product and thus the value perceived by the customers, several researchers have proposed a classification of processes based on the value chain model of Porter [POR 85]. Indeed, in his model, Porter defines two classes of activities of organization. The first class consists of the primary activities that are related to the production and the distribution of the products and the services of the organization. They include five activities: inbound logistics, operations, outbound logistics, marketing and sales. These activities create a value perceptible by the customers. The second class consists of the support activities that are necessary for the execution of the primary activities. They include four activities: firm infrastructure, human resource management, technology and procurement. This model has been adopted in management quality [ISO 00] and information system [MEL 00] to characterize the business processes that are constituted by these activities. In our context, we adopted the three categories of business process proposed by Melao and Pidd [MEL 00]:

iii) `Core Process` is a business process that has external customers and includes the primary activities of the value chain.

iv) `Support Process` is a business process that has internal customers and concerns secondary activities in the value chain.

v) `Management Process` is a business process that manages core and support processes.

4) *Strategic*: according to [LOR 93], the steering of the organizations based on the process view needs to implement mainly two types of processes, namely: the `Strategic processes` and the `Operational processes`. Any `Strategic Process` is `ControlledBy` an `Organizational intention` that `hasForContent` a `Strategic Objective`. Any `Operational Process` is `ControlledBy` an `Organizational intention` that `hasForContent` an `Operational Objective` that is an `Organizational Objective`.

5) *Repetition*: finally, to address the processes' *repetition* dimension, we rely on the project management approach that emphasizes the concept of *project* or *unique process*. According to the International Organization for Standardization [ISO 03], a *project* is "A unique process consisting of a set

of coordinated and controlled activities with start and finish dates, undertaken to achieve an objective conforming to specific requirements including constraints of time, cost and resources". We retain that a project is a single *business process* of the *business organization* that is characterized by a date of beginning and a date of end for a unique product or service. As opposed to the notion of Project, we define the notion of Repetitive Process.

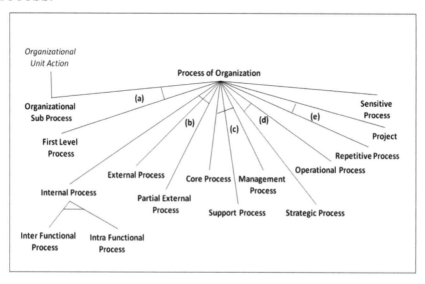

Figure 8.6. *Business Processes* *are classified according to several dimensions: (a) granularity, (b) affiliation, (c) value, (d) strategic, (e) repetition*

Motivated by practical purposes, COOP extensions are underway within two ongoing projects of development of information systems using the ontology.

In the context of the EGIDE project [TUR 11, TUR 12a, TUR 12b], our goal is to develop a decision support system for the identification of knowledge that requires capitalization. This knowledge is called "Crucial knowledge". The system will be used by the ASHMS (Association de Sauvegarde des Handicapé Moteurs de Sfax). This is an organization looking after handicapped children. COOP ontology is used to construct the criteria for the characterization and identification of sensitive processes in order to locate the knowledge mobilized and created by these processes, which may be crucial.

In addition, within the TATIN-PIC project [KEN 11], an interactive table is currently being designed to help collaborative preliminary design. COOP ontology is used to model, in detail, both the collective actions of the project team and the individual actions of the members of the team. This project leads to further analysis of the concepts of project and project team.

8.4. Discussion

As we have just seen, the COOP ontology mobilizes for its different modules multiple theories from various disciplines. For each module, in this chapter we have tried to account for the choice of these theories. The result of this work is a formal – globally consistent – ontology of organizations and their actions-processes. In this discussion, we intend to position COOP with respect to reference works in the field of formal ontologies of the organizations and their actions.

Beyond the structuring of its modules, COOP ontology consists of two separate, although dependent, parts. By scrupulously applying our precept to distinguish between the *object* and the *process*, we have defined ontological foundations for, on the one hand, the organizations and, on the other hand, the actions-processes performed by these organizations. The two are linked: once the status of agent to organizations is assigned, the identity and the structure of these organizations are key elements to explain their ways of acting.

As we have seen, our proposals are to a great extent inspired by Bottazzi and Ferrario's work [BOT 09] on the formal ontology of organizations and, like these authors, we adopt the foundational ontology DOLCE [MAS 03] and the project of the LOA to define these social objects "lacking" Searle's social ontology. The latter – the Social Objects – are defined *a minima* as Non-Physical Objects (namely objects not directly located in the physical space) dependent on a community of agents. *Organizations* are further defined by Bottazi and Ferrario [BOT 09] as Social Objects. To fill the conceptual distance between Social Objects and organizations, two tracks are followed by the LOA.

The first track corresponds to the definition of the intermediate notions of *collection* and *collective*, a *collective* being considered as a special case of *collection* [BOT 06]. As we have seen, we adopt a different position in accepting the concept `Collection` as defined by these authors, but in founding on a different basis the notion of collective and further of organization. Slater and Varzi [SLA 07] seemingly support a close position in distinguishing between the team and the team members. These authors clarify that the same group of individuals can constitute different teams, according to the roles played by the individuals in these teams. Assuming that their concept of a group of individuals coincides with our notion of a `Collection` of individuals, the precision brought does not mean that one should go through a concept of a group in order to define a notion of organization. It should be noted in this regard that in their subsequent treatment of the notion of an organization, Bottazi and Ferrario [BOT 09] did not reuse the notion of `Collection`. By contrast, according to our understanding, given an organization, an observer has all the space to conceive the `Collection` of its members, in particular if he/she wants to follow the evolution in time of this `Collection`.

The second track is an ambitious project to define a general theory of social objects and their links with the physical world. To this end, the concepts of *qua-individual* ([MAS 04, MAS 05]) and, more recently, of *perspectile* [BOT 11], have been defined. The general idea is to admit the existence of new objects, social objects, inherent in physical objects and *counting* for the latter in contexts involving particular social conventions (e.g. the social object "John *qua* (as) President of OntoBusiness Inc." *counts* for the physical object "John" in his role of President, recognized by the company). According to Bottazzi and Ferrario, the consideration of these new objects allows us to account for problems of identity of organizations, considering that these social objects (rather than their physical host) correspond to the parts of the organization[8]. It should be noted that in our case, we do not consider the members affiliated to an organization as parts of the organization: the relationship `isAffiliatedTo` is not a subrelation of the relationship `isPartOf`[9]. At the same time, the only parts of

---

8 Technically, two entities with exactly the same parts are considered identical. If individual members of an organization are identified to the parts of this organization, the identity of members should involve the identity of the organizations, which is obviously not the case.

9 To keep the homogeneous nature the relationship isPartOf, we consider that an Organization may only have as parts suborganizations, namely of Organization Units. Thus, the identity of the Organization Units leads to the identity of the Organizations.

organizations that we consider are themselves organizations (`Organization Units`). We are therefore open to the fact that *qua-individuals* (whose theorizing is still in draft form) can correspond to individual parts of an organization.

Concerning the idea that an organization is an agent, curiously, although it was presented by Bottazzi *et al.* in [BOT 07], this was not accounted for in their axiomatic presented in [BOT 09]. This same questioning was recently expressed by Robinson in his comparative analysis of the concepts of *legal person* and *organization* [ROB 10, p. 122]: "If the surface structure of natural language is intended to have ontological relevance in DOLCE, then philosophical discussion of whether or not organizations, legal persons, and other social objects are 'really' agentive is not necessary relevant [...] there is natural language surface structure evidence to consider moving the governments of states (and even organizations more generally) to the agentive category as well ('The German government condemned the attacks in Iraq', 'The Chinese government moved to suppress new reports coming out of Tibet')". We can find, about the agent status of the organization, the same caution by Boella and van der Torre [BOE 05]: "Inspired by Searle's analysis of social reality we define organizations, functional areas [a subclass of ours `Organization Units`] and roles as *socially constructed agents*. These agents do not exist in the usual sense of the term, but they are abstractions which other agents describe as if they were agents, with their own beliefs, desires and goals, and with their own autonomous behavior". These comments only remind us of the fact that an ontology is committed to a theory. We have seen in this regard that our ontology is committed to today's strong trend in the philosophy of social science recognizing a genuine agent status to organizations [TUO 05a, LIS 11]. The pseudo-agent status granted by Boella and van der Torre to *functional areas* and *roles* is accompanied by a homogeneous pseudo-part status they recognize to these entities [BOE 06, p. 83]: "The decomposition hierarchy of the organizational structure, however, is not based on the part-of relation of objects". Our conception for these entities is widely different: on the one hand, as we noted above, we consider `Organization Units` as *genuine* parts and also as `Organizations` (hence, as *genuine* agents); in contrast, roles are *concepts*, therefore non-agents, and if they can be considered to be parts of the *structure* of the organization, they are not as much parts of the organization itself. In the balance sheet, the only agents that we consider to participate in the actions of the organization are the `Organizations` (and their `Organization Units`) and the `affiliated` persons.

8.5. Conclusion

In this chapter, we have proposed an original COOP. To establish the ontological foundations of an organization's processes, the ontology COOP is structured according to three levels of abstraction (foundational, collective and organizational), which are organized around a minimum set of central concepts: (1) at the foundational level (DOLCE), the distinction between Endurants and Perdurants anchors the complementarities of the object and process views for the analysis of any reality; (2) at the collective level, Collectives are defined as Agentive Entity and the foundations for the intentional behaviors of these plural entities are laid; (3) at the organizational level, Organizations – as Collectives intentionally built and endowed with a formal structure – are introduced and their Processes – as deliberate, and structured actions culminating in a result bringing added value to a client – are defined. The originality of COOP in the field of formal ontologies of organizations (especially with respect to the work of Bottazzi and Ferrario) is the account of actions and processes of organizations.

This ontological framework constitutes, in our opinion, a solid basis for the analysis of the processes of organization. Clearly, some concepts need to be further inspected and others to be closely looked into. However, we think that we have implemented an ontological framework, which should be easy to expand and update in the future. For that matter, the fact that well-identified theories (from various disciplines) are grounding the concepts at different levels of abstraction constitutes an important asset.

On a theoretical plan, we have identified new concepts to add to COOP, as well as other concepts for which the analysis must be deepened. The concepts of goal and procedure (a kind of norm) are to be introduced as a priority in order to refine our model of process of organization as a collection of joint activities and/or subprocesses (note that this model derives from the model of social action of Tuomela). These concepts play a role in explaining the mechanisms of planning and coordination of the processes and, in fine, their structure. The concept of added value, in relation to the concepts of resource and client, is also to be introduced (the latter are to be deepened). The challenge is to better understand the nature of the process as a process of creation of new resources for a client or as a process of transformation of resources into new resources with greater added value.

8.6. Bibliography

[BER 07] BERTHIER D., "An ontology for modelling flexible business", in ELLEITHY K. (ed.), *Advances and Innovations in Systems, Computing Sciences and Software Engineering*, Springer, pp. 83–87, 2007.

[BOE 05] BOELLA G., VAN DER TORRE L., "Organizations as socially constructed agents in the agent oriented paradigm", in GLEIZES M.-P., *et al.* (eds), *Proceedings of the 5th International Workshop Engineering Societies in the Agents World*, LNAI 3451, Springer-Verlag, Berlin/Heidelberg, pp. 1–13, 2005.

[BOE 06] BOELLA G., VAN DER TORRE L., "A foundational ontology of organizations and roles", in BALDONI M., *et al.* (eds), *Proceedings of the 4th International Workshop on Declarative Agent Languages and Technologies (DALT 2006)*, LNAI 4327, Springer-Verlag, pp. 78–88, 2006.

[BOR 04] BORGO S., LEITÃO P., "The role of foundational ontologies in manufacturing domain applications", in MEERSMAN R. *et al.* (eds), *Proceedings of the OTM Confederated International Conferences*, ODBASE 2004, LNCS 3290, Springer-Verlag, pp. 670–688, 2004.

[BOT 06] BOTTAZZI E., CATENACCI C., GANGEMI A., *et al.*, "From collective intentionality to intentional collectives: an ontological perspective", *The Journal of Cognitive Systems Research*, vol. 7, nos. 2–3, pp. 192–208, 2006.

[BOT 07] BOTTAZZI E., FERRARIO R., MASOLO C., *et al.*, "Designing organizations: towards a model", in BOELLA G. *et al.* (eds), *Proceedings of the Workshop on Normative Multi-agent Systems*, pp. 244–267, 2007.

[BOT 09] BOTTAZZI E., FERRARIO R., "Preliminaries to a DOLCE ontology of organizations", *International Journal of Business Process Integration and Management*, Special Issue on Vocabularies, Ontologies and Business Rules for Enterprise Modeling, vol. 4, no. 4, pp. 225–238, 2009.

[BOT 11] BOTTAZZI E., FERRARIO R., "Introducing perspectiles in organizations", in KOKINOV B. *et al.* (eds), *Proceedings of the European Conference on Cognitive Science (EuroCog '11)*, New Bulgarian University, Sofia, 2011.

[BRA 92] BRATMAN M.E., "Shared cooperative activity", *Philosophical Review*, vol. 101, pp. 327–340, 1992.

[DAV 93] DAVENPORT T.H., *Process Innovation: Reengineering Work through Information Technology*, Harvard Business Press, Boston, MA, 1993.

[FER 04] FERRARIO R., OLTRAMARI A., "Towards a computational ontology of mind", in VARZI A.C. *et al.* (eds), *Proceedings of the International Conference Formal Ontology in Information Systems (FOIS '04)*, IOS Press, pp. 287–297, 2004.

[FOX 92] FOX M.S., "The TOVE project: towards a common-sense model of the enterprise", *Proceedings of the 5th international conference on Industrial and Engineering Applications of Artificial Intelligence and Expert Systems (IEA/AIE '92)*, Springer-Verlag, London, UK, pp. 25–34, 1992.

[FRE 84] FRENCH P., *Collective and Corporate Responsibility*, Columbia University Press, New York, 1984.

[GAL 09] GALTON A., MIZOGUCHI R., "The water falls but the waterfall does not fall: new perspectives on objects, processes and events", *Applied Ontology*, vol. 4, no. 2, pp. 71–107, 2009.

[GAN 04] GANGEMI A., BORGO S. (eds.), *Proceedings of the 14th International Conference on Knowledge Engineering and Knowledge Management (EKAW'04), Workshop on Core Ontologies in Ontology Engineering*, vol. 118, Northamptonshire, UK, 2004. Available at http://ceur-ws.org.

[HAM 93] HAMMER M., CHAMPY J., *Reengineering the Corporation: A Manifesto for Business Revolution*, Harper Business, New York, 1993.

[HEA 11] HEATH J., "Methodological individualism", in ZALTA E.N. (ed.), *The Stanford Encyclopedia of Philosophy*, Spring 2011 ed., 2011. Available at: http://plato.stanford.edu/archives/spr2005/entries/methodological-individualism/.

[HIL 04] HILPINEN R., "Artifact", *Stanford Encyclopedia of Philosophy,* 2004. Available at: http://plato.stanford.edu/entries/artifact/.

[ISO 00] INTERNATIONAL ORGANIZATION FOR STANDARDIZATION, ISO 9000:2000, "Systèmes de management de la qualité – Principes essentiels et vocabulaire", 2000. Available at: http://www.iso.org/iso/fr/catalogue_detail?csnumber=29280.

[ISO 03] INTERNATIONAL ORGANIZATION FOR STANDARDIZATION, ISO 10006:2003, "Quality management systems, Guidelines for quality management in projects", 2003. Available at: http://www.iso.org/iso/catalogue_detail.htm?csnumber=36643.

[KAS 05] KASSEL, G., "Integration of the DOLCE top-level ontology into the OntoSpec methodology", *The Computing Research Repository CoRR abs/cs/0510050*, 2005. Available at: http://arxiv.org/abs/cs/0510050.

[KAS 10] KASSEL G., "A formal ontology of artefacts", *Applied Ontology*, vol. 5, nos. 3–4, pp. 223–246, 2010.

[KAS 12] KASSEL G., TURKI M., SAAD I., *et al.*, "From collective actions to actions of organizations: an ontological analysis", *Symposium on Understanding and Modelling Collective Phenomena (UMoCop)*, University of Birmingham, UK, 2012.

[KEN 11] KENDIRA A., GIDEL T., JONES A., *et al.*, "The TATIN-PIC Project: a multimodal collaborative work environment for preliminary design", *Proceedings of the 15th International Conference on Computer Supported Cooperative Work in Design (CSCWD'11)*, Lausanne, Switzerland, 2011.

[LAU 06] LAUDON C., LAUDON J.P., *Management Information Systems*, Pearson Education, 2006.

[LIS 11] LIST C., PETI P., *Group Agency: The Possibility, Design, and Status of Corporate Agents*, Oxford University Press, 2011.

[LOR 03] LORINO P., *Méthodes et pratiques de la performance*, Editions d'Organisation, Paris, 2003.

[MAS 03] MASOLO C., BORGO S., GANGEMI A., GUARINO N., OLTRAMARI A., WonderWeb Deliverable D18: Ontology library (final), technical report, LOA-ISTC, CNR, 2003.

[MAS 04] MASOLO C., VIEU L., BOTTAZZI E., *et al.*, "Social roles and their descriptions", *Proceedings of the 9th International Conference on the Principles of Knowledge Representation and Reasoning (KR '04)*, pp. 267–277, 2004.

[MAS 05] MASOLO C., GUIZZARDI G., VIEU L., *et al.*, "Relational roles and qua-individuals", *Proceedings of the AIII Fall Symposium on Roles, an Interdisciplinary Perspective*, Hyatt Crystal City, Arlington, Virginia, 2005.

[MAY 87] MAY L., *The Morality of Groups*, University of Notre Dame Press, Notre Dame, 1987.

[MEL 00] MELAO N., PIDD M., "A conceptual framework for understanding business processes and business process modeling", *Information Systems Journal*, vol. 10, no. 2, pp. 105–130, 2000.

[MOR 07] MORLEY C., HUGUES J., LEBLANC B., *et al.*, *Processus métiers et S.I. évaluation, modélisation, mise en œuvre*, Dunod, France, 2007.

[NUR 05] NURCAN S., ETIEN A., KAABI R., *et al.*, "A strategy driven business process modelling approach", *Business Process Management Journal*, vol. 11, no. 6, pp. 628–649, 2005.

[PAC 00] PACHERIE E., "The content of intentions", *Mind and Language*, vol. 15, no. 4, pp. 400–432, 2000.

[PAC 12] PACHERIE E., "The phenomenology of joint action: self-agency vs. joint-agency", in SEEMANN A. (ed.), *Joint Attention: New Developments*, MIT Press, Cambridge, MA, 2012.

[PFE 90] PFEIFFER R.S., "The central distinction in the theory of corporate moral personhood", *Journal of Business Ethics*, vol. 9, pp. 473–480, 1990.

[POR 85] PORTER M., MILLAR V., "How information gives you competitive advantage", *Harvard Business Review*, vol. 63, no. 4, pp. 149–160, 1985.

[ROB 10] ROBINSON E.H., "An ontological analysis of states: organizations vs. legal persons", *Applied Ontology*, vol. 5, pp. 109–125, 2010.

[SEA 90] SEARLE J.R., "Collective intentions and actions", in COHEN P.R. *et al.* (eds), *Intentions in Communication*, MIT Press, Cambridge, MA, pp. 401–415, 1990.

[SEA 95] SEARLE J.R., *The Construction of Social Reality*, Free Press, New York, 1995.

[SLA 07] SLATER M.H., VARZY A.C., "Team identity and fan loyalty", in WALLS J.L., BASSHAM G. (eds), *Basketball and Philosophy*, University of Kentucky Press, 2007.

[SMI 11] SMILEY M., "Collective responsibility", in ZALTA E.N. (ed.), *The Stanford Encyclopedia of Philosophy*, Spring 2011. Available at: http://plato.stanford.edu/entries/collective-responsibility/.

[SOS 09] SOSA D., "What is it like to be a group?", *Social Philosophy and Policy*, vol. 26, no. 1, pp. 212–226, 2009.

[TRY 08] TRYPUZ R., *Formal Ontology of Action: A Unifying Approach*, Wydawnictwo Kul, Lublin, 2008.

[TUO 05a] TUOMELA R., "We-intentions revisited", *Philosophical Studies*, vol. 125, pp. 327–369, 2005.

[TUO 05b] TUOMELA R., TUOMELA M., "Cooperation and trust in group context", *Mind & Society*, vol. 4, pp. 49–84, 2005.

[TUR 11] TURKI M., SAAD I., GARGOURI F., *et al.*, "Towards identifying sensitive processes for knowledge localization", in SMARI W.W., FOX G. (eds), *Proceedings of the International Conference on Collaboration Technologies and Systems (CTS '11)*, IEEE, Philadelphia, PA, pp. 224–232, 2011.

[TUR 12a] TURKI M., SAAD I., GARGOURI F., *et al.*, "A decision support system for identifying sensitive organization's processes", *Journal of Decision Systems*, vol. 21, no. 4, pp. 275–290, 2012.

[TUR 12b] TURKI M., Proposition d'une méthode multicritère et d'une ontologie noyau des processus d'organisation pour l'aide à l'identification des processus sensible, PhD thesis, Faculté des Sciences Economiques et de Gestion de Sfax-Tunisie, Université de Picardie Jules Verne - France, 2012.

[USC 98] USCHOLD M., KING M., MORALEE S., et al., "The enterprise ontology", The Knowledge Engineering Review, vol. 13, pp. 31–89, 1998.

[WFM 99] WORKFLOW MANAGEMENT COALITION, Workflow Management Coalition terminology & glossary, 1999. Available at http://www.wfmc.org/.

[WOO 09] WOOD Z., GALTON A., "A taxonomy of collective phenomena", Applied Ontology, vol. 4, nos. 3–4, pp. 267–292, 2009.

Chapter 9

A Business Process Evaluation Methodology for Knowledge Management Based on Multicriteria Decision-Making Approach

In an organizational context, characterization and evaluation of business processes (BPs) are necessary to locate knowledge that needs to be capitalized upon. In this chapter, we propose a multicriteria methodology for identifying sensitive BPs for knowledge localization. This methodology is composed of two phases. The first phase consists of the preference model construction. The second phase aims to exploit the preference model (decision rules) to classify the "potential sensitive business processes". This methodology is based on the multicriteria decision-making approach and uses the dominance-based rough set approach (DRSA) dedicated to the sorting problem in multicriteria decision-making.

9.1. Introduction

Nowadays, the organizations have become increasingly conscious of the necessity to formalize knowledge produced and used by their BPs. As said by Ford and Staples [FOR 06], "knowledge is valuable". Firms are becoming aware of the importance of the immaterial capital owned by their employees,

Chapter written by Mohamed TURKI, Inès SAAD, Faïez GARGOURI and Gilles KASSEL.

which corresponds to their experience and the accumulated knowledge about the firm activities.

Considering the large amount of knowledge to be preserved, the organizations must first identify the sensitive BPs that are likely to mobilize knowledge on which it is necessary to capitalize. Few methods focusing on process analysis for knowledge localization have been proposed by researchers for knowledge management. We quote: the global analysis methodology (GAMETH) proposed by [GRU 00], the determining critical knowledge method [TSE 05] and the identifying crucial knowledge methodology [SAA 09].

The GAMETH$^©$ Framework [GRU 00] relies on the following three main phases:

–"The project framing" specifies the project context, defines the domain and limits of the intervention and determines the processes targeted to be deeply analyzed.

–"The identification of crucial knowledge" aims at distinguishing the problems that weaken the critical activities, i.e. the activities that might endanger the sensitive processes. The concept of a sensitive process is defined by Grundstein [GRU 00] as a process that represents the important issues collectively acknowledged. These issues concern weaknesses in the process that present a risk of not being able to meet the cost or time objectives, the required quality for the goods or services produced, obstacles to overcome, the difficulty to reach challenges and goods or services that are strategic assets of the company.

–"The determination of the axes of a knowledge management initiative" is intended to define, localize and characterize the knowledge to be capitalized upon.

In [TSE 05], a methodology is developed for modeling the knowledge requirements and the associated tasks for collecting the knowledge required to solve problems in organizations. The process of identifying requirements in designing a knowledge management system depicts the three different stages: objective exploration, requirement exploration and identification of refined requirement. Tseng and Huang used the *Delphi* method to collect the required knowledge.

The methodology proposed by Saad *et al.* [SAA 09] is a generalization of the GAMETH framework and was conducted and validated in a French automobile company. It aims at evaluating the knowledge localization within a project. It is composed of two phases: (1) constructing preference model, and (2) classifying "potential crucial knowledge". We note that the works already mentioned in the field of knowledge management aim at analyzing and identifying sensitive processes to construct a set of "reference crucial knowledge".

The scientific works mentioned above has not studied deeply the operation of sensitive processes identification. However, in these methods, the characterization phase and the BP evaluation have not been studied in depth. In addition to that, the set of the criteria has not been explicated. So, in order to provide a solution, this chapter aims to consolidate a previous work done by Saad *et al.* [SAA 09] and to optimize the operation of "sensitive processes identification". To reach this objective, we rely on multicriteria decision-making to construct a set of coherent criteria and to determine the preference model of the decision makers in order to identify the sensitive BPs.

Indeed, the organizations must identify the sensitive processes that mobilize crucial knowledge that is considered as an immaterial resource. These processes must contain at least one activity that mobilizes some tacit knowledge held by a very small number of experts or poorly mastered to solve critical problems. The proposed methodology is composed of two phases. The first phase is relative to constructive learning devoted to infer the preference model of the decision makers. Practically, it consists of inferring a set of decision rules from some holistic information in terms of assignment examples provided by the decision makers. This is done through the DRSA [GRE 01]. The previous set of rules may be used to classify the "potential sensitive business processes". In the second phase, the decision maker uses the preference models (decision rules) of the different decision makers defined in the first phase to assign the new BPs that are called "potential sensitive process" to the classes Cl1 "weakly sensitive process" or Cl2 "sensitive process" or Cl3 "very sensitive process".

The remainder of the chapter is organized as follows. Section 9.2 presents the related works to analyze the approaches that define some criteria for characterizing and evaluating the BPs. Section 9.3 presents the DRSA. Section 9.4 presents the sensitive BP identifying methodology. Section 9.5

presents a decision support system for identifying sensitive BPs (or organization's processes) entitled a decision support system for identifying a sensitive organization's processes (OP-DSS). One basic characteristic of a DSS is that it supports but does not replace the decision process [MAR 98]. An OP-DSS is based on the multicriteria decision-making approach and the DRSA to infer the decision rules that are necessary to classify potential sensitive organization's processes. Section 9.6 describes the application of the proposed methodology in the context of the association of disabled people. Section 9.7 concludes the chapter and underlines some future research topics.

9.2. Related works

In this section, we present some approaches significant for the evaluation and identification of BPs.

According to Hammer and Champy [HAM 93], the criterion "process importance" evaluates the process impact on the organization's clients (external or internal). Thus, the client satisfaction and the improvement of the organization's services are considered as a strategic objective. As informally mentioned in the Baldrige Glossary[1], the concept of strategic objectives refers to an organization's articulated aims or responses to address major change or improvement, competitiveness or social issues, and business advantages. Strategic objectives are generally focused both externally and internally and relate to significant customer, market, product, or technological opportunities and challenges (strategic challenges). Broadly stated, they are what an organization must achieve to remain or become competitive and ensure long-term sustainability. Strategic objectives set an organization's longer term directions and guide resource allocations and redistributions.

Davenport [DAV 93] proposed an approach for selecting processes for innovation, which is an important prerequisite to process change. The author states that most companies choose to address a small set of BPs in order to gain experience with innovation initiatives and focus their resources on the most critical processes. Among the criteria that have been identified to guide the process selection is the process's centrality to the execution of a firm's business strategy. It should be noted that the process centrality represents the

---

1 http://www.baldrige21.com/Baldrige_Glossary.html.

key criterion for measuring the importance of the process in terms of an organization's objective satisfaction.

In an information system engineering approach, we distinguish three BP types. According to Melao and Pidd [MEL 00], these types are based on the value chain defined by Porter and Millar [POR 85]. First, the core process is a BP that has external customers and includes the primary activities[2] of the value chain. These activities are related to the production and distribution of the products and the services of the organization. In addition, these activities create a value perceptible by customers. Second, the support process is a BP that has internal customers and concerns secondary activities[3] in the value chain. These activities are necessary to the execution of the primary activities. And finally, the management process is a BP that manages the core processes and the support processes. Similarly to Melao and Pidd [MEL 00], Morley *et al.* [MOR 07] proposed three process types: (1) the main processes produce a result; they create a value in a company. Their results are intended for a client or an external partner. These processes provide a strategic advantage and lead to detailed modeling. (2) The secondary processes produce results used by the main processes. They are sources of direct cost without creating value. (3) The steering processes are intended to control the achievement of company objectives and the implementation of its strategy. From our point of view, the core processes (respectively, the main processes) are the most important processes in terms of the organization's service quality improvement and the external client's needs satisfaction. However, the authors intentionally determined the degree of importance of the core processes.

In the quality management approach [ISO 03], strategic process identification should be made according to the impact of the process on the result and the customer satisfaction. Thus, this activity is made according to the organization strategy. For example, a customer-oriented organization will give importance to the customer listening process. A classification of process types has been given by the quality approach of the norm ISO 9000. It distinguishes three types of processes. The operational processes are those that have a direct impact on the added value of organization. This process

---

2 The primary activities include five kinds of activities: inbound logistics, operations, outbound logistics, marketing and sales.

3 They include four kinds of activities: firm infrastructure, human resource management, technology and procurement.

type constitutes the core business of the company and produces products or services that target customers (for example sales, design, procurement and purchasing, production and aftermarket support). The support processes contribute to a smooth implementation of the operational processes by providing the necessary resources (for example human resources and financial resources). They indirectly bring value to the organization and are necessary for the execution of the operational process. The management processes contribute to the determination of policy and deployment of the goals in the organization (for example listening to customers and other stakeholders, development strategy, internal communication and personnel mobilization).

The approaches presented above do not show in detail how to evaluate the importance of a BP to achieve the strategic objectives of the organization. In addition, these works lack a mathematical model or a formal procedure for computing the contribution degree of a BP according to the organization's strategic objectives.

The approaches listed above treated the problematic of process identification. Thus, the degree of importance of each process depends on the study context and the organizational needs. However, there is no approach has that presented a formal model leading to the identification of the most important processes that we call "sensitive processes".

9.3. Dominance-based rough set approach

The DRSA [GRE 01] is a rough sets based multicriteria classification method. This method has been developed to overcome the shortcomings of rough sets in multicriteria classification problems. Indeed, conventional rough set theory based on indiscernibility cannot be used to deal with multicriteria classification problems while attributes have a preference order. The basic idea of DRSA is to replace the indiscernibility principle with dominance.

Information about decision objects is often represented in an "information table", where rows correspond to "objects", columns correspond to "attributes" and entries are "attributes-values". Formally, the information table S is a four-tuple <U, Q, V, f> where:

– U is a finite set of objects;

– Q is a finite set of attributes;

– $V = \bigcup_{q \in Q} Vq$, Vq is a domain of the attribute q;

– F: U x Q → V an information function defined such that f(x, q) ∈ Vq, ∀q ∈ Q, ∀ x ∈ U.

The set of attributes Q is often divided into two subsets: subset C of "condition attributes" and subset D of "decision attributes". In this case, the information table is called the decision table.

For the purpose of this chapter, a series of assumptions, which are appropriate in multicriteria classification problems, is established. The domain (or scale) of condition attributes is supposed to be ordered to decrease or increase preference. Such attributes are called "criteria". Without the loss of generality, we assume that the preference is increasing with a value of f (x, q) for every q ∈ C. We also assume that the set of decision attributes D is a singleton {d}. Decision attribute d makes a partition of U into a finite number of decision classes Cl = {Clt, t ∈ T}, T = {0,..., n}, such that each x ∈ U belongs to one and only one class in Cl. Furthermore, we suppose that the classes are preference-ordered, i.e. for all r, s ∈ T, such that r > s, the objects from Clr are preferred to the objects from Cls.

The basic idea of the rough set approach is the approximation of knowledge generated by the decision attributes and the "granules of knowledge" generated by condition attributes. The sets to be approximated are defined as follows:

$$Cl_t^{\geq} = \bigcup_{s \geq t} Cl_s, Cl_t^{\leq} = \bigcup_{s \leq t} Cl_s, t = 0,...,n$$

The set $Cl^{\geq}$ is $Cl_t^{\geq} = \bigcup_{s \geq t} Cl_s, Cl_t^{\leq} = \bigcup_{s \leq t} Cl_s, t = 0,...,n$ called the upward union. The assertion x ∈ $Cl^{\geq}$ means that x belongs to at least class Clt. The set $Cl^{\leq}$ is called the downward union. The assertion x ∈ $Cl^{\leq}$ means that x belongs to at most Clt.

The P-lower approximation of $Cl^{\geq}$ contains all the objects with a P-dominating set that are assigned with certitude to classes at most as good as Clt. The P-upper approximation of $Cl^{\geq}$ contains all the objects with a P-dominating set that are assigned to a class at least as good as Clt. We can also define that the P-boundary sets of $Cl^{\geq}$Bnp(Clt) contain all the objects that are assigned both to a class better than Clt and to one or several classes worse than Clt. The quality of classification is defined by the following ratio:

$$\gamma_P = \frac{card(U - (\bigcup_{t=1,...,n} Bn_p(Cl_t^{\geq})))}{card(U)} = \frac{card(U - (\bigcup_{t=1,...,n} Bn_p(Cl_t^{\leq}))}{card(U)} \qquad [9.1]$$

The ratio expresses the percentage of objects that are assigned with certitude to a given class.

The decision attributes induce a partition of U in a way that is independent from the condition attributes. Accordingly, a decision table may be seen as a set of "if...then..." decision rules, where the condition part specifies values assumed by one or more condition attributes and the decision part specifies an assignment to one or more decision classes. In DRSA, three types of decision rules may be considered: (1) certain rules generated from lower approximations of unions of classes, (2) possible rules generated from upper approximations of unions of classes and (3) approximate rules generated from boundary regions.

9.4. BP evaluation methodology

The methodology that we propose for evaluating BPs is composed of two phases (see Figure 9.1): (1) construction of the preference model in terms of decision rules, and (2) exploitation of the preference model to classify the "potential sensitive business processes"[4]. The term "potential sensitive business process" should be mapped to the concept of "potential alternatives" as defined by [ROY 93] in multicriteria decision-making, that is a real or virtual alternative of action considered by at least one decision maker as a realistic one. Thus, a "potential sensitive business process" is a process that has been identified as sensitive by at least one decision maker.

The first phase is to determine some decision rules based on the decision makers preference information on a set of BPs that are examples of learning and that we call "reference business processes". The preference information is related to the decision to assign the BP to one decision class. We distinguish three decision classes as follow: (1) the decision class Cl1 "weakly sensitive business processes", (2) the decision class Cl2 "sensitive business processes" and (3) the decision class Cl3 "very sensitive business

---

4 We define a sensitive business process as a process that is susceptible to mobilizing knowledge on which we can capitalize.

processes". The preferences model results in the form of decision rules like "if conditions then conclusion".

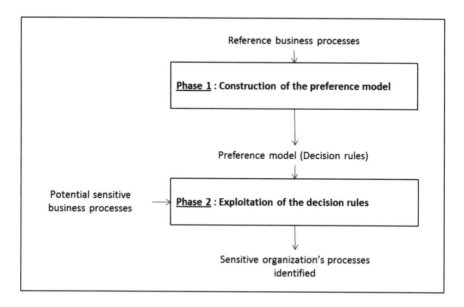

Figure 9.1. *Business process evaluation methodology*

In the second phase, the decision makers use the preference models (decision rules) defined in the first phase in order to assign the rest of the BPs to be evaluated in the three decision classes. These processes are called "potential sensitive business processes".

9.4.1. *Phase 1: preference model construction*

This phase consists of four steps (see Figure 9.2). The first step is to identify a set of "reference business processes". In the second step, we analyze in depth these processes by studying the following dimensions: the structural complexity, the dysfunction, the cost and the duration. In the third step, we construct a set of criteria in order to evaluate the reference BPs. The fourth step is to infer the decision rules from the example assignment of the reference BPs in the decision classes.

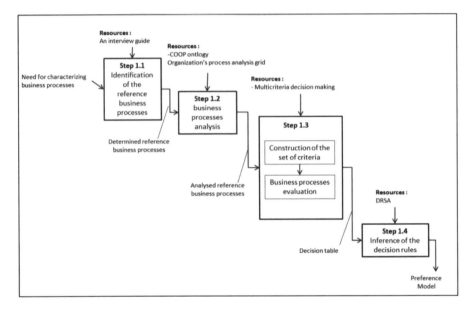

Figure 9.2. *Construction of the preference model*

9.4.1.1. *Step 1.1: reference BP identification*

Given the large number of BPs in an organization, it is difficult and expensive to analyze and evaluate them entirely. So, the analyst in collaboration with the decision makers should choose a set of representative BPs to be assigned in one of the decision classes.

To conform to the terminology used in multicriteria decision aid [GRE 01], we call this learning set "a list of reference business processes". This list is used to infer the decision rules based on the decision makers preferences. Such rules are then used to classify new BPs.

The application of this step should be based on interview guidelines, which must be realized and validated with the stakeholders.

9.4.1.2. *Step 1.2: BP analysis*

This step aims at modeling and analyzing the reference BPs. Therefore, we have adopted a constructivist approach that consists of representing the activities really performed by the actors involved in the processes.

The process analysis is to characterize the processes in terms of: the activities that compose them, the affiliated actors, the organizational units, the cost, the time, the mobilized resources and the provided results.

9.4.1.3. *Step 1.3: construction of evaluation criteria*

We built the set of criteria in collaboration with the decision makers in order to identify the sensitive BPs (see Appendix 1). The analysis of these processes is necessary to locate knowledge that needs to be capitalized. We follow both the top-down and bottom-up approach. Our approach is the result of experiments conducted over several months. It should be noted that the final formulation of these criteria and the scales are underapproved by the association president and some doctors. The top-down approach consists of decreasing one or more general goals as a view or dimension. The bottom-up approach consists of building a criteria family from a list of indicators that could influence the opinion makers about the importance of the processes. These indicators are designated by the term "consequence" in the multicriteria decision-making approach [ROY 93]. The construction of the list of consequences is determined partly from a literature review [HAM 93, DAV 93, ISO 03, LOR 03] and partly from the information collected with decision makers during the sensitive BP identification.

Seven criteria have been identified: (1) degree of contribution of the BP to achieve the strategic objective, (2) structural complexity, (3) number of business domains, (4) externalization degree, (5) number of critical activities, (6) cost and (7) duration. Each criterion has a scale that is composed of a set of qualitative levels used for the BP evaluation.

To measure the degree of contribution of the reference BPs, we have proposed a model [TUR 12a] on four levels. This number of levels depends on our study context. As is shown in Figure 9.2, from right to left, the first level corresponds to the first-level process (FLP) also named the strategic process or macroprocess. Each FLP is divided into a set of subprocesses named the second-level process (SLP). The SLPs are divided into a set of subprocesses named the third-level process (TLP). Finally, the TLPs are composed of a set of BPs. Thus, there are three types of arc: (1) the arcs connecting BP to TLP (BP $\rightarrow$ TLP$_i$) where $(1 \leq i \leq m3)$, (2) the arcs connecting TLP to SLP (TLPi $\rightarrow$ SLP$_j$) where $(1 \leq i \leq m3)$ and $(1 \leq j \leq m2)$ and (3) the arcs connecting SLP to FLP (SLP$_j$ $\rightarrow$ FLP) where $(1 \leq j \leq m2)$.

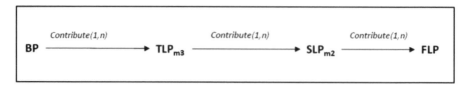

Figure 9.3. *Model for computing degrees of contribution*

To show how to calculate the degree of contribution of each BP to an FLP, referred as V(BP-FLP), we consider Figure 9.4.

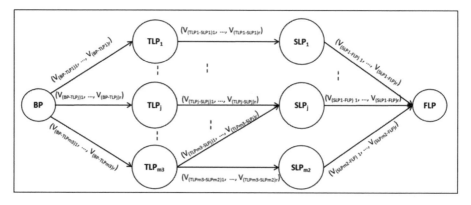

Figure 9.4. *Graph with four levels for computing degrees of contribution*

The algorithm for computing degrees of contribution consists of the following two steps (see Appendix 1):

– *Step 1:* we determine in this step the degree of contribution of (BP → SLP). For each project, we proceed in the following way: we enumerate all the possible paths (BP → TLP → SLP) and we retain the way that maximizes the minimal contribution degree of BP compared to each process of level 2.

– *Step 2:* in this step, we proceed similarly to step 1; we use the subgraph BP-SLP. We enumerate all the possible ways (BP → SLP → FLP) and we select the one that maximizes the minimal contribution degree of BP to FLP.

9.4.1.4. *Step 1.4: decision rule inference*

We propose an iterative procedure for inferring decision rules that are collectively accepted by the decision makers. The different steps of this procedure are shown in Figure 9.5.

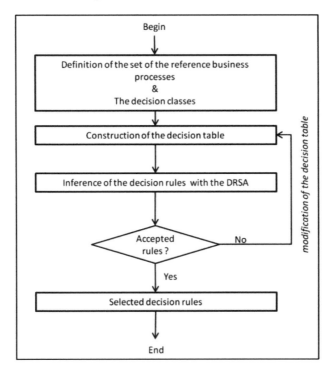

Figure 9.5. *Decision rule inference procedure*

First, we must identify the set of "reference business processes" and the list of decision classes. Second, we must construct the decision table (see Table 9.1) by introducing the necessary data determined by the decision makers. Third, we must apply the DRSA and particularly the dominance learning from examples module (DOMLEM) algorithm [GRE 01] in order to infer the decision rules. The result is presented in terms of approximation quality (see Table 9.2). This allows us to verify the inconsistencies of decision rules. These decision rules are inferred by comparison between the information related to the assignment examples given intuitively by each decision maker and the results of the classification given by the DOMLEM inference algorithm.

Reference sensitive business processes	Criteria			Decision makers
	g_1	$\cdots$	g_m	D_1
BP_1	$f(BP_1, g_1)$	$\cdots$	$f(BP_1, g_m)$	Cl1/Cl2/Cl3
$\cdots$	$\cdots$	$\cdots$	$\cdots$	$\cdots$
BP_n	$f(BP_n, g_1)$	$\cdots$	$f(BP_n, g_m)$	Cl1/Cl2/Cl3

Table 9.1. *Schematic representation of a decision table*

Classes	P-lower approximations	P-upper approximations	P-Boundary
$Cl_1^\leq$ At most "weakly sensitive process"	BP_6, BP_{11}, BP_{15}	$BP_6, BP_{11}, BP_{14}, BP_{15}, BP_{16}$	BP_{14}, BP_{16}
$Cl_2^\leq$ At most "sensitive process"	$BP_3, BP_5, BP_6, BP_9, BP_{19},$ $BP_{11}, BP_{12}, BP_{14}, BP_{15}, BP_{16}$	$BP_3, BP_5, BP_6, BP_9,$ $BP_{19}, BP_{11}, BP_{12},$ $BP_{14}, BP_{15}, BP_{16}$	$\varnothing$
$Cl_2^\geq$ At least "sensitive process"	$BP_1, BP_2, BP_3, BP_4, BP_5,$ $BP_7, BP_8, BP_9, BP_{10}, BP_{12},$ BP_{13}, BP_{17}	$BP_1, BP_2, BP_3, BP_4,$ $BP_5, BP_7, BP_8, BP_9,$ $BP_{10}, BP_{12}, BP_{13},$ $BP_{14}, BP_{16}, BP_{17}$	BP_{14}, BP_{16}
$Cl_3^\geq$ At least "very sensitive process"	$BP_1, BP_2, BP_4, BP_7, BP_8,$ BP_{13}, BP_{17}	$BP_1, BP_2, BP_4, BP_7,$ BP_8, BP_{13}, BP_{17}	$\varnothing$

Table 9.2. *The approximations of the decision classes Cl1, Cl2 and Cl3 according to the decision maker*

9.4.2. *Phase 2: exploitation of the preference model*

In this phase, the analyst uses the preference model constructed in the first phase to assign the new BP called "potential sensitive business processes" to three decision classes: Cl1 "very sensitive business processes", Cl2 "sensitive business processes" and Cl3 "weakly sensitive business processes". Similarly to the previous one (see Figure 9.6), the second phase starts by identifying the algorithm to compute the contribution degrees of potential sensitive BPs to each strategic objective. This algorithm uses as an input the information of the performance of the "potential sensitive business processes" previously introduced in the matrices BP-TLP, TLP-SLP and SLP-FLP. The results are introduced in the "performance table" (see Table 9.3). After this, we must verify if there is at least one rule that covers the performance vector. We must affect each "potential sensitive business process" BP_i characterized by the performance $(BP_i, g_1), \ldots, (BP_i, g_n)$ to the classes Cl1 or Cl2 or Cl3.

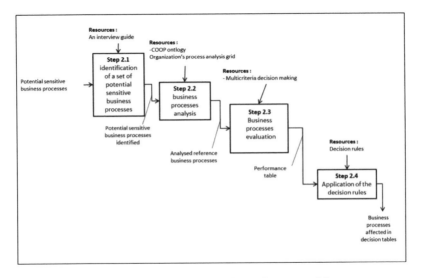

Figure 9.6. *Exploitation of the preference model*

Potentially sensitive business processes	Criteria		
	g_1	$\cdots$	g_m
BP_1	$f(BP_1, g_1)$	$\ldots$	$f(BP_1, g_m)$
$\ldots$	$\ldots$	$\ldots$	$\ldots$
BP_n	$f(BP_n, g_1)$	$\ldots$	$f(BP_n, g_m)$

Table 9.3. *Schematic representation of a performance table*

9.5. The decision support system for identifying sensitive processes OP-DSS

OP-DSS is mainly composed of four parts (see Figure 9.7): (1) graphical interface, (2) model base, (3) database and (4) knowledge base.

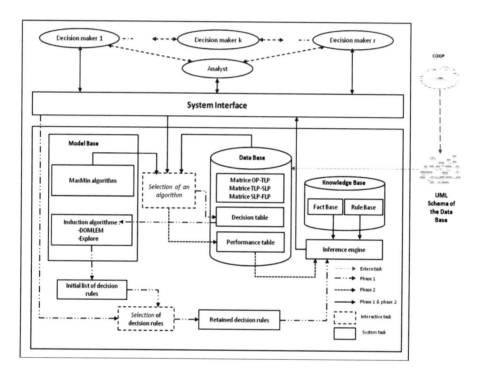

Figure 9.7. *OP-DSS architecture*

9.5.1. *Graphical interface*

The graphical interface defines how different resources of OP-DSS (algorithms, database and knowledge base) are used. The interface of OP-DSS is based on a graphical user interface (GUI) environment, i.e. a hierarchy of menus and submenus offering the user transparency, simplicity and user-friendliness in the exploitation of the system.

9.5.2. *Model base*

The model base of OP-DSS contains: (1) the algorithms for computing the contribution degrees of the set of processes to the strategic objectives (see section 9.4.1.3); (2) algorithm for the inference of decision rules.

The model base part contains two algorithms for decision rule induction. On the one hand, the DOMLEM algorithm [GRE 01] produces a minimal covering set of decision rules, i.e. a subset of non-redundant and complete decision rules. On the other hand, the explore algorithm produces a set containing all the decision rules [STE 93]. It should be noted that the explore algorithm is implemented in the DRSA approach. OP-DSS uses the DOMLEM and explore algorithms that use the rough set theory.

9.5.3. *Database*

The modeling of the conceptual schema of the OP-DSS database was carried out using unified modeling language (UML). This conceptual schema is based on the core ontology of organization's processes (COOP) defined in [TUR 13]. The idea consists of transforming the ontological concepts into UML classes. The concept taxonomy of COOP has been formalized with OntoSpec language [KAS 05] and published online at http://home.mis.u-picardie.fr/~site-ic/site/IMG/pdf/action_of_organization-v1.0-os.pdf.

Figure 9.8 shows the conceptual schema of the database. We characterize the "process of organization" as a central concept in the conceptual schema. A semi-informal characterization of the concept "process of organization"[5] is given in [TUR 12b, TUR 13] as follows: (1) A "process of organization" is a "deliberate action of organization" composed of "organizational activities" that can have for agent either a "human" or an "organization unit". (2) A "process of organization" is more precisely a "culminated process" that, when successfully carried out, culminates in a "result" that is useful for a "client".

As is shown in Figure 9.8, each process of organization has one organization for an agent; each process of organization has an organizational objective, which can be a strategic objective or an operational objective; each process of the organization has one or more organizational activities for each part.

---

5 "Business process" and "process of organization" refer to the same concept.

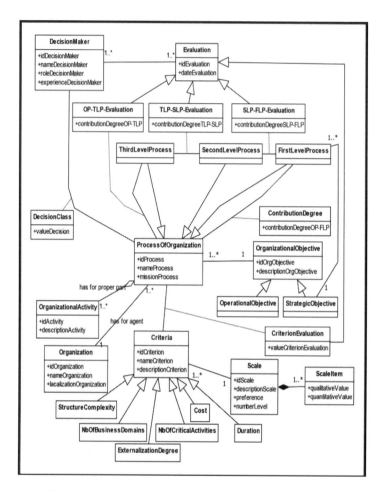

Figure 9.8. *UML-based conceptual schema of the database*

To model the multicriteria evaluation of the organization's processes, we propose six classes that represent the criteria: "structural complexity", "number of business domains", "externalization degree", "number of critical activities", "cost" and "duration". The evaluation of each organization's process begins by computing the degree of contribution of the organization's process to performing the "strategic objective". For this reason, we define the three association classes: (1) "OP-TLP evaluation", which is necessary to save the value of computing the degree of contribution of OP to TLP; (2) "TLP-SLP evaluation", which is necessary to save the value of computing the degree of contribution of TLP to SLP; and (3) "SLP-FLP evaluation", which is necessary to save the value of computing the degree of contribution of SLP to FLP. Each "criteria" have one "scale", which is composed of one or more scale items. Moreover, each process of organization must be evaluated according to the set of criteria mentioned above. Thus, the evaluation value is saved in the association class "criterion evaluation". The classification of each process of organization is made by the decision maker in only one decision class.

9.5.4. *Knowledge base*

To construct the knowledge base, we used the expert system generator JESS[6] (Java expert system shell). Since we are interested in "very sensitive processes" and "sensitive processes", the rules base contains only the rules permitting us to assign with certainty "potential sensitive processes" to the class Cl3 and the class Cl2.

A rule in JESS is defined through the function **defrule**. An example relative to our application is depicted in Figure 9.9. The fact base contains the initial facts relative to the reference organization's processes. A fact in JESS is defined through the function **defacts**. Figure 9.10 presents a JESS definition of a fact relative to the application.

```
(defrule rule1
(Organization-Process
  (OP-Num ?OP)
  (OP-Name ?OPN)
  (OP-Mission ?OPM)
  (SO1 VeryImportant)
  (SO2 VeryImportant)
  (SO3 VeryImportant)
  (SO4 VeryImportant)
  (Structural-Complexity VeryComplex)
  (Business-Domain VeryHigh)
  (Externalization VeryHigh)
  (Critical-Activity VeryHigh)
  (Cost VeryHigh)
  (Duration VeryHigh)
=> (printout outfile "very sensitive organization's
process")))
```

Figure 9.9. *Example of a rule definition*

6 JESS is a free package, which is available at http://www.jessrules.com/.

```
(defacts   Process
(Organization-Process
  (OP-Num OP1)
  (OP-Name Neonatolgy process)
  (OP-Mission healthcare support made by a neonatologist)
  (SO1 VeryImportant)
  (SO2 VeryImportant)
  (SO3 VeryImportant)
  (SO4 VeryImportant)
  (Structural-Complexity VeryComplex)
  (Business-Domain VeryHigh)
  (Externalization VeryHigh)
  (Critical-Activity VeryHigh)
  (Cost VeryHigh)
  (Duration VeryHigh)))
```

Figure 9.10. *Example of a fact definition*

9.5.5. *Implementation*

In the following, we present a brief description of the prototype implementing OP-DSS. We used the JAVA language to implement the interfaces of OP-DSS. Through the GUI of the system, the user can introduce data or infer decision rules or classify the OP into Cl1, Cl2 or Cl3.

Figures 9.11–9.14 show four printed screens from OP-DSS. The screen in Figure 9.11 permits us to generate matrix OP-TLP containing the evaluation of each OP with respect to each TLP. As is shown in this screen, the user introduces OP for evaluation and then introduces the evaluation directly. The user may also add/remove a TLP from the list initially shown. Similar interfaces are used for TLP-SLP and SLP-FLP evaluations. They permit us to generate matrix TLP-SLP and matrix SLP-FLP, respectively.

Once all the data are introduced in the interfaces, OP-ILP evaluation and ILP-DLP evaluation, the user may use the interface shown in Figure 9.12 to compute the degrees of contribution of each OP to each strategic objective.

Once all decision rules are generated, the user may use the interface shown in Figure 9.14 to visualize the evaluation of each OP with respect to each criterion. Then, he/she should classify these processes into Cl1, Cl2 or Cl3.

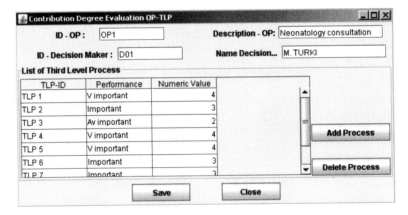

Figure 9.11. *OP-TLP evaluation*

Contribution Degree Evaluation TLP-SLP				
ID - OP : OP01			Description OP : Neonatology Consultation	
ID - Decision Maker : D01			Name Decision Maker : M. TURKI	
	SLP 1	SLP 2	SLP 3	SLP 4
TLP 1	V important	V important	A important	V important
TLP 2	V important	Important	A important	V important
TLP 3	V important	V important	Important	V important
TLP 4	V important	V important	Important	Important
TLP 5	V important	V important	Important	Important
TLP 6	V important	V important	Important	Important
TLP 7	V important	V important	Important	Important
TLP 8	A important	W important	W important	M important

Save   Close

Figure 9.12. *TLP-SLP evaluation*

Contribution Degree Evaluation SLP - FLP				
ID - OP : OP1			Description OP : Neonatology consultation	
ID - FLP : FLP1			Description FLP : impact on the medical care	
ID Decision Maker : D01			Name Decision Maker : M. TURKI	
List of SLP				
ID - SLP	Performance	Valeur numérique		
SLP1	V Important	4		
SLP2	Important	3		Add SLP
SLP3	W Important	1		
SLP4	W Important	1		
				Computing the contribution degree OP-FLP

Save   Close

Figure 9.13. *SLP-FLP evaluation*

ID - OP	g6	g7	g8	g9	g10	Decision
OP1	Complex	Complex	High	Average	Weak	CI3
OP2	V Complex	Complex	Average	Average	Weak	CI3
OP3	Complex	A Complex	Average	Average	Weak	CI3
OP4	Complex	Complex	High	Average	Weak	CI2
OP5	Complex	Complex	Average	Average	Weak	CI2
OP6	A Complex	Complex	Average	Average	Weak	CI1
OP7	V Complex	Complex	Average	High	Average	CI3
OP8	V Complex	A Complex	Average	High	High	CI3

ID - Decision Maker: D01   **Name Decision Maker :** M. TURKI

Save   Close

Figure 9.14. *Decision table interface*

Appendix 1, section 9.9, provides the general schema of the degree of contribution algorithm. To incorporate JESS in our system, we have developed an executable file (inference.exe) in JAVA to import JESS DLLs (see Figure 9.15). OP-DSS and JAVA dialog is completely transparent to users. As shown in Figure 9.11, OP-DSS automatically generates an input text file (input.txt) that is used by inference.exe. The results generated by JAVA are then stored by inference.exe in an output text file (output.txt). The latter is then used by O-DSS to provide results (in terms of decision rules) to the user.

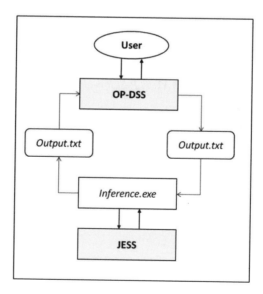

Figure 9.15. *OP-DSS and JESS dialog system*

The decision rules are first generated by DOMLEM. These rules are initially expressed in the following form (for example for the organization's process OP1):

if $f(x, g5) \leq 2 \wedge f(x, g6) \leq 2 \wedge f(x, g7) \leq 2 \wedge f(x, g8) \leq 2 \wedge f(x, g10) \leq 2$, then $x \in Cl1^{\leq}$

The rules are automatically converted, by OP-DSS, to apply to the syntax of JESS. For example, the rule cited above is translated as follows:

if OP1.Structural-Complexity is "at most averagely complex" and OP1.Number-of-Critical-Activity is "at most average" and OP1.Externalization-Degree is "at most internal" and OP1.Cost is "at most average" and OP1.Number-of-Business-Domain is "at most average" then OP1 is at most in Cl1.

9.6. Case study

The model presented above for computing the degree of contribution has been performed in the Association de Sauvegarde des Handicapés Moteurs de Sfax (ASHMS – Association for the protection of people with mobility disabilities). Particularly, we are interested in the early care of disabled children with cerebral palsy. This care consists of several actions in terms of medical and paramedical consultations in different specialties. Among these specialties, we quote: neonatology, neuropediatrics, physical medicine, orthopedics, psychiatry, physiotherapy and occupational therapy. An in-depth analysis of the care process has been made in the context of ASHMS. Thus, some strategic objectives have been identified and a processes map has been presented. Taking into account the granularity of the identified processes and their detail levels in terms of modeling, we have identified with the stakeholders some processes classified as follows: 17 BP, 14 TLP, 9 SLP and 4 FLP. All these processes are validated through some interviews made with seven stakeholders: the president of ASHMS, the neuropediatrician, the neonatologist, the physiotherapist, the occupational therapist, the speech therapist and the psychologist.

Initially, a scoping meeting was conducted with the steering committee of ASHMS in order to determine the FLP corresponding to the strategic objectives. This committee comprises the association president, the executive director and two doctors (neuropediatrician and neonatologist). Subsequently, we conducted three interviews with each stakeholder. During the first interview, an initial list of processes was proposed by each actor. After this, we made a description of the identified processes in order to validate them with the stakeholders during the second interview. During the third interview, we gathered the decision makers in order to evaluate each BP for computing the contribution degree to the FLP. We noted that the evaluations made by the decision makers were very close. This is why we retained a single value per graph arc. The list of the decision makers is as follows: the president of ASHMS, the neuropediatrician, the neonatologist, the physiotherapist, the occupational therapist, the speech therapist and the psychologist. These actors confirmed that in practice, it is very difficult to determine the contribution degree of a given BP to the FLP of the ASHMS. For this reason, we used the model for measuring the contribution degrees.

To illustrate the application of the MaxMin algorithm for computing the contribution degree of the BP, we present the result of the evaluation of BP_1, "process of neonatology consultation", to reach the FLP_1, "the global process of care of the disabled children with cerebral palsy". On the basis of the data introduced in the matrices BP-TLP, TLP-SLP and SLP-FLP, the execution of the *MaxMin* algorithm returns the value 4. This result means that BP_1 is qualified as "a very sensitive process". This qualification was validated by the decision makers involved in the decision process. It should be noted that we verified with the decision makers the consistency of the values generated by the algorithm.

However, we note that some qualifications were not consistent. This inconsistency leads us to re-examine with the decision makers the data introduced during the evaluation.

9.7. Conclusion and futures works

Sensitive BP is a complex operation since it involves a large number of actors from various business domains. In this chapter, we have addressed a methodology for identifying sensitive BP to knowledge localization. This methodology is based on the multicriteria decision-making approach and DRSA approach. It is composed of two phases: (1) construction of the preference model, and (2) exploitation of the preference model to classify the "potential sensitive business processes". In the first phase, we have addressed a model for computing the contribution degrees of the BPs to reach the strategic objectives. Finally, we have illustrated the experimentation of the proposed methodology in the context of ASHMS.

One important finding of the proposed methodology is the use of multicriteria analysis and rough set theory in the field of knowledge management. The multicriteria analysis is mainly used to define the evaluation criteria and to identify potential sensitive BPs. Rough set theory and, more precisely, the DRSA are used during the inference of decision rules.

There are some open research topics that are related to the methodology. The first is related to the dynamicity and changes of the BPs. Then, it will be necessary to predict the impact of the disappearance or the addition of one or more processes to the model of computing the contribution degrees. The second is related to the nature of BP. However, in our research, we do not take into account the interorganizational processes that involve more than one organization and the processes of the extended organization.

9.8. Bibliography

[DAV 93] DAVENPORT T.H., *Process Innovation: Reengineering Work through Information Technology*, Harvard Business Press, Boston, MA, 1993.

[FOR 06] FORD D.P, STAPLES D.S., "Perceived value of knowledge: the potential informer's perception", *Knowledge Management in Research and Practice*, vol. 4, pp. 3–16, 2006.

[GRE 01] GRECO S., MATARAZZO B., SLOWINSKI R., "Rough sets theory for multicriteria decision analysis", *European Journal of Operational Research*, vol. 129, no. 1, pp. 1–47, 2001.

[GRU 00] GRUNDSTEIN M., "From capitalizing on company knowledge to knowledge management", in MOREY D., MAYBURY M., THURAISINGHAM B., *Knowledge Management, Classic and Contemporary Works*, Chapter 12, The MIT Press, Cambridge, MA, pp. 261–287, 2000.

[HAM 93] HAMMER M., CHAMPY J., *Reengineering the Corporation: A Manifesto for Business Revolution*, Harper Business, New York, 1993.

[ISO 03] INTERNATIONAL ORGANIZATION FOR STANDARDIZATION, ISO 10006, Quality management systems, Guidelines for quality management in projects, 2003.

[KAS 05] KASSEL G., Integration of the DOLCE top-level ontology into the OntoSpecmethodology, The Computing Research Repository CoRR abs/cs/0510050, 2005. Available at http://arxiv.org/abs/cs/0510050.

[LOR 03] LORINO P., *Méthodes et pratiques de la performance*, Editions d'Organisation, Paris, 2003.

[MAR 98] MARAKAS G.M., *Decision Support Systems in the 21st Century*, Prentice-Hall, Upper Saddle River, NJ, 1998.

[MEL 00] MELAO N., PIDD M., "A conceptual framework for understanding business processes and business process modeling", *Information Systems Journal*, vol. 10, no. 2, pp. 105–130, 2000.

[MOR 07] MORLEY C., HUGUES J., LEBLANC B., *et al.*, *Processus métiers et S.I. évaluation, modélisation, mise en œuvre*, Dunod, France, 2007.

[POR 85] PORTER M., MILLAR V., "How information gives you competitive advantage", *Harvard Business Review*, vol. 63, no. 4, pp. 149–160, 1985.

[ROY 93] ROY B., BOUYSSOU D., *Aide multicritère à la décision: méthodes et cas*, Economica, Paris, 1993.

[SAA 09] SAAD I., GRUNDSTEIN M., SABROUX C., "Une méthode d'aide à l'identification des connaissances cruciales pour l'entreprise", *Revue systèmes d'information et management*, vol. 14, no. 3, pp. 43–78, 2009.

[STE 93] STEFANOWSKI J., VANDERPOOTEN D., "A general two stages approaches to rule induction from examples", in ZIARKO W., *Rough Sets, Fuzzy Sets and Knowledge Discovery*, Springer, Berlin, pp. 317–325, 1993.

[TSE 05] TSENG B., HUANG C., "Capitalizing on knowledge: a novel approach to crucial knowledge determination", *IEEE Transactions on Systems, Man, and Cybernetics Part A: Systems and Humans*, vol. 35, pp. 919–931, 2005.

[TUR 12a] TURKI M., SAAD I., GARGOURI F., *et al.*, "A model to measure the contribution degrees of the organization's processes for knowledge management", *Proceedings of the 5th World Summit on Knowledge Society*, Rome, Italy, 2012.

[TUR 12b] TURKI M., Proposition d'une méthode multicritère et d'une ontologie noyau des processus d'organisation pour l'aide à l'identification des processus sensible, PhD thesis, University Picardie Jules Verne, France, 2012.

[TUR 13] TURKI M., KASSEL G., SAAD I., *et al.*, "A core ontology of organization's processes", *Conference on Knowledge Management, Information and Knowledge Systems (KMIKS '13)*, Hammamet, Tunisia, 2013.

9.9. Appendix 1. The set of criteria

	Criteria	Description	Scale	Preference
g1	Impact on improving the medical care of a disabled child	Measure the impact on improving the medical care of a disabled child	Very important = 4; Important = 3; Averagely important = 2; Weakly important = 1	↑
g2	Impact on social care of a disabled child	Measure the impact on social care of a disabled child	Very important = 4; Important = 3; Averagely important = 2; Weakly important = 1	↑
g3	Impact on educational care of a disabled child	Measure the impact on educational care of a disabled child	Very important = 4; Important = 3; Averagely important = 2; Weakly important = 1	↑
g4	Impact on scientific research in the medical filed	Measure the impact on scientific research in the medical filed	Very important = 4; Important = 3; Averagely important = 2; Weakly important = 1	↑
g5	Structural complexity	Measure the structural complexity of the OP	Very complex = 4; Complex = 3; Averagely complex = 2; Weakly complex = 1	↑

g6	Number of business domains	Measure the number of business domains	High = 3; Average = 2; Weak = 1	↑
g7	Externalization degree	Evaluate the externalization degree in term of the actors affiliation	External = 3; Mixed = 2; Internal = 3	↑
g8	Number of critical activities	Measure the number of critical activities	High = 3; Average = 2; Weak = 1	↑
g9	Duration	Measure the duration of the OP	Short = 1; Average = 2; High = 3	↑
g10	Cost	Measure the cost of the OP	Low = 1; Average = 2; High = 3	↑

9.10. Appendix 2. Contribution degree computing algorithm

```
Algorithm contribution Degrees
BEGIN
--OP: a given organization's process
--FLP: a given FLP
--m2: number of SLP
--m3: number of TLP
--V_OP_TLP[j]: a vector which contains the valuation V(OP-TLPj)
--MAT_TLP_SLP: a matrix which contains the valuation V(TLPj-SLPi)
--V_SLP_FLP: a vector which contains the valuation V(SLPi-FLP)
--V_Res: an intermediate vector which contains the result of
the step 1
--Step 1: the contribution degrees computing OP-SLP
int max=0; int min=0;
for(inti=1;i<=m2;i++)
{
  for(int j=1;j<=m3;j++)
  {
    if (V_OP_TLP[j]<MAT_TLP_SLP[j][i])
    min = V_OP_TLP[j];
    else
    min = MAT_TLP_SLP [j][i];
    if (max<min)
    max=min;
  }
  V_Res[i]=max;
}
--Step 2: the contribution degrees computing OP-FLP
int max=0; int min=0;
for(inti=1;i<=m2;i++)
{
  if (V_SLP_FLP[i] <V_Res [i])
  min = V_SLP_FLP [i];
  else
  min = V_Res [i];
  if (min > max)
  max =min;
}
return max;
END
```

Chapter 10

A Collaborative Approach for Optimizing Continuity between Knowledge Codification with Knowledge Engineering Methods and Knowledge Transfer

10.1. Introduction

Knowledge transfer is a real challenge for organizations and particularly for those who have based their strategy on experts' knowledge codification using knowledge engineering methods. These organizations are facing one major problem: their knowledge repository is used by few people.

The concept of knowledge transfer was first introduced by Teece [TEE 77]. Knowledge transfer can be defined as a process in which an organization recreates and maintains a complex, causally ambiguous set of routines in a new setting [SZU 96]. This process is a key part of the knowledge management cycle and allows organizations to absorb and make optimal use of crucial knowledge.

Research on knowledge transfer focuses on three subjects [HAR 12, DAL 11, ALA 01, GUP 00, ZAC 99, SIM 99, SZU 96, MOW 96, ZAN 95]:

Chapter written by Thierno TOUNKARA.

– factors that affect knowledge transfer; there are dimensions for measuring the degree to which knowledge can be easily communicated, understood and transferred;

– modes or processes of knowledge transfer that deal with mutual transformation between tacit knowledge and explicit knowledge;

– evaluation and measurement of the performance of knowledge transfer; the goal is to elaborate indicators to measure the efficiency of knowledge transfer.

Our research deals with the first two themes. We refer to knowledge transfer models that consider knowledge elicitation as a possible stage for sharing and transferring knowledge. Focusing on knowledge engineering techniques for knowledge elicitation and organizational memory elaboration, we explore their limits analyzing codification effects on factors that affect knowledge transfer. Then, we derive practical implications for knowledge elicitation by:

– elaborating criteria for the identification of characteristics of different sets of knowledge;

– defining the good level of knowledge description in regard to its characteristics;

– proposing guidelines to adapt the knowledge presentation to recipients' preferences.

Relying on the SECI model of Nonaka and Takeuchi [NON 95], we propose a framework that leads to a shared context for knowledge interpretation. This framework defines and formalizes the different situations of exchange between groups of actors involved in the transfer process.

Our approach allows an optimal continuity between knowledge capture using knowledge engineering methods and knowledge transfer at individual and organizational levels.

10.2. Factors influencing knowledge transfer

Relying on the literature review, we can classify the factors that influence knowledge transfer into four types:

– characteristics of knowledge;

– knowledge transfer channels;

– absorptive capacity of receivers;

– cultural and organizational contexts.

10.2.1. *Characteristics of knowledge*

With characteristics of knowledge, we can measure different aspects that may be facilitators or barriers for knowledge transfer.

Relying on the work of Zander and Kogut [ZAN 95] and Simonin [SIM 99], we highlight three characteristics that would affect knowledge transfer: tacitness, complexity and specificity (or degree of contextualization).

– Codifiability (tacitness vs. explicitness)

Codifiability expresses the degree to which the knowledge could be articulated in documents and software [ZAN 95].

Tacit knowledge is not easily codifiable. Polanyi described tacit knowledge as "things that we know but cannot tell" [POL 67] and thus can only be transferred through interaction. Tacit knowledge is not easily articulated or formalized and is difficult to put into words, text, drawings or other symbolic forms. In fact, tacitness is a property of the knower: it is easily articulated by one person but may be very difficult to externalize by another.

Tacit knowledge is typically considered to be more valuable than explicit knowledge and requires more cognitive efforts of a sender and receiver to be transferred [DAL 11, HAR 12].

When knowledge is more codifiable, it can be divided into specific components that are easily understood and articulated. Highly codifiable knowledge is known as explicit knowledge. Explicit knowledge is associated with declarative knowledge and "know why". Declarative knowledge and "know why" consist of descriptive elements [GAR 97]. Explicit knowledge represents content that has been captured in some tangible form such as words, audio recordings or images. It is the process for transforming knowledge into a format that makes it possible for it to be stored or transferred as information.

– Complexity

Knowledge complexity can be defined as the number of tools and routines used in the process of knowledge transfer [REE 90]. Routines are actions based on unstated conventions that were derived from previous experiences and can embody the application of knowledge within an organization [SZU 96]. A complementary definition of complexity is the number of distinctive skills or competencies needed to understand the knowledge application.

Consequently, the more the routines are needed to interpret and appropriate knowledge, the more difficult its transfer can be [ARG 00].

– Specificity or degree of contextualization

Specificity describes the degree to which knowledge and routines in which it is embedded can satisfy the knowledge receiver. In other terms, "specificity" captures the degree to which knowledge is dependent or not on many different contexts of use [ZAN 95].

The more the knowledge can be adapted to the context of the receiver and the more it is absorbed and understood by the receiver, the more valuable it is.

For example, knowledge strongly connected with local experiences and culture can be a barrier to transfer and difficult to transplant to other environments.

– Causal ambiguity

The notion of causal ambiguity was introduced by Lippman and Rumelt [LIP 82]. They argued that when the precise reasons for success or failure in applying/replicating a capability/sets of knowledge in a new setting cannot be determined even *ex post*, causal ambiguity is present. It is the "basic ambiguity concerning the nature of the causal connections between actions and results" (p. 420).

So, causal ambiguity can be a great barrier for knowledge transfer because knowledge receivers (recipients) do not understand the relationships between knowledge application and outcomes.

From the literature, we can infer that high (low) degrees of tacitness, complexity, or specificity will produce high (low) degrees of ambiguity [SZU 96, DEF 90, BAR 85, WIL 85].

Highly tacit knowledge generates ambiguity through the skilled operator's own level of unawareness of the actions that he or she undertakes. Consequently, the causal relationship between actions and results remains less than apparent or is not understandable to knowledge receivers.

A high level of complexity arises from large numbers of technologies, organization routines and individual or team-based experience. Barney [BAR 85, p. 12] stated that "in complex, highly inter-dependent human or technological systems, the causes of success and failure are often difficult to assign . . . and . . . the establishment of cause-effect relationships can be very difficult, and the concomitant assessment of performance may be highly ambiguous". So, causal ambiguity can be derived from complexity and the potential for knowledge transfer is limited.

Williamson's research [WIL 85, pp. 53, 96] shows that human asset specificity is highly correlated with tacitness. The more tacit the knowledge, the higher the risk of having a high degree of specificity. Consequently, the relationship between high level of specificity and ambiguity will be similar to that of tacitness (i.e. high degree of specificity may cause ambiguity).

Although tacitness, complexity and specificity can each generate ambiguity, they can also act in combination. Interaction effects of tacitness, complexity and specificity should increase ambiguity beyond the simple sum of individual effects from each characteristic and create a barrier for knowledge transfer.

Considering causal ambiguity as an effect, we will focus our research on the causal variables: tacitness/explicitness, complexity and specificity.

10.2.2. *Knowledge transfer channels*

Communication processes and information flows drive knowledge transfer in organizations. The existence and richness of transmission channels are success factors for knowledge transfer [GUP 00].

Knowledge transfer channels can be informal or formal, personal or impersonal [HOL 98].

Informal mechanisms (such as informal seminars or coffee break conversations) refer to socialization and may be more effective in small organizations [FAH 98]. Socialization mechanisms refer to those organizational mechanisms that build interpersonal familiarity and personal affinity. However, such mechanisms may involve certain amounts of knowledge loss due to the lack of formal coding of the knowledge [ALA 01].

Formal transfer mechanisms (such as training sessions) may ensure greater distribution of knowledge but may inhibit creativity.

Personal channels (such as apprenticeships) may be more effective for distributing highly contextual knowledge, whereas impersonal channels (such as knowledge repositories) may be most effective for knowledge that can be readily codified and generalized to other contexts.

Daft and Lengel [DAF 86] showed that personal and more open communication increases the richness of communication channels. Gupta and Govindarajan [GUP 00] argued that greater participation in corporate socialization mechanisms would have a positive impact on the richness of transmission channels. Information technologies can support all four forms of knowledge transfer channels.

10.2.3. *Absorptive capacity of knowledge receivers*

Gupta and Govindarajan [GUP 00] identified absorptive capacity as a key element for the knowledge transfer process.

Absorptive capacity can be defined as "the ability of a firm to recognize the value of new, external information, assimilate it, and apply it" [COH 90]. For an individual, such a capacity is largely a function of its pre-existing stock of knowledge (background related with the knowledge domain, familiarity with knowledge engineering models, understanding profiles, etc.).

So, absorptive capacity is a characteristic of the recipient of the knowledge. In the absence of such an ability, difficulties during the integration of received knowledge may become an excuse for discontinuing its use.

It seems very difficult to control the absorptive capacity because knowledge must go through a recombination process in the mind of the knowledge receiver. This recombination depends on the recipient's cognitive capacity to process the incoming stimuli [VAN 98].

10.2.4. *Cultural and organizational contexts*

Prior research shows that the formal organizational context (structure and systems, sources of coordination and expertise) and cultural attributes of the organization affect efficiency of knowledge transfer [BUR 83, GHO 94, WIE 13].

Gibson and Birkinshaw [GIB 04] referred the cultural and organizational context to the systems, processes, values and beliefs, which collectively shape individual-level behaviors in any organization.

Maier [MAI 10, pp. 159–160] suggested that the organizational structure has an impact on knowledge management approaches. He discussed different organizational forms that aim at accelerating organizational learning and transfer, and thus the development, combination and use of organizational knowledge [MAI 10].

Various studies provide evidence to suggest that cultural values influence knowledge sharing behaviors by shaping patterns and qualities of interactions needed to leverage knowledge among individuals [ALA 06, DE 00, GRA 05]. It seems that culture creates an organizational context for social interaction and provides norms regarding what is "right" and "wrong" [AJM 08, DE 00]. Therefore, it can influence the way knowledge is transferred in the organization. De Long and Fahey [DE 00] argue that:

– different cultural attributes influence knowledge sharing and transfer across the organization (horizontal) and throughout the various levels of an organization (vertical);

– in contrast to functionally driven organizations, the predominantly horizontal structures (project-based organizations for example) are more likely to promote horizontal knowledge sharing of specific knowledge;

– cultures that reward individuals for knowledge sharing and encourage the use of existing knowledge create different knowledge sharing patterns than cultures that do not promote such activities.

Interorganizational knowledge transfer (across organizational boundaries) seems to be more complex compared to knowledge transfer within the organization. There are many reasons:

– Cultural distance can raise barriers for understanding partners and transferability of knowledge-based assets.

– Organizational distance (centralized vs. decentralized, innovators vs. followers, entrepreneurial vs. bureaucratic) can accentuate the difficulty of transferring knowledge through interorganizational relationships [SIM 99].

In our study, we limit the scope to a context of knowledge transfer within the organization.

10.3. Modes of knowledge transfer

For a better understanding of knowledge transfer, it is important to explore the first two complementary approaches: social exchange and codification.

10.3.1. *Social exchange versus codification*

We can share and transfer knowledge through social exchange, which is a process of personal communication and interaction. It is a socialization process (focusing on tacit knowledge) as described by Nonaka and Takeuchi [NON 95] in their SECI knowledge management model.

Knowledge codification is the process for transforming knowledge into a tangible, explicit form such as a document so that knowledge can then be communicated much more widely and with low cost.

In this chapter, we analyze knowledge transfer strategy based on knowledge codification using knowledge engineering methods.

10.3.2. *Knowledge transfer models*

We present here three theoretical models with distinct perspectives. These models bring a conceptual framework for many knowledge transfer processes. They have been reviewed and discussed by scholars and practitioners [DAL 11, HAR 12].

These three models give us a better understanding of the knowledge codification role in knowledge transfer process.

– SECI model

The SECI model of Nonaka and Takeuchi [NON 95] has proven to be one of the more robust in the field of knowledge management (KM). This model focuses on the knowledge conversion between tacit and explicit knowledge. It describes how knowledge is accumulated and transferred in organizations following the four modes: socialization, externalization, combination and internalization.

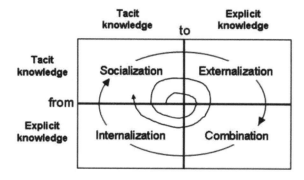

Figure 10.1. *The SECI model [NON 95]*

Socialization is the sharing of tacit knowledge through social interactions such as face-to-face interaction.

Externalization is the process of converting tacit knowledge in a visible form: explicit knowledge. It is a way for organizations to make knowledge tangible and store it in manuals and databases in order to be easily shared. In this mode, knowledge engineering methods are useful.

Combination is the process through which discrete pieces of explicit knowledge are recombined into a new form.

Internalization is the last conversion process (from explicit knowledge to tacit knowledge) where knowledge is converted into personal mental models and can then be used in an optimal way to achieve tasks.

One point of criticism of the SECI model is that knowledge development does not necessarily need to begin with socialization [LI 03].

– BOISOT I-space KM model

The BOISOT KM model is a conceptual framework incorporating a theoretical foundation of social learning. Boisot [BOI 98] suggested that knowledge is structured, understood and transferred through three dimensions: codification, abstraction and diffusion.

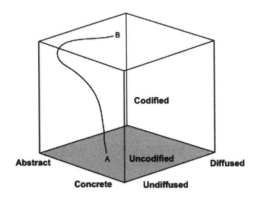

Figure 10.2. *The BOISOT I-space KM model*

Codification refers to the degree to which knowledge can be encoded (even if the receiver does not have the facility to understand it) while abstraction refers to a low level of knowledge contextualization (easy to generalize to other contexts).

The assumption is that well-codified and abstract knowledge is much easier to understand than highly contextual knowledge. Consequently, for tacit knowledge with a high contextual level (high degree of specificity) there is a risk of loss of context due to codification, which is a barrier for knowledge transfer. That is one of the limits of the knowledge transfer process relying on organizational memories built with knowledge codified principally using knowledge engineering techniques.

Highly contextual knowledge needs a shared context for its interpretation and that implies face-to-face interaction and in a general way a socialization approach as in the SECI model of Nonaka and Takeuchi [NON 95].

In this model, codification and abstraction work together and facilitate the knowledge diffusion and transfer.

The Boisot model has been criticized for its lack of practical applications [DAL 11]. More extensive field testing of this knowledge transfer model would provide feedback regarding its applicability as well as provide more guidelines on how best to implement the I-space approach.

– Alavi and Leidner knowledge transfer model

The knowledge transfer model of Alavi and Leidner (Figure 10.3) depicts the transfer of knowledge among individuals and groups [ALA 01]. Their model contains core elements of knowledge management research: the distinction between tacit and explicit knowledge, knowledge application mechanisms [GRA 96] and the SECI process [NON 95].

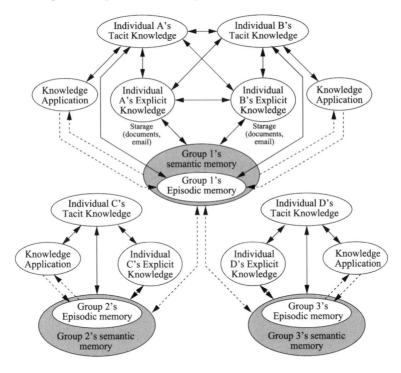

Figure 10.3. *The Alavi and Leidner knowledge transfer model [ALA 01]*

In their model, an individual is connected to the group processes through transfer (an individual may share knowledge with the group during a decision-making meeting for example) or through a centralized storage mechanism (e.g. computer files or regular meetings). Individuals can then call on the centralized memory to make decisions, if needed (arrows H). Individuals learn from the application of knowledge and their learning becomes embedded into their tacit knowledge space and the group's episodic memory (arrows I). Organizational knowledge processes would then consist of the summation of the individual and group knowledge processes. In this case, one group may have acquired and applied knowledge to a given situation and coded this knowledge in the form of a certain routine. This best practice may then be shared with other groups by allowing access to group memory systems (arrows J) or by facilitating intergroup dialogue.

Alavi and Leidner [ALA 01] focus on the interaction between knowledge applications and tacit knowledge. They do not represent explicit knowledge transferred through directives (i.e. rules, standards and procedures). It seems that they do not consider that the application of knowledge can also occur through directives. As stated by Harrison and Hu [HAR 12], it is possible to acquire and share explicit knowledge without performing the deeper levels of cognition required for developing a tacit understanding.

10.4. Research methodology

In this research, we have a constructivist approach mixing theoretical and empirical points of view.

10.4.1. *Literature review*

The literature review helps us identify factors influencing knowledge transfer (section 10.2). We focus our study on three dimensions (Table 10.1): characteristics of knowledge, absorptive capacity and knowledge transfer channels.

We have used these factors as a grid for interviewing groups of users in four different organizations to understand barriers for the transfer of codified expert knowledge.

10.4.2. *Focus groups for data collection and generation of testable propositions*

Focus groups have been frequently used in market research to collect data concerning products, advertising, price setting and other marketing issues.

We define focus groups as a qualitative collection of data that involves a facilitator or moderator leading a discussion between a number of knowledgeable informants of similar status on a topic that will facilitate the development of the understanding required to answer the research question [REM 12].

| | Characteristics of knowledge | | | | |
	Codifiability (tacitness vs. Explicitness	Complexity	Specificity	Absorptive capacity	Knowledge transfer channels
[ALA 01]				X	X
[ARG 00]		X			
[BOI 98]	X		X		
[COH 90]				X	
[DAL 11]	X				
[GAR 97]	X				
[GUP 00]				X	
[FAH 98]	X				X
[HAR 12]	X				
[HOL 98]					X
[NON 95]	X				
[POL 67]	X				
[REE 90]		X			
[STU 98]					
[SZU 96]		X			
[TEE 77]					
[TUR 06]	X	X	X		
[VAN 98]				X	
[ZAC 99]	X				
[ZAN 95]	X	X	X		

Table 10.1. *Factors influencing knowledge transfer discussed in prior research*

– Collecting qualitative data with focus groups technique

In our research, we have created four focus groups in four different organizations (Table 10.2) to understand barriers for codified knowledge transfer. Data were captured by note taking and voice recording during group discussions.

Organization field	Focus groups (users of the codified experts' knowledge)
Radio telecommunication (France)	Five audio technicians working in the recording, manipulation, mixing and reproduction of sound.
Electricity producer (Canada)	Five managers involved in contracts negotiation with companies for electricity distribution.
Pension plans and retirement administration (Canada)	Four program designers involved in the elaboration of programs for pension plans financing.
Verification of: – safety of the buildings – professional qualifications of owner builders	Three engineers in charge of verifications of under pressure devices in buildings.

Table 10.2. *Focus groups for our research*

– Focus groups to generate propositions for an optimal methodology of knowledge transfer

Using the focus groups technique, we also generate testable propositions:

– to enrich the content, readability, accessibility of the codified knowledge referential;

– to facilitate its appropriation and assimilation.

These propositions lead us to a new methodology for optimizing the transfer of expert codified knowledge.

– A case study to experiment the proposed methodology for knowledge transfer.

We experimented with our methodology for codified knowledge transfer at the Hydro Quebec Company. Lessons learned with this case study are described at the end of this chapter.

10.5. Codifying with knowledge engineering methods: barriers for knowledge transfer

After qualitative data collection with focus groups, we analyzed arguments and classified identified barriers (Figure 10.4) in categories corresponding to the three dimensions influencing knowledge transfer that we pointed out in our literature review (characteristics of knowledge, absorptive capacity of knowledge receivers and knowledge transfer channels).

Characteristics of knowledge	Absorptive capacity of knowledge receivers
•High degree of specificity (strong linked to situations expert experienced) •High degree of complexity (important number of routines needed to interpret knowledge)	•Great distance between the receiver's context of use and the described one •*logical structuring not adapted* to the receiver's preferences •*Multiplicity of formalisms* (accessibility, readability, understandability)

Knowledge transfer channels
•*No formalized channel:* -to exchange about contexts of use -to manage, in a collaborative approach, the evolution of the codified referential •*No incitation for informal exchange* (informal seminars, coffee break conversations,...)

Figure 10.4. *Barriers for codified knowledge transfer identified with focus groups*

These identified barriers make it very difficult:

– to assimilate the content of the codified knowledge;

– to adapt and interpret codified expert knowledge;

– to create a shared context for knowledge interpretation.

These empirical results confirm that, as underlined in the literature review, the understandability and diffusibility of codified knowledge with knowledge engineering techniques depend on many factors:

– Accessibility and readability of used formalisms for the knowledge receivers [DAL 11].

– Knowledge receivers' profiles (background, context of knowledge use, preferences for logical structuring and understanding profiles) [TOU 02].

– Level of description of complex and specific knowledge [STU 98].

– Exchange channels between knowledge sources (experts or specialists) and potential future users.

10.5.1. *Multiplicity of formalisms*

Knowledge engineering methods lead to a set of models and each of them corresponds to a specific type of knowledge. For example, the Common KADS methodology proposes five types of model [DIE 00]:

– Task model of the business process of the organization.

– Agent model of the use of knowledge by executors to carry out the various tasks in the organization.

– Knowledge model that explains in detail the knowledge structures and types required for performing tasks.

– Communication model that represents the communicative transactions between agents.

– Design model that specifies the architectures and technical requirements needed to implement a system including functions detailed by the knowledge and communication models.

So, expertise is codified through formalisms (which are often diagrams) depending on the type of knowledge.

We can point out many difficulties associated with the multiplicity of models: accessibility, readability and understandability/intelligibility. The profile of knowledge receivers can accentuate those barriers: are they familiar to the use of models? What about their cognitive preferences of apprenticeship: are they more textual than visual?

Knowledge engineering methods only focus on the codification of the tacit knowledge of knowledgeable staff (experts or specialists) but they do not take into account the appropriation and organizational learning capabilities of readers (potential future users).

10.5.2. *Heterogeneity of readers profiles*

In an organization, readers do not have the same level of expertise and their profiles can be heterogeneous (background, contexts of knowledge use, preferences for logical structuring, understanding profile, familiarity with models, etc.).

However, the logical structuring and the presentation of the tacit knowledge codified are not guided by learning levels of future readers, but only by the concepts tackled when interviewing experts/specialists and by the model structure.

10.5.3. *Background*

A knowledge receiver with important prior knowledge (related to the knowledge domain) and familiar with the use of models may have a greater absorptive capacity. It may be easier for such a receiver to decode and assimilate knowledge with a high level of complexity.

10.5.4. *Contexts of use*

The greater the distance between the receiver's context of use and the described one, the more the knowledge receiver will make important cognitive efforts to adapt knowledge. This case happens when the codified knowledge is very specific to the knowledge source's context.

10.5.5. *Preferences for logical structuring and understanding profile*

Preferences for logical structuring depend on the learning level of the knowledge receiver. For a novice, understanding concepts before procedural tasks could be more logical. However, an expert would perhaps prefer a structuring guided by problem solving.

The understanding profile can be assimilated into the cognitive preferences of the reader when learning: textual and/or visual preferences.

When the knowledge domain is codified, taking into account the logical structuring and cognitive preferences of the reader, knowledge transfer can be accelerated because the knowledge receiver makes less cognitive effort.

10.5.6. *Level of description of complex knowledge*

The more complex the knowledge, the more difficult its transfer can be.

To reduce complexity, we propose the following complementary activities to enrich codified knowledge referential:

– Identifying sets of complex knowledge already codified.

– Describing and illustrating routines in which identified complex knowledge is embedded.

– Organizing exchange (with adequate knowledge transfer channels: informal or formal) between experts and users to help them build a shared context for interpretation.

10.5.7. *Level of description of specific knowledge*

It may be difficult for experts to explain some sets of knowledge without strong links to situations they have experienced. For those sets of knowledge with a high degree of specificity, the knowledge receiver has to make an important cognitive effort to generalize (abstract) the knowledge and recontextualize it for his/her personal use.

We propose the following three activities to facilitate this abstraction step:

– Identifying sets of specific knowledge already codified.

– Eliciting with experts general principles that guide the use of identified specific knowledge.

– Identifying and illustrating with experts other possible contexts of use.

10.5.8. *Exchange channels to increase diffusion/transfer*

Communication and transmission channels are necessary to accelerate knowledge transfer. They are an important basis for:

– elaboration of a shared context for interpretation;

– legitimization of captured knowledge as best practice;

– evolution of codified knowledge through social interactions.

In Table 10.3, we summarize key points (derived from the focus groups) to analyze codified knowledge transfer efficiency.

	Activities for efficiency of codified knowledge transfer
Codified knowledge	*Complex knowledge* Identify sets of knowledge with high level of complexity Explicit and illustrate associated routines Create a shared context for interpretation (develop interactions between experts and knowledge receivers)
	Specific knowledge Identify sets of knowledge with high degree of dependence with the knowledge source's context of use Explicit general principles associated to specific knowledge Identify and illustrate other possible contexts of use
Reader's profiles	*Background* Professional background Level of expertise of the reader in the knowledge domain Degree of familiarity with knowledge engineering models
	Contexts of use Identify various work situations where the codified knowledge would be useful for the reader
	Identify preferences for logical structuring
	Preferences for his/her understanding profile Visual representation of knowledge? Textual representation of knowledge? Audio preference (multimedia)? Illustration with concrete case studies?
Exchange channels	Identify existing communication and transmission channels Stimulate social interactions between knowledge sources (experts) and readers

Table 10.3. *Analysis grid for codified knowledge transfer*

10.6. Methodology for knowledge transfer efficiency

We propose here an empirical methodology for the transfer and appropriation of a codified knowledge referential at individual and organizational levels. It is a four-step approach, guided by the previous analysis grid (Table 10.3). Executing this four-step transfer methodology supposes, first, that identification and codification of tacit knowledge are well performed.

10.6.1. *Capturing and codifying tacit knowledge domain*

First, we identify experts to interview for capturing tacit knowledge: they are knowledge sources and will be authors of the codified knowledge referential. We carry out individual interviews.

We define the goal and scope of the codification sessions. During these 2 h sessions, there are strong interactions with experts to identify and formalize the different types of tacit sets of knowledge. Using knowledge engineering techniques (such as Common Kads for example) and their associated knowledge models, we codify tacit knowledge models.

The codified knowledge referential is then read by other experts who will add comments and is then revalidated by authors (knowledge sources) of the codified knowledge referential.

The result is a codified knowledge referential:

– reflecting the knowledge domain and the tacit experience of one or many experts;

– structured into chapters corresponding to crucial tacit sets of knowledge identified with experts.

10.6.2. *Defining and formalizing exchanges between groups of actors involved in the knowledge transfer process*

The focus groups have directed our research toward two propositions to build a methodology for optimizing the transfer of codified experts' knowledge:

– Define groups of actors to be involved in the transfer process and define precisely the role of each of them.

– Identify and formalize situations of exchange between groups of actors involved in the transfer process.

10.6.2.1. *A clear vision of groups of actors involved in the transfer process*

Our transfer methodology relies on three groups of key actors:

– Knowledge sources who are experts or specialists interviewed to capture tacit knowledge; they are authors of the codified knowledge referential.

– Knowledge readers are knowledge receivers selected to contribute to the adaptation of the codified knowledge referential; they are in charge of the rewriting of the codified referential.

– Other knowledge receivers who are potential future users (other team members, new employees, etc.).

10.6.2.2. *An adequate structuring of exchanges between groups of actors*

The goal is to formalize situations of exchange that will lead to a collective good appropriation and a legitimization of captured knowledge. Clear and precise objectives must be defined for each formalized situation (Table 10.4).

We rely on the SECI model [NON 95] as a framework to identify each situation of exchange between groups of actors involved in the transfer process.

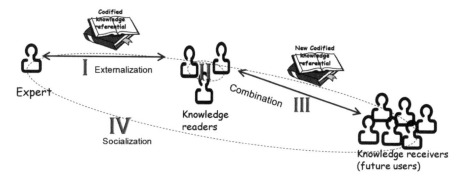

Figure 10.5. *Situations of exchange between groups of actors involved in the transfer process*

Situation of exchange	Objectives	Transmission channel
Presentation of the codified referential to knowledge readers	The goal is, for knowledge readers, to understand the objectives, scope and content of the captured knowledge. Knowledge sources (experts/specialists) present and comment the referential to clarify sets of complex/specific knowledge by giving examples and different contexts of use. This presentation initiates the process of elaboration of a "shared context for knowledge interpretation" and is important for its success. Many sessions can be useful to have a collective understanding of the codified referential.	– Formal seminars
Exchanges between knowledge readers to adapt the codified referential	Knowledge readers are involved in a collaborative work that will lead to the adaptation of the codified knowledge referential. Here, they identify complex and specific sets of knowledge and try to make them more explicit: – building case studies collectively; – illustrating other contexts of use relying on their own experiences; – changing the logical structuring of some chapters.	– Formal seminars – Groupware – Other collaborative platforms
Sharing the rewritten referential with potential future users	The goal is to share the rewritten and stabilized codified referential with other knowledge receivers who are potential future users. The pool of rewriters has to define apprenticeship objectives and delimit the appropriate sets of knowledge they will have to focus on. Training sessions can be appropriate to exchange with potential future users.	– Face-to-face training sessions – Online training sessions
Sharing learned lessons when using the codified referential	The objective is to facilitate future evolutions of the codified knowledge referential by capitalizing learned lessons of actors using it. Exchanges (even informal) between the different groups of actors must be organized periodically to identify: – new ways of doing more efficient (evolutions); – new applications/new contexts of use; – difficulties met.	– Informal and formal seminars – Coffee break conversations – Online forums – Blogs – Knowledge portals

Table 10.4. *Formalization of exchanges to develop a shared context for knowledge interpretation*

– *The externalization mode* (I): knowledge experts and knowledge readers interact to make the codified knowledge referential more explicit.

– *Combination mode* (II and III): first, knowledge readers interact among themselves to adapt and re-write the codified referential. Then, exchanges are organized with future users to share the rewritten referential.

– *Socialization mode* (IV): in this mode, social interactions are encouraged between all the groups to facilitate the evolution of the codified knowledge referential and its application in other contexts of use.

10.6.2.3. *Using adequate channels with regard to the purpose of the knowledge transfer*

For each situation of exchange, we recommend to select the most suitable transmission channel (informal or formal, personal or impersonal) to increase appropriation and transferability (Table 10.4).

Fahey and Prusak [FAH 98] define a "shared context" as a "shared understanding of an organization's external and internal worlds and how these worlds are connected" [FAH 98]. They insist on the fact that a disregard for shared context means that the generation, transmission and use of knowledge are not seen as activities that bring individuals to deeper understanding through dialogue. As a result, information remains simply a pattern of disjointed and ill-structured data points or events. Without a shared understanding, the path from information to knowledge is difficult to traverse.

Elaborating a shared context for knowledge transfer must be a dynamic activity because knowledge as a flow implies that any shared understanding is likely to change over time, and sometimes may do so suddenly.

10.6.2.4. *The four steps of the knowledge transfer methodology*

Figure 10.6 shows our two-step methodology for knowledge transfer efficiency.

– Characterization of readers

This is an important step for defining readers' profiles (background, contexts of use and preferences for logical structuring).

– Elaboration of specifications for rewriting

The goal, here, is to define:

– additional contents for the description of highly complex and specific knowledge;

– additional illustrations (case studies, videos) to elaborate;

– a logical structuring for the codified knowledge referential.

– Sharing the knowledge referential

Our sharing approach has one main goal: create a shared context for knowledge interpretation to make easier and accelerate organizational learning.

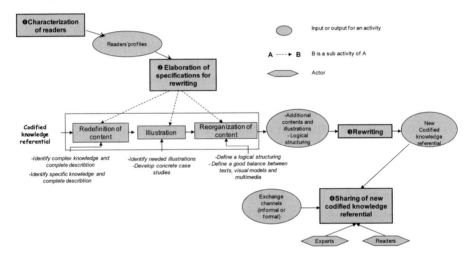

Figure 10.6. *Methodology for codified knowledge transfer*

10.7. Hydro Quebec case study

Hydro Quebec is one of the biggest electricity producers and distributors in North America. Hydro Quebec is a public company and its principal shareholder is the Quebec Government.

The Hydro Quebec study is part of a bigger project called "support for critical knowledge capture" led by the Human Resources Department. The study lasted 2 months and concerned one operational unity. It was motivated by the future retirement of one of the unity's experts. The project took place in the "Distribution network" entity with five managers involved in contract negotiation with companies for electricity distribution

Interviewing the expert and using knowledge engineering techniques, a codified knowledge referential was elaborated in a first stage. There were three types of knowledge in this referential:

– Technical knowledge about the types of distribution networks (overhead and underground distribution networks), the supply modes and the connection to the system.

– Economical knowledge dealing with cost regulations (electricity service contracts, billing and payment).

– Juridical knowledge that covers rights and obligations of customers and the distributor.

The following two objectives were assigned to our study:

– Optimize the use of the codified knowledge referential.

– Accelerate the transfer of the knowledge referential to five future experts of the same unity.

10.7.1. *Approach*

We mixed questionnaires and interviews to implement our knowledge transfer methodology.

Questionnaires were used with the five managers (readers of the codified knowledge referential) to characterize their profiles (professional and study background, contexts of use of the referential, etc.). Four of them had a technical background and the fifth had a managerial background.

Interviewing the five future experts helped us to identify additional needs for the codified knowledge referential in detail. Interviews were guided by our analysis grid for codified knowledge transfer.

10.7.2. *Results and implications*

Our study led to new specifications for the codified knowledge referential to increase its transferability (Table 10.5).

	New specifications for the codified knowledge referential
About the content	A list of additional descriptions to write A list of missing critical knowledge to integrate in the referential (needing new interviews of the expert) A list of sets of knowledge to complete by concrete case studies
About the structuring	Despite the multiplicity of models in the codified knowledge referential, readers *find models readable* because each of them was associated with a textual description For the logical structuring of the referential, they preferred a *problem-solving approach*
About the new referential sharing	It was proposed: – a *collective and collaborative rewriting* of the codified knowledge referential (with the expert); – a *"knowledge management facilitator"* who will drive the sharing step and coordinate the evolution of the referential.

Table 10.5. *Summary of new specifications for the codified knowledge referential*

10.7.2.1. *Knowledge transfer as a collaborative process*

The first implication of Hydro Quebec case study is that the methodology for knowledge transfer must be performed as a collective and collaborative process, which involves three categories of actors (and roles must be clearly defined):

– knowledge sources (experts/specialists);

– knowledge management facilitators;

– knowledge readers.

10.7.2.2. *Codified knowledge referential versus not stable decision situations*

Managers pointed out the fact that, in the contract negotiation field, decision situations are not stable. When the attributes of the decision-making situation vary, the knowledge required to make effective decisions changes correspondingly. For this reason, they need access to a wider range of knowledge coming from external sources. So, it would be interesting to integrate in the codified knowledge referential, a list of internal and external sources recommended by the expert.

10.8. Discussion

10.8.1. *About completeness of knowledge*

In our research, it seems important to integrate the notion of completeness as a characteristic of knowledge, which plays an important role in the absorptive capacity of decision makers.

The notion of completeness refers to the degree to which the knowledge for making decisions or completing tasks is entirely sufficient for the decisions maker's use [TUR 06]. Knowledge is less likely to be complete when decision situations are not predictable [GRE 90]. Because of such uncertainty, individuals have to engage in search processes to obtain the necessary information to accomplish tasks.

Identifying "incomplete" sets of knowledge in the codified referential will lead to the identification (with experts) of pertinent internal and external sources of information, which may supply the "bits" required to complete knowledge sets [GAZ 86].

10.8.2. *Exploring ontologies for knowledge transfer*

Classical knowledge engineering methods formalize domain concepts in an elementary way (simple categorization, poor formal relations between concepts). For this reason:

– we can hardly implement efficient information retrieval systems in knowledge portals for example;

– it is difficult to update the knowledge referential in a collaborative way and in a distributed context;

– the dictionary on concepts is not reusable with efficiency for other related domains.

A central technical aspect of knowledge management is the construction and maintenance of an organizational memory as a means for knowledge conservation, distribution and reuse.

In this context, ontologies may be an alternative because they allow a shared and common understanding of a domain that can be communicated across people and computers. They facilitate sharing and reuse of knowledge in a computational form.

Ontologies are interesting candidates to facilitate communication between people in organizations. They provide the terms, their meanings, their relations and constraints [STU 98]. They may be used for supporting the users in finding relevant knowledge, for example by offering the appropriate concepts for posing queries.

Coupled to intranets and knowledge portals, ontologies are good candidates to improve knowledge management.

10.8.3. *About costs*

The economic aspect can be a limitation of the knowledge transfer model that we propose. Implementing such a process transfer can be a heavy investment for companies:

– An organization (it can be a formal community) must be settled and this involves identifying actors and defining roles and responsibilities for them.

– Actors must be available for the codification, rewriting and evolution of the knowledge referential.

10.9. Conclusion

In our research, we propose to create continuity between knowledge codification and knowledge transfer. In fact, our methodology is an attempt to reconcile two perspectives in knowledge management [COU 01]: the functional and interpretive perspectives.

In the functional perspective, knowledge management is defined as the way that organizations create, capture, store, reuse and protect knowledge to achieve organizational objectives. This reflects the belief that the world is factual and that the facts can be known and captured. From this view, our approach gives tools for having a good understanding of the characteristics of knowledge to be captured and for having a good level of knowledge description to make the appropriation and transfer easier.

The interpretive perspective is based on the belief that social reality is constructed socially, and attention is directed to interpretation, distributed cognition, communications and social processes. In this perspective, our methodology leads to a social construct with a broad shared understanding by defining and encouraging suitable situations of exchange between groups of actors involved in the knowledge transfer process.

Organizational knowledge is viewed as existing in a collective mind, developed through interpretation, communication and shared meanings. Organizational knowledge is in a constant state of flux as new experiences are evaluated and shared. Knowledge management in this environment consists of fostering communications between individuals, sharing and enriching interpretations, and coordinating actions.

The transfer methodology, we propose, relies on a robust theoretical framework: the SECI model of Nonaka and Takeuchi [NON 95]. Integrated with knowledge engineering techniques, the methodology can enhance knowledge transfer by leading to the elaboration of a pertinent shared context for knowledge interpretation.

The Hydro Quebec casestudy highlights the importance of defining an appropriate organization to support the knowledge transfer process.

In the next steps of our research, we will focus on the following two aspects:

– The experimentation of the "sharing approach". This is an important step we must perform to identify precisely actionable tasks and suitable channels for each situation of exchange between groups of actors.

– The evaluation of knowledge transfer efficiency after an implementation of the proposed methodology.

10.10. Bibliography

[AJM 08] AJMAL M.M., KOSKINEN K.U., "Knowledge transfer in project-based organizations: an organizational culture perspective", *Project Management Journal*, vol. 39, no. 1, pp. 7–15, 2008.

[ALA 01] ALAVI M., LEIDNER D.E., "Review: knowledge management and knowledge management systems: conceptual foundations and research issues", *MIS Quarterly*, vol. 25, no. 1, pp. 107–136, 2001.

[ARG 00] ARGOTE L., INGRAM P., LEVINE J.M., *et al.*, "Knowledge transfer in organizations: learning from the experience of others", *Organizational Behavior and Human Decision Processes*, vol. 82, no. 1, pp. 1–8, 2000.

[BAR 85] BARNEY J.B., "Information cost and the governance of economic transactions", in NACAMALLL R.D., RUGIADINI A. (eds.), *Organizations and Markets*, Societa Editrice it Milano, Milan Italy, pp. 347–372, 1985.

[BOI 98] BOISOT M., *Knowledge Assets: Securing Competitive Advantage, in the Information Economy*, Oxford University Press, Oxford, 1998.

[BUR 83] BURGELMAN R.A., "A process model of internal corporate venturing in the diversified major firm", *Administrative Science Quarterly*, vol. 28, pp. 223–244, 1983.

[COH 90] COHEN W.M., LEVINTHAL D.A., "Absorptive capacity: a new perspective on learning and innovation", *Administrative Science Quarterty*, vol. 35, pp. 128–152, 1990.

[COU 01] COURTNEY J.F., "Decision and knowledge management in inquiring organizations: toward a new decision-making paradigm for DSS", *Decision Support Systems*, vol. 31, pp. 17–38, 2001.

[DAF 86] DAFT R.L., LENGEL R.H., "Organizational information requirements, media richness, and structural design", *Management Science*, vol. 32, pp. 554–571, 1986.

[DAL 11] DALKIR K., *Knowledge Management in Theory and Practice*, 2nd ed., The MIT Press, Cambridge, MA, 2011.

[DE 00] DE LONG D., FAHEY L., "Diagnosing cultural barriers to knowledge management", *The Academy of Management Executive*, vol. 14, no. 4, pp. 113–127, 2000.

[DIE 00] DIENG R., CORBY O., GIBOIN A., *et al.*, *Méthodes et outils pour la gestion des connaissances*, Dunod, 2000.

[FAH 98] FAHEY L., PRUSAK L., "The eleven deadliest sins of knowledge management", *California Management Review*, vol. 40, no. 3, pp. 265–276, 1998.

[GAR 97] GARUD R., "On the distinction between know-how, know-what, and know-why", in HUFF A. WALSH J. (eds), *Advances in Strategic Management*, JAI Press, Greenwich, CT, 1997.

[GAZ 86] GAZDIK I., "Stimulation enhances inventiveness on the shop floor", *Technovation*, vol. 4, no. 2, pp. 131–141, 1986.

[GHO 94] GHOSHAL S., BARTLETT C.A., "Linking organizational context and managerial action: the dimensions of quality of management", *Strategic Management Journal*, vol. 15, pp. 91–112, 1994.

[GIB 04] GIBSON C.B., BIRKINSHAW J., "The antecedents, consequences, and mediating role of organizational ambidexterity", *Academy of Management Journal*, vol. 47, no. 2, pp. 209–226, 2004.

[GRA 96] GRANT R.M., "Towards a knowledge-based theory of the firm", *Strategic Management Journal*, vol. 17, no. 10, pp. 109–122, 1996.

[GRA 05] GRAY J.H., DENSTEN I.L., "Towards an integrative model of organizational culture and knowledge management", *International Journal of Organisational Behaviour*, vol. 9, no. 2, pp. 594–603, 2005.

[GRE 90] GRESOV C., "Effects of dependence and tasks on unit design and efficiency", *Organization Studies*, vol. 11, pp. 503–529, 1990.

[GUP 00] GUPTA A., GOVINDARAJAN V., "Knowledge flows within multinational corporations", *Strategic Management Journal*, vol. 21, pp. 473–496, 2000.

[HAR 12] HARRISON A., HU Q., "Knowledge transfer within organizations: a social network perspective", *45th Hawaii International Conference on System Sciences*, Grand Wailea, Maui, Hawaii, January 4–7 2012.

[HOL 98] HOLTHAM C., COURTNEY N., "The executive learning ladder: a knowledge creation pro-cess grounded in the strategic information systems domain", in HOADLEY, BENBASAT I. (eds), *This article was edited in the proceedings of AMCIS (Americas Conference on Information Systems)*, Baltimore, MD, pp. 594-597, 1998.

[LI 03] LI M., GAO F., "Why Nonaka highlights tacit knowledge: a critical review", *Journal of Knowledge Management*, vol. 7, no. 4, pp. 6–14, 2003.

[LIP 82] LIPPMAN S.A., RUMELT R.P., "Uncertain imitability: an analysis of interfirm differences in efficiency under competition", *Bell Journal of Economics*, vol. 13, pp. 418–438, 1982.

[MAI 10] MAIER R., *Knowledge Management Systems: Information and Communication Technologies for Knowledge Management*, 3rd ed., Springer, 2010.

[MOW 96] MOWERY D.C., OXLEY J.E., SILVERMAN B.S., "Strategic alliances and inter-organizational knowledge transfer", *Strategic Management Journal*, vol. 17, pp. 77–91, 1996.

[NON 95] NONAKA I., TAKEUCHI H., *The Knowledge-Creating Company: How Japanese Companies Create the Dynamics of Innovation*, Oxford University Press, New York, 1995.

[POL 67] POLANYI M., *The Tacit Dimension*, Routledge and Kean Paul, London, 1967.

[REE 90] REED R., DEFILLIPPI R.J., "Causal ambiguity, barriers to imitation, and sustainable competitive advantage", *Academy of Management Review*, vol. 15, no. 1, pp. 88–102, 1990.

[REM 12] REMENYI D., *Field Methods for Academic Research: Interviews, Focus Groups & Questionnaires*, 2nd ed., Academic Publishing International, March 2012.

[SIM 99] SIMONIN B.L., "Ambiguity and the process of knowledge transfer in strategic alliances", *Strategic Management Journal*, pp.595–623, 1999.

[STU 98] STUDER R., BENJAMINS R., FENSEL D., "Knowledge engineering: principles and methods", *Data & Knowledge Engineering*, vol. 25, pp.161–167, 1998.

[SZU 96] SZULANSKI G., "Exploring internal stickiness: impediments to the transfer of best practice within the firm", *Strategic Management Journal*, vol. 17, pp. 27–43, 1996.

[TEE 77] TEECE D., "Technology transfer by multinational firms: the resource cost of international technology transfer", *Economic Journal*, vol. 87, pp. 242–261, 1977.

[TOU 02] TOUNKARA T., MATTA N., ERMINE J.L., *et al.*, *L'appropriation des connaissances avec MASK*, EGC, Montpellier, 2002.

[TUR 06] TURNER L., MAKHIJA V., "The role of organizational controls in managing knowledge", *Academy of Management Review*, vol. 31, no. 1, pp. 197–217, 2006.

[VAN 98] VANCE D., EYNON J., "On the requirements of knowledge-transfer using IS: a schema whereby such transfer is enhanced", in HOADLEY E., BENBASAT I. (eds), *Proceedings of the 4th Americas Conference on Information Systems*, Baltimore, MD, pp. 632–634, August 1998.

[WIE 13] WIEWIORA A., TRIGUNARSYAH B., MURPHY C., *et al.*, "Organizational culture and willingness to share knowledge: a competing values perspective in Australian context", *International Journal of Project Management*, vol. 31, pp. 1163–1174, 2013.

[WIL 85] WILLIAMSON O.E., *The Economic Institutions of Capitalism*, Free Press, New York, 1985.

[ZAC 99] ZACK M.H., "Managing codified knowledge", *Sloan Management Review*, vol. 40, no. 4, pp. 45–58, 1999.

[ZAN 95] ZANDER U., KOGUT B., "Knowledge and the speed of the transfer and imitation of organization capabilities", *Organization Science*, vol. 6, pp.76–92, 1995.

List of Authors

Marie-Hélène ABEL
Heudiasyc
University of Technology of
Compiègne
France

Pierre-Emmanuel ARDUIN
LAMSADE
Paris-Dauphine University
France

Henda Hajjami BEN GHÉZALA
RIADI Laboratory
Ecole Nationale des Sciences de
l'Informatique
University of Manouba
Tunisia

Narjès Bellamine BEN SAOUD
Institut supérieur d'informatique
University of Tunis El Manar
and
RIADI Laboratory
Ecole Nationale des Sciences de
l'Informatique
University of Manouba
Tunisia

Imed BOUGHZALA
Telecom Ecole de Management
Institut Mines-Telecom
France

Sarra BOUZAYANE
MIRACL Laboratory
Higher Institute of Computer
Science and Multimedia
Sfax
Tunisia

Imène BRIGUI-CHTIOUI
International Business School
Paris
France

Soumaya CHERICHI
LARODEC
IHEC Carthage
University of Carthage
Tunisia

Karima DHOUIB
MIRACL Laboratory
University of Sfax
Higher Institute of Technological
Studies of Sfax
Tunisia

Rim FAIZ
LARODEC
IHEC Carthage
University of Carthage
Tunisia

Faïez GARGOURI
MIRACL Laboratory
University of Sfax
Tunisia

Michel GRUNDSTEIN
LAMSADE
Paris-Dauphine University
France

Gilles KASSEL
MIS Laboratory
University of Picardie Jules Verne
Amiens
France

Pierre MORIZET-MAHOUDEAUX
Heudiasyc
University of Technology of
Compiègne
France

Fadoua OUAMANI
RIADI Laboratory
Ecole Nationale des Sciences de
l'Informatique
University of Manouba
Tunisia

Camille ROSENTHAL-SABROUX
LAMSADE
Paris-Dauphine University
France

Inès SAAD
MIS Laboratory
University of Picardie Jules Verne
France Business School
Amiens
France

Thierno TOUNKARA
Telecom Ecole de Management
Institut Mines-Telecom
France

Mohamed TURKI
ISIMS
MIRACL Laboratory
University of Sfax
Higher Institute of Technological
Studies of Sfax
Tunisia
and
MIS Laboratory
University of Picardie Jules Verne
Amiens
France

Xuan Truong VU
Heudiasyc
University of Technology of
Compiègne
France

Index

A, B

action of collective, 194, 234
agentive entity, 197, 202, 223, 237, 243
annotation rules, 208, 210
argument and counter-argument
 construction, 93, 116–122, 125
argumentation, 97–104
ashms, 239, 271
business process, 215, 249
 evaluation, 249

C, D

collaborative decision making, 108, 131
collaborative learning, 62, 71, 72, 74,
 76, 82
collective,
communication,
community
 assessment, 17
 of practice, 2
conflict resolution, 72, 111, 113
cross-cultural interaction, 74
culture, models of culture, 66, 67, 70,
 76
decision
 structuring, 184, 189, 190, 194, 202,
  204, 208–210

support systems, 187
 table, 255
design science, 4, 9, 24, 25
DOLCE, 79, 188
DRSA, 95–97

E, F, G

evaluation process, 121
extraction patterns, 185, 206, 207,
 210
features set, 164–172
field study, 23
focus group, 1, 3, 9–14, 24, 31, 290–
 293, 297, 298
formal ontology of organization, 197,
 215, 232, 240

I, J, K

incommensurability, 131, 133, 134,
 136–138, 154
interaction protocol, 116–117
interpretative framework, 131, 134,
 153, 155
jurisprudence, 184–190, 194, 202,
 204
knowledge localization, 249, 250, 251,
 272

knowledge sharing, 1, 2, 6, 14, 17, 20–22, 34, 36, 50, 57, 61, 71, 73, 132, 136, 149, 188, 285

L, M

legal knowledge management, 183
legal ontology, 188
linguistic analysis, 185, 192–194, 203, 204–206
linguistic markers, 204, 205, 815
maturity model, 4–5
measuring impact, 2, 78, 126, 155, 159, 161–163, 168, 176, 275
microblog, 159
multi-criteria decision making approach, 249
multicriteria decision aid, 258

O, P, R

ontology engineering, 192

preference model, 108, 110, 111, 219, 231, 256–258, 262, 263, 272
relevant tweets, 159, 160, 169–172

S

sensitive process, 106
social network
    collaborative system, 48
    group decision making, 113, 115
    knowledge management, 40
    knowledge sharing, 57
    social network aggregation, 35–40
    user profiling, 39
    user social data, 44
social relation, 39, 40, 160, 162, 163

T, U

tacit knowledge, 6
Twitter, 34
user profile, 39, 43, 63, 78–82